Great
Planning
Disasters

Great Planning Disasters

Peter Hall

Weidenfeld and Nicolson
London

First published in Great Britain by
George Weidenfeld and Nicolson Limited
91 Clapham High Street
London SW4 7TA

ISBN 0 297 77627 4

Printed in Great Britain by
Butler & Tanner Ltd
Frome and London

CONTENTS

Contents

List of Tables

List of Figures

Preface

Writing this proved far from easy. I have tried to make it digestible, so I hope that reading it will be easier.

My problem has been this. I wanted to do two things: first, to tell some tales about a few selected 'Great Planning Disasters'; secondly, to help explain them in terms of an eclectic body of theory culled from the borderland of political science, welfare economics, social psychology and ethics. The first was simple enough, but without the second it was just higher journalism; and the second was very difficult.

This could be simply because I was unable to handle the necessary level of theoretical abstraction. I am reminded of a story about Alfred Hitchcock, who back in the 1930s made a musical: 'I hate this sort of thing,' he is reputed to have said; 'melodrama is the only thing I can do.' But I think that the problem is more elusive: it is that I wanted to make the theory accessible to a group of readers, including planners, bureaucrats and officials, who otherwise would almost certainly never hear of it. And the theory proved not merely eclectic, but in many places highly esoteric.

I've done my best with it. If even just a few practical people come to realize that the theory helps to illuminate what they are doing, and even call this into question, then perhaps it will all have been worth while.

I have been powerfully aided over a five-year stint by a number of people. First, as always, by the anonymous librarians in many places: the British Library Reference Division (or, as it will always be for most of its devotees, the BM Reading Room), the British Library of Political and Economic Science, the University

Preface

of California library at Berkeley, the New South Wales Public
Library in Sydney, the University of Reading Library and others.

Secondly, to those colleagues and friends who read all or part
of the manuscript: Douglas Hart, Andrew Sharman, Andrew
Wilson and Melvin Webber. I owe a particular debt to Gila
Falkus at Weidenfeld and Nicolson for reading the whole text
in draft and for making helpful suggestions on improving the
book's readability.

Thirdly, I owe deep thanks to the secretaries at the University
of Reading who produced the manuscript, in particular to
Patricia Hobson and Elizabeth Hodgson who typed the first
draft, and to Chris Holland for a heroic feat in finishing the
revised draft in almost impossible circumstances. Sheila Dance
and Brian Rodgers did a characteristically professional job on
the maps and diagrams.

Fourthly, I would like to recognize the encouragement of Har-
vey Perloff as we worked side by side, in loose but warm contact,
on parallel projects in the same area. As ever, his inspiration and
advice have been invaluable.

Lastly, as ever, my thanks go to Magda for putting up with
me.

PETER HALL
London
1 June 1979

CHAPTER I

Overview

Great Planning Disasters as a title sounds sensational – even sensationalist. But it is meant to be a reasonably exact description, so let us start with some definitions.

Great A major planning decision, involving an investment (or a set of related investments) costing a great deal of money by almost anyone's standard: at least millions of pounds or dollars, more commonly tens or hundreds or even thousands of millions. This is the kind of decision that should call for an elaborate effort of analysis and evaluation before it is finally made. This book concentrates on big decisions for two reasons: first, because most people would think it more important to get these right; secondly, because they are much better documented, whether officially, in the reports and minutes of Select Committees, or unofficially, in the work of independent critics. Doubtless, if the small decisions were as well reported, many of the same conclusions would emerge.

Planning This word is confusing in that it has two rather different but related meanings.[1] First, it can refer to a set of *processes* whereby decision-makers engage in logical foresight before committing themselves. These include problem definition, problem analysis, goal and objective setting, forecasting, problem projection, design of alternative solutions, evaluation of alternative solutions, decision processes, implementation processes, monitoring, control and updating. Such processes are common to the planning of many public activities: defence, economic development, education, public order and welfare. Many of them are used in part, within different parameters and with different objective functions, by large private corporations. But secondly, the word can refer to processes that result in a *physical plan* showing the distribution of activities and their related structures (houses, factories, offices, schools) in geographical space. When we talk about 'planning' or 'planners' we often mean this kind of planning, otherwise known as physical planning, or town and country planning, or urban and regional planning. In this book, most but not all of the cases refer to this second kind of planning: they are about how much of what is put where. One or two will stray outside that strict definition, though they too will have a clear relation to questions of physical planning, in particular, the quality of the physical environment. But in any event, all the cases by definition involve the *processes* of planning. To analyse these, especially when they appear to go wrong, is the object of this book.

Disasters This is the really emotive word that is likely to cause misunderstanding. It is used in this book to refer to *any planning process that is perceived by many people to have gone wrong*. This I believe is the only reasonable starting-point, for – as will become evident in every case – opinions differ, and every project will continue to be defended. Disasters, thus defined, can be of two kinds. First, *negative disasters*: decisions to take a course of action, culminating in a physical result, that were later substantially modified (or reversed, or abandoned) after considerable commitment of effort and resources. Secondly, *positive disasters*: decisions to take a course of action, with a physical result, that were implemented despite much criticism and even opposition, and which were later felt by many informed people to have been a mistake. Since they are great, the case studies in this book all refer to large (and generally discrete) physical investments. Since they are concerned with planning, most deal in part with locating these investments in space. Since they are negative or positive disasters, they have all involved great public controversy. Because the 1960s in the Western world were a period of rapid economic growth and high investment levels, there are numerous examples. Negative disasters (abandonments) include the third London airport, the Channel tunnel and its associated high-speed rail links, motorways for London and many other European and

2

American cities, successive comprehensive redevelopment schemes for places like Piccadilly Circus and Covent Garden in London, and many other large investments. Positive disasters (criticized commitments) include the Concorde supersonic airplane, the Bay Area Rapid Transit System (BART) in San Francisco and some similar schemes in other cities, many motorway systems almost everywhere, nuclear power plants in Britain and France and Austria, the Sydney Opera House and many others. Again, it is necessary to stress that the judgement is subjective. I may think that the Channel tunnel was thoroughly desirable and its abandonment was a disaster; you may think that BART is the finest rapid transport system in the world or that the Sydney Opera House is the twentieth century's most distinquished building, but many people criticized these projects and in some cases that criticism led to their abandonment. And that is the starting-point of the book.

The objective, then, is to begin a discussion of the pathology of the planning process: how such decisions are made, and then abandoned or continued in the face of criticism. The method of approach is a three-layered one. First, in this chapter, I make a general overview of the territory and look at some possibly promising explanations that are common to all or most of the cases. Secondly, in Part One (Chapters 2–7), I come down to the ground and make a series of detailed case studies. Necessarily, for reasons of space, this involves an invidious choice. I have chosen examples that were reasonably varied in subject matter or in geographical location, but that were above all well documented in official or unofficial accounts. As will be all too evident, I have not sought or claimed to do original work here: I have shamelessly borrowed, with appropriate acknowledgement, from the many excellent sources that were available. A number of these, indeed, deserve to become better known as case studies in the pathology of decision-making.[2] Finally in Part One I have included a chapter on two cases that once appeared to be disasters but which turned into apparent successes (the new Californian campuses and the British national library), since these may offer important pointers for policy.

In Part Two (Chapters 8–13) – and this is by far the most difficult part, for both author and reader – I have tried to interpret
the lessons from these case studies in the light of general theory.
This theory is highly eclectic; it has been pillaged from work over
the last two decades in the social sciences and related disciplines.
Much of it, significantly, has been at the borders of two or more
of these fields, thus economics-psychology, psychology-socio-
logy, economics-ethics. So some of it has remained obscure to
all but a few specialists, though one of the key authors in the
area, Kenneth Arrow, was belatedly recognized through the
award of the Nobel Prize for economics while this book was
being written. I hope this material will not be as obscure or as
difficult as it once seemed. I use it in trying to provide some
explanatory guidelines to the understanding of plan-making
pathology.

As explained at the start of Part Two, most of this theory is
positive: it seeks to explain how and why people behave as they
do when they affect the process of decision-making, not how
they ought to behave. But in the final chapter, I turn to elements
of a *normative* theory of decision-making, in an attempt to start
a discussion about how the processes might be improved. It does
not go far enough: that would be the subject matter of some
future book.

A FIRST APPROACH: THREE TYPES OF UNCERTAINTY

How to approach the problem, to gain sufficient understanding
and if possible some significant interpretative clauses, is the aim
of this preliminary chapter. One obvious starting-point is that
many of these planning disasters seem to have been initiated on
the basis of forecasts that were later found inadequate and mis-
leading. Thus Concorde was started on the basis of inflated estimates of the demands of airlines for supersonic travel, and thus,
indirectly, of the demand for supersonic travel itself. The London
ringways were planned on the basis of estimates of population,
economic activity and car ownership which were later seen to
be too generous. The BART system in San Francisco was based

on travel forecasts that proved to be hopelessly over-optimistic. Almost all the cases were started on the basis of cost estimates that were soon exceeded, some by a very large amount. But all the cases we are considering are examples of forecasting and planning in uncertainty, and it is helpful to turn to the classic analysis of this problem in the work of Friend and Jessop.[3] They distinguish three kinds of uncertainty in planning:

UE: *Uncertainty about the relevant planning environment*, i.e. everything outside the immediate decision-making system. This is the conventional kind of uncertainty, which expresses itself in bad forecasts of behaviour within the system that is being planned for. Planners cannot in practice easily predict the mass behaviour of people in society, whether the particular subject is their propensity to have children, to move about, or to demand different goods and services.

UR: *Uncertainty about decisions in related decision areas*, including decisions that are within the decision-making system but relate to areas of discretion beyond the immediate problem. This is much more specific and small-scale than the first kind of uncertainty. It deals with the behaviour of other individual decision-makers, or these same decision-makers in groups or organizations. They may be in other organizations, or in other parts of the same organization. The important point is that they have some area of discretion outside the area of our decision-makers, which makes them to some degree independent agents; therefore our decision-makers have to take regard of their actions.

UV: *Uncertainty about value judgements*, which includes all the problems where information has been assembled, but where the final decision turns upon questions of value. In any democratic society, however manipulated, it must include the problem of gauging the values of the client population (or, since this is seldom homogenous, different client sub-populations) and, moreover, trying to predict how these may change over time. Finally, it includes the problem of how to compare value weightings on different dimensions among different groups, in situations where, quite often, these values are in conflict.

An important piece of insight, which will recur in our case

studies, is that at first glance the problem of uncertainty seems to lie in the UE area, but that on closer analysis it proves to lie in UR or UV or both. Though it is possible to break into the chain at any point in terms of increasing depth of explanation it is most useful to start with the UE problems and then go logically, first to the UR level of analysis and then to the UV.

Uncertainty in the environment

UE failures, as already seen, consist essentially of bad forecasts – invariably of a quantitative kind – of the system that is being planned, or planned for. And most prove to be of two kinds: first, bad forecasts of demand; secondly, bad cost forecasts.

Poor demand forecasts are a problem because they directly affect the evaluation of the project in terms of its rate of return, whether this evaluation is made in conventional finance-accounting terms or in terms of some social cost-benefit framework. Many of the case studies in this book deal with transport investments, and the demand forecasts for these tend to be a product of two forecasts themselves both notoriously prone to error: population and economic growth. In Britain population projections tended to be underestimates from 1955 to 1965, as the birthrate grew; subsequently, at any rate down to the late 1970s, they tend to have been overestimates. So for a decade future population estimates have been reduced for the country as a whole and for similar areas within it; but these latter have also been affected by unexpected developments, like the rapid migration out of the older inner-city areas. Economic forecasts in Britain, on the other hand, tend to have been consistently over-optimistic. This is probably because they were not true forecasts at all, but rather in the nature of exhortations to the public which, if believed, might somehow prove to be self-fulfilling prophecies. [4] So by the late 1970s most forecasts of demand for goods and services based on 'discretionary income', made a decade or less before, already appeared too high, as in the case of the London motorways or the third London airport. Yet planners in practice were still dangerously dependent on official projections that might at any point again be changed. Everyone was taken by surprise, for instance, when in 1977–8 the British birth-rate began to rise again.

The cost-escalation problem is equally serious, especially where it is exacerbated by a failure of demand forecasting. Among the case studies in this book, several are strong contenders for an unfortunate world record: they include the Sydney Opera House, which escalated from $A7,000,000 to $A102,000,000 in fifteen years, and Concorde, which escalated from £150,000,000–£170,000,000 to about £1,200,000,000 in fourteen years (all at current prices). One project (British Rail's high-speed link from London to the Channel tunnel, not discussed here) was reported as having doubled in cost, to £350,000,000 in only six months; it was then axed by the British government.

We shall discover some general rules about these cases, and hence some hints on their avoidance in future. First, some degree of cost escalation is in fact usual on major civil projects: the careful analysis by Merewitz[5] suggests that the average is a little over 50 per cent. But secondly, the average escalation tends to be particularly high where the project involves the development and/or application of novel technologies. Concorde applied a known technique (supersonic flight) to commercial flying with its basic problem of carrying an economic payload. BART applied system-wide automatic train control and aircraft construction techniques in a context where they had never before been used. The Sydney Opera House depended on a dome structure that was not fully understood when the design won an open competition. Though there may be an element of deliberate under-costing in some projects (especially those derived from military technology), in many others there may be no way of precisely costing the bill; the risk allowance must be very great.

This suggests certain rules. First, to avoid risk, adaptations of existing technology should be used, rather than totally new ones. (British Rail's High-speed Train and Advanced Passenger Trains, both relatively cheap and effective developments of very traditional technology, are good examples.) Secondly, cost-escalation rules for different classes of project should be developed, based on systematic analysis of actual escalation in previous cases, as was already being done by military procurement authorities, after bitter experience, in the late 1950s. And thirdly, if possible, a political commitment to preliminary estimates, which may in practice be pure guesswork, should be avoided. Lastly, planners should try to incorporate some allowance for the unforeseen factor, termed by the economist Albert Hirschman 'the Principle of the Hiding Hand': that some undercosted projects succeed unexpectedly, because of circumstances that were never considered when the original decision was taken.[6] Hirschman quotes the Troy and Albany railroad in nineteenth-century New England: tunnelled through a mountain, it escalated in cost because of inadequate geological knowledge and resultant engineering problems, but was translated almost overnight from a commercial disaster to a success when it became part of a transcontinental system after the Civil War. Planners need to develop scenarios that will incorporate these possibilities in their final process of decision.

Uncertainty in related decision areas

Many problems, which at first sight appear to fall in the UE category, at second analysis can be more precisely explained in terms of UR or UV problems. The decisions on Concorde and the third London airport – the first a positive disaster, the second a negative one – were both affected by the decisions of American aircraft manufacturers to develop a new generation of wide-bodied jets with quiet by-pass engines. These planes made Concorde seem relatively less economic, and more noisy, than had appeared in 1962. They fundamentally altered airport planning, by allowing much higher volumes of traffic to be handled by fewer planes with less noise impact. The American manufacturers – Boeing, Douglas, Lockheed – were located 6,000 or more miles from London, where the Concorde and airport decisions were being made. Yet in the case of Concorde the concept of the big jet was already understood in 1962, when it was the critical element in that decision; while in the case of the airport, there was already abundant information about the sales of the new jets. So distance does not really provide an adequate explanation even in this case.

It does so even less when the related decision units are not distant at all, but are in fact part of the same machine. One extraordinary example, not treated among the case studies in this book, is the rebuilding of Piccadilly Circus, in the heart of London. It first became a major public issue when an outcry arose over the proposed design for a large office and shopping development on one of the three main sites on the Circus, the so-called Monico site, in 1958. The proposal was 'called in' for decision by the then Minister of Housing and Local Government, and after a public inquiry conducted by Colin Buchanan (who was later to achieve greater fame as the author of the report *Traffic in Towns*) the proposal was rejected. It was decided instead to prepare a comprehensive development plan for the whole Circus. A first consultant's exercise was rejected in 1963, the year of the Buchanan report, on the ground that it did not provide enough space for traffic circulation. A second, prepared specifically to deal with this objection, was produced in 1966 but was questioned in 1967, ironically on the ground that by this time government policy had changed, and that the objective now was to restrain traffic growth in London. A development brief produced an apparently acceptable solution, but this could not be implemented because yet another government department was operating a policy of restriction on office development in central London. Then finally, when an agreed compromise was reached in 1972, the property boom had collapsed and developers had lost interest. Finally, in 1979, the Monico site is being developed and it is certain that the London Pavilion site is to begin redevelopment.

Uncertainty in value systems
However, on closer examination the UR problems in the Piccadilly Circus case do prove to turn in large measure on shifts in values. As we shall see in the case of London's motorways, the prevailing value system of the early 1960s was in favour of greater freedom for people to drive their own cars, even in central London. By the late 1960s, and subsequently, the prevailing values were in favour of restraint on traffic in central London and of better

9

public transport. Similarly, the restriction on office development arose from a new perception in the early 1960s that the regional problem was being exacerbated by the growth of service employment in London. All this suggests that it is the UV area that is the most important in understanding the problem of decision-making in uncertainty.

In some sense, indeed, shifts in values provide the final explanation of everything else: apparent UE or UR problems can all be traced finally to UV explanations. Thus population projections are reduced (UE) because the birth-rate falls, partly because of changes like abortion law reform (UR); but in turn this reflects changes in social values such as women's liberation or even pessimism about the future (UV). Economic growth falls partly because of changing expectations of businessmen (also UV). But, in a more specific sense than this, we can see from many of the case studies that UV shifts are often the direct reason for a planning disaster, especially for the negative ones, though sometimes also for the public perception of other cases as positive disasters.

Consider for instance the London motorways. They failed partly because of inadequate demand forecasts (UE) and partly because of shifts in general policy that made investment in public transport more attractive relative to investment in urban roads (UR). But the main reason was without doubt a massive shift in values and the expression of these changed values in the political arena. As we shall see, when the motorway plans were unveiled in 1965-7 both political parties, together with the media and a wide spectrum of public opinion, were publicly and enthusiastically in favour. By the time they were abandoned, in 1973, there was hardly a voice left in support. The questions must be how such an extraordinary shift comes about, and how it then communicates itself from the public (or rather a section of the public, the community activists) to the politicians, often in the face of rooted policy maintenance on the part of the professionals and bureaucrats at central and local government level. We shall later find that recent academic work in Britain and the United States provides an important set of insights into this process,[7] although only at a certain level of analysis. It can show, for instance, how activists come to exact leverage on the political process, and how the power of the policy maintainers can be bent or broken. It can draw, for instance, on Anthony Downs's concept of the Passionate Minority[8] to show how such a small group, greatly concerned about an issue in a largely apathetic world, can overcome the one-man-one-vote tyranny of the ballot box to achieve the outcome it wants. What it cannot yet do, what it has not really tried to do, is to explain the sudden quantum jumps in values which triggered off the whole process.

Consider the case of Concorde. It is now condemned because of a massive shift in values against this kind of technologically speculative measure and in favour of resource conservation and environmental protection. But when the critical Concorde decision was made in 1962, very few people publicly cared either about noise around airports or about fuel conservation; these people, like the Swede Bo Lundberg, were regarded as, if anything, slightly eccentric. Yet, in the succeeding decade, their views swept the thinking world and shifted the political spectrum. Writers like Lundberg, Schumacher and Mishan were all pleading their case in the early 1960s; but until some point later in that decade few people cared to read the message. Why did the change come when it did? How, in Donald Schon's phrase, does an idea get into 'good currency'?[9] Partly, the process may be dialectic: economic growth and technological development will hurt minorities, who will respond by fighting motorways or airports or even new aircraft. (Partly, also, there were vested interests – rival aircraft manufacturers, for instance – willing to use the support thus offered.) More widely, and indirectly, a new generation grew up amidst affluence, and some of it did not like what it saw. Then, the energy crisis of the early 1970s – artificial and short-lived as it was – appeared for many people to confirm the idea, suggested by the Club of Rome,[10] that this path of development led only to destruction. Such explanations are almost trite. Behind them, the suddenness of the value shift perhaps denies any tidy, rational explanation. It lies at the heart of our reason for considering certain decisions as planning disasters.

Overview

I do not want to seem to promise more than this book can deliver. There will be no grand overarching model which will explain all previous disasters and guarantee how to avoid new ones. The object is to begin an exploration, not to end one. By applying different kinds of explanatory theory, we may gain an eclectic kind of understanding, which will then suggest some rules of thumb that future planners may use in their efforts to avoid, or at least minimize, their mistakes. If the book can go some way in that direction, then it will have achieved its modest purpose.

So we shall now let the case studies tell their own tales. Here, theory will be kept to a minimum, although at the end of each chapter there will be an attempt to sum up the main lessons. But for the most part, these stories are the raw material for the latter half of the book.

PART ONE

CASE STUDIES

London's Third Airport

The main point about London's third airport is that, like Thurber's unicorn, it does not exist. True, scattered across the face of England are no less than seventy-eight sites once considered in 1970 by a government commission of inquiry for the role. One, Cublington in Buckinghamshire, was the final choice of all but one of its members. Another, Maplin on the North Sea coast of Essex, was resolutely supported by that last member and was finally picked by the government of the day, in 1971. Yet another, dropped by the commission after only seven months' work, had been proposed by an expert committee and then accepted by the government, in 1967, before public outcry forced a reversal. That site, Stansted in Essex, is a recurrent theme of this chapter. For many believe and fear that in the end, despite everything, it will become London's third airport almost imperceptibly.

Still in 1979 there is no third airport. After three sites have been accepted by government and later abandoned, after the expenditure of millions of pounds on inquiries and commissions, government policy is to wait and see. The story of the third London airport is an extraordinary history of policy reversals, last-minute abandonments, contradictions and inconsistencies in forecasts. It has all the ingredients of a great planning disaster.

To understand the story, a first essential is to follow it as contemporaries saw it, but then to use the benefit of hindsight. It is a long and tortuous history, difficult to follow in detail – after the biggest inquiry, by the Roskill Commission in 1968–71, someone unkindly said that the documentation, suitably pulped and compressed, could provide all the material needed for the runways. But there is one essential clue to understanding: throughout the controversy there has been an intimate and sometimes confusing relationship between two aspects, *the timing of the need* and *the size and location of the airport*. As estimates of timing have changed, sometimes radically and suddenly, so has the perception of the right solution – a theme to which we shall return.

THE BEGINNINGS

The story really begins in 1943, in the middle of World War Two. For at that point the government decided to build a new heavy military transport airfield at a site called Heath Row, fifteen miles west of London on the edge of the built-up area, where, as long ago as 1931, the Fairey Aviation company had laid out a small grass field. From the start, this new site was designed for conversion to peacetime use. For it was evident that London's major airport between the two world wars, at Croydon, was too small and too constrained by suburban development on all sides to serve the needs of expanding air traffic. In fact work took longer than expected – thus setting an unfortunate precedent for the whole subsequent history of London airport planning – and London Heathrow had its first flight on 1 January 1946, opening officially as London Airport on 25 February.

Heathrow had some obvious advantages. It was close to central London. It had one of the few really good road connections towards the centre (the six-lane Great West Road, or Brentford–Hounslow bypass, opened in the 1920s) and already preliminary work had begun on an extension inwards to central London, a project not fully completed until the 1970s. The land was almost perfectly flat and meteorological conditions were reasonably good. But the airport took several square miles of what was left of some of the best agricultural soil in all Britain: the market gardening lands on the Taplow terrace gravels, whose loss to suburban development the geographer Dudley Stamp had bemoaned in the 1930s.[2] And, perhaps even more important, because of the prevailing westerly winds it was clear that the main approach paths would be directly over west London. Yet the Minister Lord Winster said, when it opened, that a main consideration in its choice was that it would cause the minimum of disturbance to householders.[3] It was clear that no one at the time, including Patrick Abercrombie when he prepared his *Greater London Plan* in 1944, had any appreciation of the potential noise problem in the jet age, even though Abercrombie himself must have heard the first jet aircraft overhead as he finalized his report.[4]

Traffic at Heathrow built up rapidly as expected, and even by the late 1940s the government had to contemplate a second airport to relieve it at peak periods. There were two leading candidates. One, Gatwick, had opened as long ago as 1930; twenty-seven miles south of central London on the main Brighton road and railway, it had been used as a bad-weather relief for Croydon in the 1930s. It was taken over in 1945 by the government, who first announced that it would not develop it, then that it would, then again that it would not – this last in 1949. The other candidate, Stansted in Essex, some thirty-four miles north-east of central London, had been built during World War Two as an American air base and was a military airfield until 1949, when the Air Ministry sold it to the Ministry of Civil Aviation with the firm understanding that it would be London's second airport.[5]

Ironically, at this point the Cold War intervened. American air strength built up rapidly in East Anglia, since this was the optimal location within Britain for penetrating deep into the Continent. In consequence Stansted lost its potential role, for it would have presented difficult air traffic control problems. So the government, in a White Paper of July 1953, proposed that Gatwick should become the second airport – mainly, it appears, at the peak season – with Blackbushe in Hampshire acting as a reserve. A quick public inquiry followed; it had very limited terms of reference, and the inspector refused to accept evidence on the possibility of other sites, so, despite some local protest, expansion at Gatwick was approved in a government statement of October

Figure 1: London Airports.

1954.[6] Blackbushe closed in 1960, and therefore the overspill from Heathrow became concentrated on Gatwick.

Like Heathrow, Gatwick was far from optimally sited. True, it was on the flat lands of the Sussex Weald, and it had a good direct train service to Victoria. But it was too close to built-up areas, and as early as 1947 the government had determined to build a new town at nearby Crawley. Additionally, the land to the north and west, especially around Leith Hill, was, and is, a traditional pleasure-ground for Londoners. It is ironic to think that, had either site been evaluated by the rigorous criteria of the 1960s or 1970s there is little chance that it would have passed the test.

Gatwick in the 1950s, as at the end of the 1970s, was a one-runway airport. But the possibility always existed of giving it a second runway, thus making it eventually as important as Heathrow. The government in 1953 had given certain pledges that Gatwick would not be developed to its fullest extent, but a House of Commons subcommittee in 1960 found officials evasive on this question. This was significant, because by then the question of a third airport was emerging. The committee members were worried that in due course Stansted might develop on the Gatwick pattern, but despite pressure the Ministry of Aviation officials refused to be drawn: they said that they continually looked ahead as far as they could, but that they could not see indefinitely ahead and they must avoid costly error. The committee, fearing that Stansted might become the third airport by stealth, condemned Ministry of Aviation experts for indecision and inactivity. David McKie, commenting on this episode, concludes that even then officials had determined on a strategy: a quick decision would be taken in 1965, at a time when the need for the third airport was so manifest that Stansted would be the only choice.[7] In view of the history of the late 1970s, this is particularly significant.

The subcommittee recommended that an early decision should be taken in principle on whether Stansted should become London's third airport.[8] In response, the government in November 1961 set up an inter-departmental – that is, purely official –

Table 1

THIRD LONDON AIRPORT: CHRONOLOGY

January 1946	Heathrow opens for traffic.
July 1953	White Paper (Cmd. 8902) confirms Heathrow as first airport, Gatwick as second with Blackbushe supplementing it; Stansted in reserve.
June 1963	Inter-departmental committee report proposes Stansted as third airport.
December 1965 } February 1966	Public inquiry on Stansted proposal.
May 1966	Inspector's report on inquiry (not then published) finds Stansted case non-proven, recommends look at alternatives.
May 1967	White Paper (Cmnd. 3259) announces government intention to proceed with Stansted; Inspector's report made public for the first time.
February 1968	Government announces independent commission into third airport timing and location.
May 1968 December 1970 }	Roskill Commission inquiry.
January 1971	Roskill Commission report recommends third airport at Cublington, Buckinghamshire.
April 1971	Government announces that airport will be built at Maplin, Essex.
August 1973	Maplin Development Act establishes Development Authority.
July 1974	Labour government announces abandonment of Maplin project; publishes *Maplin: Review of Airport Project*.
November 1975/ } June 1976	Government consultation document *Airport Strategy for Great Britain* suggests alternative scenarios precluding Maplin.
February 1978	White Paper Airports Policy (Cmnd. 7084) re-affirms Maplin.
August 1978	Setting-up of Advisory Committee on Airports Policy.

committee to consider requirements for a third London airport, including timing and location, the two key phrases that were afterwards to recur. Significantly, of its fifteen members, eight were officials from the Ministry of Aviation, five others represented air traffic in one way or another, one represented ground transport, and there was a sole representative from the planning division of the Ministry of Housing and Local Government. (At this time planning was at a low ebb both within government generally and within the Ministry.) It was perhaps small wonder that when the committee reported to the Minister of Aviation, Julian Amery, in June 1963 they found that Heathrow and Gatwick, even with two runways at the latter, would be unable to handle all London's air traffic from about 1973; that a third airport to relieve them should be built on the Heathrow model with two parallel and independent runways; and that, of a dozen sites examined, Stansted seemed to be the only suitable one.[9] The committee's forecasts are difficult to compare with those made in subsequent inquiries, because they are mainly in terms of SBR (Standard Busy Rate – the hourly rate of traffic movement, passengers or aircraft, reached or exceeded on thirty occasions during the summer). On this basis they calculated that Heathrow would run out of capacity by 1971; Heathrow and Gatwick considered together would have an overspill problem by 1973. The committee also gave forecasts down to 1970 in terms of the conventional measures (air traffic movements and passengers) used by later forecasters. They are shown in Table 2 but they cannot reliably be projected beyond 1970 because they do not have a simple linear relationship to the SBR forecasts. For the same reason it is difficult to reconstruct the Committee's estimate of airport capacity in conventional terms (Table 3), except that Heathrow was predicted to overspill after 1970, when it was forecast to have 15,000,000 passengers (229,000 air traffic movements) a year. (Heathrow in 1976 actually carried 23,200,000 passengers.) Gatwick was estimated to overspill in 1980, even with two runways; a 'guesstimate' is that it might carry about 3,200,000 passengers then. (In 1976, with one runway, it carried 5,700,000.) The two airports together would have an overspill

Table 2

LONDON AIRPORTS: TRAFFIC FORECASTS 1963–79

(1) *Air Traffic Movements* (000s)

		1965	1970	1975	1980	1985	19
Inter-dept. Committee 1963		210	279	?	?	?	
White Paper 1967	Lower		277	327	327	?	
	Middle	221	283	353	430		
	Upper		302	402	525	?	
Roskill Commission 1971		225	347	392	470	545	
Maplin review 1973 (No Tunnel)	Low	225	347				3
	Assessment						4
	High						5
Consultation documents 1975	Low						
	High						5
White Paper 1978							

(2) *Passengers* (Mill.)

		1965	1970	1975	1980	1985	19
Inter-dept. Committee 1963		11.4	17.4	?	?	?	
White Paper 1967	Lower		18.4	25.6	33.0	?	
	Middle	11.9	19.3	29.6	43.6	?	
	Upper		21.7	37.8	63.7	?	
Roskill Commission 1971		12.7	22.0	36.1	56.6*	82.7	
Maplin review 1974 (No Tunnel)	Low	12.7	22.0		58.1*		78
	Assessment				62.0*		89
	High				75.8*		11.
Consultation documents 1975	Low	12.7	22.0		33.9*	47.7*	6?
	High				46.2*	72.8*	10(
White Paper 1978	Low	12.7	22.0	28.8	36.7	51.1	6?
	High				41.9	63.5	8

Sources: Documents listed
*Interpolated

Table 3

LONDON AIRPORTS: ESTIMATED CAPACITY 1963–78

	Heathrow			Gatwick			London Airport system without third airport		
	Air traffic movements 000	Passengers mill.	Saturation Date	Air traffic movements 000	Passengers mill.	Saturation Date	Air movements traffic 000	Passengers mill.	Saturation Date
Inter-dept. Committee 1963	229+	15+	1971	?67	?3	1980	?315*	?20*	1973*
White Paper 1967 { Lower		16.3	1970				354	30	1978
Middle		15.7	1969		?6.6	1972–4	353	30	1975
Upper		15.2	1968				359	30	1973
Roskill Commission 1971	314			110			478	61	1981
Maplin review 1975	338	38–53	1983–1990	168	16–25		620	61–104	After 1990
Consultation documents 1975/6	308	38–53		168	16–25	1983–90	590	50–104	1988–90
White Paper 1978	275	38		160	25		555	72	1990 or after

Sources: Documents listed.   * Heathrow + Gatwick only

by 1973, at which point – again on a very rough estimate from SBR – they would have rather less than 20,000,000 passengers; in actuality, they had 28,900,000 passengers by 1976. So the main conclusion – an urgent need for the third airport in 1973 – was based on a hopeless underestimate of both Heathrow's and Gatwick's capacity. The main reason was a failure to appreciate the increased size and capacity of planes (a point stressed by the consultants Halcrow and Partners in their evidence for the County Councils at the Stansted inquiry).

The committee went on to forecast that by 1980 the overspill problem would demand two runways at the new airport. But, because of air traffic control problems, any airport within reasonable distance of London (50 miles) could not operate planes in all directions. Even with this constraint, air traffic control would make it impossible to site the third airport south of London, or north-west of London (the area the Roskill Commission chose, after a more detailed investigation of the problem, in 1971). This, plus ground access constraints – the requirement that the site be within one hour of central London by rail or road – narrowed the choice to about a dozen sites east and west of London. To the west, there was no site with the desired capacity within an hour's ride. To the east, Stansted, though not perfect, in the committee's words, seemed the only possible site. It satisfied air traffic control constraints. It was an operational airport with a 10,000-foot runway. Parallel runways could be laid, and so it was suggested that the noise problem should not be severe. It was reasonably close to London, and with completion of the planned MII would have good access. True, it could not operate omnidirectionally, it would interfere somewhat with East Anglian military flying and it would take a lot of good agricultural land, but these disadvantages were outweighed by its merits. Therefore, the committee predictably concluded, Stansted should be developed by the early 1970s to become, eventually, a two-runway airport with a similar level and type of traffic to Heathrow's.

Equally predictably, the recommendation met with a storm of local protest. When the public inquiry into Stansted development opened in Chelmsford in December 1965 – itself a concession by the government in the face of political pressure, for as a development within existing airport limits it did not demand a statutory inquiry at all – the North West Essex and Herts Preservation Association had raised more than £23,500 from 13,000 people to produce an excellently reasoned technically competent counter-case. It was skilfully based not on opposition to the Stansted development *per se*, but on the need for a prior independent inquiry into a national airport policy, which was demonstrably lacking. The Essex County Council was at first resigned to the Stansted proposal, but later it agreed to appoint independent consultants, who reported that before a firm conclusion could be reached a more detailed study would be needed. The evidence produced by the consultants at the inquiry called for a comprehensive cost–benefit analysis such as was used with major World Bank proposals, for instance. The local protestors naturally concentrated on the environmental impact.

The inquiry proved uncomfortable for the government. Under examination, officials were found to be shaky on critical points, such as whether Stansted really fell within the critical one-hour travel time to central London. The inquiry ended in February 1966 and the inspector, Mr G.D. Blake, reported to the President of the Board of Trade by the end of May. But the report was not published for a whole year, and only then did the reason for delay become apparent. For the inspector concluded that the Stansted proposal succeeded only on the ground of air traffic control. On a series of other criteria, there were strong arguments against it. On planning, the evidence was that Stansted was not the right place for a traffic focus of this kind and the urban development that would go with it. On access, the proposals would be unacceptable to passengers and airlines. On noise, restrictions would have to be imposed that would materially restrict full operation. On amenity, noise and traffic nuisance would greatly change the character of the neighbourhood and cause great local resentment. Lastly, the scheme would take many thousands of acres of good agricultural land. He concluded: 'It would be a calamity for the neighbourhood if a major airport were placed at Stansted. Such a decision could only be justified by national necessity. Necessity was not proved by evidence at this inquiry.'[10] He therefore recommended that: 'a review of the whole problem should be undertaken by a committee equally interested in traffic in the air, traffic on the ground, regional planning and national planning'.[11]

This suggested either an independent commission or yet another government review. But the government was against an independent inquiry, both on the ground of urgency and because it thought that all the facts had been fully explored. Accordingly it set in train its own review, covering aviation, surface transport, planning, economics and agriculture. The findings were published in a government White Paper in May 1967, when the inspector's report was also released to the public.

With total predictability, the White Paper confirmed that the government was sticking to the Stansted decision. One main reason, as before, was the belief that a third airport was urgently necessary. Once again, the government had gone through the forecasting exercise, this time using upper and lower limits as well as a 'most likely' forecast, and incorporating new factors like the advent of the 'jumbo' jets then on the drawing-boards. This (Tables 2 and 3) again showed that Heathrow would have an overspill problem by 1970 and Gatwick between 1974 and 1976, depending on whether or not it got a second runway. In practice it might not be possible to stretch capacity to the limit, so there was a need to have a new airport by the middle of the 1970s, and possibly earlier than that. The White Paper gave short shrift to the notion, canvassed by the inspector, that this date might be pushed back by vigorous development of provincial airports: too much of the total demand was concentrated in the south east, it concluded, for this policy to have much impact.

So an airport was needed. The question was whether there was a better alternative than Stansted. The review looked at a series of possible sites in the sector north, east and west of London, including locations as far afield as Ferrybridge in Yorkshire and Castle Donington in Leicestershire, but also Foulness, near Southend, on the Essex coast. This was important because Foulness was already emerging at the Chelmsford inquiry as the favoured alternative site. Nevertheless the review concluded against all the alternatives, including Foulness, on the grounds of the difficulty of removing the army firing range at Shoebury-ness, the closure of Southend Airport, and not least the cost, then estimated at £15,000,000 or more. It also rejected Thurleigh near Bedford, chiefly on the ground of conflict with military operations. Both Foulness and Thurleigh were to reappear on the Roskill Commission's short list of sites.

So, the White Paper concluded, Stansted remained the first choice. As the inspector had recognized, it was satisfactory in terms of air traffic control; the flat terrain meant low construction costs; road and rail access were satisfactory (though seventy minutes was now the quoted time); noise was not as serious as the inspector had suggested. Agricultural land would be a serious loss, but so it would be at alternative sites. Regional planning was the strongest objection since the airport would invade one of the biggest wedges of green land close to London; but on balance this was outweighed by Stansted's advantages. Therefore the British Airports Authority, which by then had acquired Stansted (as well as Heathrow and Gatwick) from the Ministry, should go ahead with a plan for major development, which would require planning permission in the normal way.

The White Paper released a new storm. It was the subject of an impassioned Commons debate on 29 June 1967. This was strongly influenced by the publication a few days before of *The Case for Reappraisal*, issued by a Stansted Working Party composed of prominent local people, including MPs. The basic analysis came from the Essex Deputy Clerk and his officers. Apart from questioning many of the technical judgements in the White Paper, it raised an important constitutional point: had the Chelmsford inquiry been a normal one under the rules for planning inquiries, it would have had to be reopened because new facts had been introduced and the proposal was now different, since in the White Paper it had been said that the airport should be capable of expansion to a four-runway basis, twice as large as Heathrow. Further, there was a suspicion that the same officials who had appeared for the inquiry in support of Stansted had actually conducted the subsequent review.[12] Indeed, Essex County Council challenged the government on these grounds in the High Court, but lost because the inquiry was a non-statutory one.

The Cabinet held its position in June, but then new and damaging evidence appeared. In July a letter appeared in *The Times* from J.W.S. Brancker, the technical assessor to the inspector at the Chelmsford inquiry, pointing to the noise aspect. In October he published a fuller account, *The Stansted Black Book*, through the local Preservation Association.[13] It challenged the White Paper on both technical and constitutional grounds, and concluded:

> ... one of the more disconcerting aspects of the White Paper is that it has doubled the potential size of the project without giving very much weight to the possible effects on such things as noise, access, industrial development, land required, etc. ... the Government seems to have retreated from the minimum conditions which it imposed in the first instance and on which the choice of Stansted was predicted. ... As a public document, the White Paper fails to give the impression of being impartial ... until alternative solutions have been examined in depth, and comparative costs are available, I cannot feel the case is proven.[14]

This was accompanied by a damning series of quotations, in which the association made it clear that it had received repeated ministerial assurances that the government would not overrule its inspector's recommendation on Stansted.[15]

By this time, a critical change had occurred in government ranks. Douglas Jay, who had defended the Stansted choice, resigned as President of the Board of Trade at the end of August 1967, and was replaced by Anthony Crosland. Crosland was vitally concerned with the emerging theme of quality of the environment. He also strongly believed in systematic economic evaluation through cost–benefit analysis, which had been conspicuously lacking in the government review. Even so, he might not have pushed the Cabinet to reverse its decision. But in November the Council on Tribunals took the unprecedented step of calling for an entirely new inquiry, on the ground that the government was by then proposing a realignment of the runways. Whether or not this was a tactical device prompted by Crosland and/or Richard Crossman, as some suspected, it had the desired effect, as did a highly critical Lords debate early in December 1967. In February 1968, Crosland announced that a new independent inquiry into the third London airport would take place.[16] This was precisely the inquiry for which the objectors had asked.

THE ROSKILL COMMISSION INQUIRY

The inquiry by the Commission on the Third London Airport, under the chairmanship of the Hon. Mr Justice Roskill, was surely the most exhaustive of its kind ever held, and perhaps ever likely to be held. (Indeed, for sheer scale only the Greater London Development Plan, shortly afterwards, would begin to compete.) It took over two and a half years, from May 1968 to December 1970, and cost over £1,000,000 in direct costs plus an unknown amount spent by those who appeared at it. However what distinguished it was not merely its scale, but, even more, its method. Even its most severe critics (such as Professor Peter Self) had to admit that it was a model of its kind.[17] It represents a high-water mark of a certain kind of rational comprehensive planning based on the attempt to qualify. So it is particularly interesting to look at the methodology, to help understand both why the commission reached the conclusion it did, and why then the government rejected a large part of it.

The commission started by drawing up a short list of sites for comparison. In this it was determined to keep a completely open mind – unfettered, as it said in its final report, by the past. It started with a long list of seventy-eight sites, and within seven months it had narrowed the choice down to four, upon which the whole of the rest of the work was concentrated. These were Thurleigh near Bedford, Cublington in Buckinghamshire, Nuthampstead in northern Hertfordshire, and Foulness, or, as it later became known, Maplin. Conspicuously, Stansted was missing, and in its final report the commission explained why. It was inferior to Nuthampstead, a site about ten miles to the north-west, in terms of air traffic control, of noise impact on urban areas, and of surface access. Therefore, logically, it had to go. On Foulness, however the commission finally admitted a failure of logic: it ranked best on noise, defence and air traffic control, but it was expensive to prepare and it involved very high surface-access costs. So it finally went in, though overall it ranked thirteenth out of fifteen: four places, ironically, behind Stansted. The reason was that it seemed to offer a particularly novel solution, and the commission thought it should be tested.

Logically, as with all previous (and subsequent) inquiries, the Roskill Commission had to look at the timing of the need. Here, some argued that they were constrained by their terms of reference, which asked them to 'inquire into the timing of the need for a four-runway airport to cater for the growth of traffic at existing airports serving the London area'. In other words, these critics argued, they were precluded from looking at the national airports policy and the possibility of large-scale diversion to provincial airports. But, in view of the fact that the commission's subsequent traffic model ranged as far as Manchester, this is perhaps hardly fair. Impressed from the start by the weaknesses of earlier forecasting efforts, the commission asked its research staff to make their own, as well as using those of the British Airports Authority, the Civil Aviation Authority and others. It had a problem with Gatwick, where it had to make alternative assumptions – one with a second runway, one without it. It concluded that there was no reason to open a third airport before traffic growth made it necessary, and it assumed that there would be no artificial control over the growth of traffic at Heathrow or Gatwick (apart from the runway decision at the latter). It concluded also that Heathrow, Gatwick with one runway, Stansted and Luton could together accommodate about 475,000 air movements by the end of the 1970s, and on balance it thought that this figure would be exceeded by demand in 1980 or 1981. Significantly in view of later events, it emphasized that expedients at existing airports would not greatly modify this: even a second Gatwick runway would postpone the need for the new airport by about two years.[18]

Table 4 LONDON THIRD AIRPORT SITES: SUMMARY COST/BENEFIT ANALYSIS

Differences from lowest-cost site (£ million discounted to 1982)

	Cublington		Foulness		Nuthamp-stead		Thurleigh	
	High time values	Low time values	High time values	Low time values	High time values	Low time values	High time values	Low time values
Row 1 Airport construction	18		32		14		0	
2 Extension of Luton	0		18		0		0	
3 Airport services	23	22	0	0	17	17	7	7
4 Meteorology	5		0		2		1	
5 Airspace movements	0	0	7	5	35	31	30	26
6 Passenger user costs	0	0	207	167	41	35	39	22
7 Freight user costs	0		14		5		1	
8 Road capital	0		4		4		5	
9 Rail capital	3		26		12		0	
10 Air safety	0		2		0		0	
11 Defence	29		0		5		61	
12 Public scientific establishments	1		0		21		27	
13 Private airfields	7		0		13		15	
14 Residential conditions (noise, off-site)	13		0		62		5	
15 Residential conditions (on site)	11		0		8		6	
16 Luton noise costs	0		11		0		0	
17 Schools, hospitals and public authority buildings (including noise)	7		0		11		9	
18 Agriculture	0		4		9		3	
19 Commerce and industry (including noise)	0		2		1		2	
20 Recreation (including noise)	13		0		7		7	
Aggregate of inter-site differences (costed items only) high and low time values	0	0	197	156	137	128	88	68

Source: GB Commission on the Third London Airport, *Report*, p. 119.

Roskill's forecasts of demand and capacity are set out in Tables 2 and 3, where they can be compared with earlier and later estimates. In so far as direct comparison is possible, they show a distinct increase on earlier forecasts in both passenger numbers and air traffic movements. But on the other hand they also posit a bigger ultimate capacity both at Heathrow, and, especially, at Gatwick (which was the more remarkable as this assumed only one runway against two earlier). So the total effect is to put back the date of opening of the third airport from the early to mid-1970s, as commonly assumed in earlier studies, to the start of the 1980s.

These basic studies done, the commission could concentrate on its main task of comparison and evaluation of the four sites. This was done on a far more elaborate scale than ever previously considered. The aim from the start was to quantify advantages and disadvantages by the use of cost–benefit analysis, then a relatively new tool in planning, which had been used with some success for new roads and new public transport facilities such as London's Underground Victoria Line. The commission decided to use the method because it saw no other way of avoiding arbitrary and subjective judgements.

This analysis was without doubt the largest and most complex of its kind ever attempted anywhere. For it involved not merely computing some of the principal direct impacts of the airport (on capital costs or travellers' time, for instance), but also estimating indirect impacts, such as urban development and its effects on agricultural land. For this last aspect, indeed, special subconsultants had to be employed to produce what were in effect subregional plans of the area around each of the four short-listed sites. These, together with the overall cost–benefit analysis by the commission's research team, were first published early in 1970 and were subject to extraordinarily detailed critical examination in the fifth and final stage of the commission's work, the public hearings in the spring and summer of 1970. Modified, but only in detail, they provided the essential basis of the commission's final evaluation. They are expressed in terms of differences in costs as compared with the cheapest site, for, as the commission argued in its final report, in an inter-site comparison the absolute money values are irrelevant. Overall, Cublington emerged as the best site from the analysis, so the other three sites were compared with it. Thurleigh, the next best, was £68,000,000 to £88,000,000 more expensive to the community, in terms of 1982 values. Nut-hampstead, the next best, was £128,000,000–137,000,000 dearer than Cublington. And the most expensive of all was Foulness, which was between £156,000,000 and £197,000,000 more costly than Cublington in real resource terms to the community (Table 4).

Table 4 makes it clear that the differences are dominated by a few items. By far the most important of these is passenger-user costs, which, for instance, represent £167,000,000 to £207,000,000 of the difference between Cublington and Foulness, or more than the overall difference (meaning that on other aspects, Foulness was on balance better than Cublington). Because of this, the commission's research team had performed elaborate exercises to see what would happen if certain critical assumptions, particularly on the value of time, were changed. It was argued, for instance, that leisure travellers put a very low (or nil) valuation on their time, and that this should be reflected in the analysis. The research team's sensitivity analysis showed that no amount of variation could alter the substantial differences between the sites, which reflected real differences in money costs and time valuation. Foulness emerged as the worst site overall fundamentally because it was the farthest from London (and from most of the rest of the population of England); conversely, Cublington emerged as best because it was well sited on the London–Birmingham axis. These access costs far outweighed differences in construction costs – where the most expensive site, Foulness on the drained Essex marshes, emerged as only £32,000,000 more expensive than Thurleigh, the cheapest on this criterion.

The cost–benefit analysis attracted an enormous volume of critical comment. One main line of argument was that it omitted some important items, either in whole or in part. The most important were planning considerations. Noise and agricultural land loss could be measured in money terms; the loss of landscape and rural amenity could also be measured, through house prices, but that would not allow for the losses to non-residents. Local employment benefits were similarly ignored. A second argument was that the valuations themselves were wrong, especially those concerning the value of time. The commission finally sought to deal with this by giving a range of values, from £1.46 to £2.58 an hour for business travel and from 11½p to 34½p an hour for leisure travel. There was also much argument about the valuation of noise, which was made through house prices and compensation costs. Finally, there was criticism that the use of money in the analysis was itself distorting, because a sum of money meant different things to different people: £1 meant more to a poor person than to a rich one, so some form of weighting should be used. On this point the commission refused to produce a formula, declaring instead that this was yet another matter to be included in the final judgement.

In that judgement, therefore, the commission accepted that the cost-benefit analysis could never include all the factors relevant to the decision. But it could provide a framework within which all the evidence could be brought together and weighed. In fact, the final verdict of the majority of the commissioners could be fairly described as cost-benefit analysis modified by judgement. It involved weighing advantages and disadvantages, through a carefully balanced judgement process. The needs of the air traveller had to be balanced against the hardship and disadvantage to those living under the flight paths. Thus the commission deliberately refused to set planning considerations as some kind of absolute constraint.

This balanced judgement led the commission to dismiss Nuthampstead straight away: though it had good access and was cheap to construct, it was worst for noise and general planning considerations and it would mean substantial agricultural land losses. Foulness (the site the commission admitted was by far the most popular among witnesses) was good for airport services, air traffic control and (surprisingly, in view of the earlier arguments about the Shoeburyness ranges) defence. It was outstandingly good on the noise criterion, but this would be cancelled out by extra traffic at Luton. On balance it was also good on planning grounds. But the commission also stressed that there were disadvantages here too: the destruction of wild life and coastline, as well as the danger of overcrowding in the southern peninsula, which the associated urban development would bring. Further, it would involve very heavy and disruptive provision of extra surface access to London. And not only would it lead to increased traffic at Luton, but because of its inaccessibility compared with the other sites it would lead to more traffic also at Manchester and Birmingham airports, with resulting environmental damage. The commission concluded that though Foulness had an advantage on planning grounds, it was by no means as big as many supposed. And this had to be weighed against its clear disadvantages: its high cost of construction, and above all its inaccessibility. Because it would attract less traffic than the other sites, there was a danger that it would never produce an adequate return on capital, and would thus be a liability to the taxpayer. However the reckoning was done, users of the airport would overall pay a heavy financial penalty.

The commission majority therefore repeated its earlier argument:

A third London airport must be able to succeed as an airport. To this end, it must meet the needs of those whom it is designed to serve. But it could succeed as an airport and yet fail in some wider social purpose. This in essence is the case made against an airport at Cublington or Thurleigh. Unfortunately the converse is not equally true. An airport cannot serve any social purpose unless it first succeeds as an airport.[19]

Because there was too great a danger that Foulness would fail as an airport, the commission rejected it. It was therefore left with Cublington and Thurleigh, two inland sites with finely balanced advantages and disadvantages. They found that Cublington was better for access and for defence. It was rather worse for planning and environment, though both imposed a burden on those living in their local areas. Cublington made a smaller claim on the nation's resources; it also offered a better prospect of reducing the noise burden around Heathrow. Therefore, despite the undoubted environmental disadvantages, the commissioners plumped for Cublington.

They did so with one exception. Almost at the very end of their work, Professor Colin Buchanan announced that he could not accept the choice of Cublington. To the surprise of his fellow commissioners, he then announced that he could not accept the rest of the report either, except for a small section on the timing of the need. He produced instead an eleven-page note of dissent. It makes an extraordinary contrast to the main report. Against their cool, logical, detached and carefully measured analysis, he contraposes a passionate, highly emotional personal testament. He explains how, almost from the start, he had developed a deep distrust of the cost-benefit approach used by the commission and its research team. He takes his stand on a principle that good planning considerations must be absolutely paramount, an approach which had been specifically rejected by the rest of the commission.[20] A central planning principle, he argues, has been the preservation of open rural background around London. A new airport in that open area would involve enormous destruction of its character and threaten the whole principle. Finally, three of the four sites are there; only Foulness is not.

Behind the sanctity of planning principles, however, lies a deeper consideration, which Buchanan makes explicit. It is that preservation of the national heritage, and in particular its traditional landscapes, is a sacred trust for present and future generations.

I see many examples of the way present day life has been enriched as a result of decisions taken years ago with sure-sighted anticipation of our needs; I see other cases where the exercise of but a little foresight would have prevented losses over which we today can merely wring our hands. Human nature does not change so quickly that it is impossible or even difficult to distinguish the things that successive generations commonly find of value. I have no doubt that the things I find of interest in the open background of London are things that will interest many generations to come. I am profoundly certain that they are *good* things.[21]

Buchanan thus took issue with his colleagues on a central issue of principle. He concluded that:

it would be nothing less than an environmental disaster if the airport were to be built at any of the inland sites, but nowhere more serious than at Cublington where it would lie athwart the critically important belt of open country between London and Birmingham.[22]

He confessed he still doubted the cost-benefit analysis on the grounds of the basis of the costings – which he did not fully understand – as well as the way they were aggregated; but above all, he felt that any such analysis must be constrained by planning considerations. So he remained adamant that Foulness was the only acceptable site.

The result was perhaps predictable. Immediately on publication of the report, the split within the commission was replicated in the wider reading (and thinking) public. The critical difference was that the Buchanan view was no longer in a minority. All those who felt intuitively, as he did, that Cublington would be an 'environmental disaster' naturally turned to his testimony for support.

One group especially did so. The Roskill Commission had been right when it predicted that its recommendation would be received with abhorrence by the majority of those living in the Cublington area. Immediately after publication the Wing Resistance Association was formed. It modelled its campaign on the highly successful one at Stansted and it did so with resources supplied by some very affluent residents. It was estimated that the Roskill Commission spent a million pounds to produce its recommendation and the Wing Resistance Association spent three quarters of a million trying to overturn it.

Again, perhaps as expected, they succeeded. The forces of economic reason may have declared for Cublington, but the forces of environmental emotion were in favour only of Foulness, and they proved far stronger both in number and in intensity. The weight of the planning profession, of the media, of general middle-class public opinion as reflected in letters to *The Times*, and finally of MPs, shared the views of Buchanan:

Time and again since the end of Stage V, I have recalled Mr Niall MacDermot's words in his closing address when he said that anyone standing on one of the famous vantage points of the Chilterns and looking out over the Vale of Aylesbury would say, 'It simply is unthinkable that an airport and all it implies should be brought here.'[23]

In April 1971 John Davies, President of the Board of Trade, told the House of Commons that the third London airport would be built at Maplin Sands (or Foulness) in Essex.

THE RETREAT FROM MAPLIN

The government meant what it said. It was convinced by the Roskill argument that the new airport would be needed very early in the 1980s, and it was conscious that the complex problem of draining the marshes at Maplin involved an abnormal lead time. In the parliamentary session 1972–3 it introduced a Maplin Development Bill, which duly became law. It established a Maplin Development Authority charged with reclaiming and managing the land at Maplin and making land available not merely for an airport, but for an associated seaport. While this was passing through parliament, in July 1973, the government published two consultation documents: one on the choice of the surface access corridor to carry new rail and road routes from London to the new airport complex, the other on a proposed designation area for the new town that would be needed to house airport and associated workers.[24]

Already, however, opposition to the Maplin proposal – barely audible at the time of the government's 1971 decision – was building up. Even at the time of the Roskill inquiry and the subsequent controversy over its finding, a local group, the Defenders of Essex, led by a local politician, Derek Wood, had sedulously fought the idea of a Maplin airport. Its voice had been drowned in the furore over Cublington. But now it began to be heard, and local Essex and Kent MPs, mainly conservationist, joined the chorus.

The 1973 consultation documents helped, for they showed the potential impact of Maplin outside the immediate airport-seaport boundaries. The new town would eventually cover over eighty-two square miles and would house 600,000 people. The surface access to the airport might need a band some hundred yards in width and over thirty miles long, with inevitable impact on local communities. Of course, similar provision would have been needed for the other Roskill sites. The point was that the image of the unique 'environmental airport', with minimal impact on quality of environment or on the lives of local people, began to fade.[25] At the same time the estimated cost rose to £825,000,000, a greater sum than the British share of Concorde, and a feeling, perpetuated in the title of Peter Bromhead's book, began to develop that here was yet another example of a prestigious white elephant.[26]

One group of people who undoubtedly thought this was the Roskill majority and those who had accepted their arguments – especially those with a concern for the economics of the case. They included influential people both inside and outside government. Perhaps the most influential of all was Anthony Crossland, who as President of the Board of Trade had been mainly responsible for the creation of the Roskill Commission in 1968. He was particularly concerned about the potential waste of national resources, which could be put to better uses. As early as March 1971, in a Commons debate two months before the announcement that Maplin would be the site, he was arguing for a strategy that would maximize the use of existing airports – plus, perhaps, the development of a new two-runway airport, possibly at Cublington. His opposition moved the Labour Party almost perceptibly; without formal debate, they adopted the position that Maplin was a Tory prestige project, using resources that would be better employed on programmes of social relevance.[27]

So, by the start of 1974, there was both a local political opposition and a national climate of opinion turning against Maplin. The oil crisis of 1973–4 undoubtedly helped this by creating a feeling that a new age of austerity was dawning, in which it made no sense to provide for massive increases in mobility. Irrational as this may have been, it did have an important psychological impact. In February 1974, the incoming Labour government immediately announced a review of the Maplin project. In July 1974 it published the review and immediately cancelled the project, dissolving the Maplin Development Corporation.

The Maplin review bore all the signs of a hasty exercise. (Indeed, in that regard it resembled the 1967 White Paper.) Parts of it were presumably inherited from an earlier study: the previous Conservative government, faced with rising opposition within its own ranks, had already announced a similar review. Significantly, like the studies of the 1960s, the 1974 Maplin review was a wholly internal exercise by the Department of Trade in association with other government departments. It also clearly had a major technical input from the British Airports Authority and the Civil Aviation Authority, both of which had been bitterly opposed to the Maplin project from the start.

This is immediately clear from the first critical step in the argument: the recalculation of the traffic forecasts. These are set out in Table 2 where they can be compared with earlier ones (including Roskill's) and later ones. As compared with Roskill they show a big drop. The review authors explain that this is due to higher oil prices, a notion that leisure passengers would become more sensitive to costs, and a more pessimistic view of future incomes. The increases forecast for the period 1972–90 range between 6.1 and 8.6 per cent – or a little more than half the actual increases over the period from 1963 to 1973.[28] Further, they stop in 1990 (a feature of this and all subsequent government forecasts). The review makes it quite clear that the forecasts are based on the work of the British Airports Authority, who ironically at the time of Roskill were forecasting much more rapid growth than the commission's research team. The comparison is striking:

TABLE 5 LONDON AREA AIRPORTS: COMPARISON OF FORECASTS OF TRAFFIC FOR 1985

	Passengers *millions*
Roskill research team, 1971	82.7
British Airports Authority to Roskill, 1971	75.7–100.2
British Airports Authority, 1972	87
Maplin review, 1974 (without Channel Tunnel)	58–76

Source: GB Commission on the Third London Airport, 1971; GB Department of Trade, *Maplin: Review of Airport Project* (1974), p. 76.

Big as the reduction is, it becomes even bigger when concerted into air traffic movements. For the review assumed a loading of 225 passengers per aircraft by 1990, as compared with 162 in the Roskill report. The justification was the arrival of bigger aircraft, plus the fact that airlines would want to achieve higher load factors. Oddly, the review sets out the figures in such a way that they cannot be compared directly with Roskill's forecasts. But the extent of the reduction is guaged by the fact that the review expects only 450,000 traffic movements in the London area in 1990, compared with Roskill's assumption of 555,000 in 1985.[29]

The next critical alteration was in forecasts of airport capacity. As shown in Table 3, Roskill had assumed that by 1981 Heathrow would be able to take between 310,000 and 330,000 movements a year (represented there as 314,000); Gatwick with its one runway could take 110,000. The review raises these figures to 338,000 at Heathrow using the most efficient traffic control methods, and at Gatwick to 168,000 – a marked rise, due to more even spreading of the load throughout the year. Thus the two together might take 500,000 movements a year as against Roskill's estimate of 440,000. For Stansted and Luton, Roskill had assumed a restricted number of movements on planning and environmental grounds, which they put at about 54,000. But the review, using information from the British Airports Authority and the Civil Aviation Authority, assumed that they could handle up to 120,000 movements during the 1980s. The net result was that the four airports would have a total capacity of 620,000 air traffic movements a year (comfortably above the 1990 traffic forecasts of 450,000) compared with a Roskill forecast of only 578,000.[30]

Thus, the review argued, down to 1990 the critical constraint would be not air traffic capacity but terminal capacity. If only this latter could be provided, the four existing airports could cope. At this point the review adopted a device that was used also in the subsequent 1975–6 national airports review; the presentation of alternative scenarios. (Strictly these are not scenarios, but alternative strategies for coping with the passenger forecasts.) The projected 1990 traffic demand (85,000,000 passengers by 1990) could be met in a variety of ways, as shown in Table 6. All assumed that Heathrow would be developed to take 38,000,000 passengers a year with a fourth terminal, and that Gatwick would go up to 16 million passengers with a second terminal (but not a second runway). In the first, Maplin would take all the rest of the traffic. In the second, Stansted and Luton would take the load. In the third, most of the excess would go to provincial airports. In the fourth, Heathrow's traffic would

Table 6
MAPLIN REVIEW: 1990 SCENARIOS

	1973 actual	1990 Scenarios			
		I	II	III	IV
		millions of passengers			
Heathrow	20.3	38	38	38	53
Gatwick	5.7	16	16	16	25
Stansted	0.2	—	16	4	4
Luton	3.2	—	10	3	3
Maplin	—	28	—	—	—
Provincial Airports	—	—	5	24	—
Total	29.4	82*	85	85	85

Source: GB Department of Trade, 1974, 17.

* Lower total, because Maplin is assumed to attract fewer passengers.

rise to 53,000,000 passengers through a fifth terminal, and Gatwick would be taken up to 25,000,000; there would be small flows through Luton and Stansted.

In comparing these scenarios, the main consideration had to be resource costs. Nowhere did the review try to emulate the elaborate cost–benefit analysis of the Roskill report. But it did conclude that both direct airport development costs, and the costs of the associated transportation links, would be higher at Maplin than elsewhere. However, the combined costs of the links at the four existing airports could be higher than the cost of the Maplin link alone.

The review also contained some figures on access costs for travellers, both in the air and on the ground, produced by consultants. This found that the two most economic scenarios were IV (Heathrow–Gatwick) and II (Stansted–Luton). In comparison, I (Maplin) imposed additional travel costs of about £21,000,000 a year in 1990, while III (provincial airports) imposed costs of £52,000,000 a year; even this, the report emphasized, would require tough restrictive measures at London airports.

Table 7
AIRPORT DEVELOPMENT COSTS AND ACCESS COSTS

	Capacity Increase from to (pass./yr)	Airport Development Costs	Transportation Capital Costs
Heathrow	38m 53m	£115m	£90m
Gatwick	16m 25m	£70m	£60m
Stansted	1m 4m	£15m	nil
	4m 16m	£110m	£47m
Luton	3m 10m	£70m	£10m
Maplin	0m 28m	£400m	£235m

Source: GB Department of Trade, 1974, 39–43, 48–9.

The report therefore clearly indicated the Luton–Stansted scenario as an economic one, though it refrained from saying so. Against that had to be set problems of noise and planning. But the noise problem, the report argued, was well on the way to dramatic improvement. Under all the scenarios, it was claimed, at all the London airports the problem would be markedly less by 1990. In particular, the Luton–Stansted scenario would bring only 2,000 people at each airport within the zone of slight annoyance (35–45 Noise and Number Index) and virtually no one within the area of moderate annoyance (45 NNI and above). This was actually better than the current situation.

Urbanization and planning did present a problem. Development at Stansted to 16,000,000 might mean an urban development of 50,000 to 60,000 in an area where the strategic plan suggested preservation of a rural wedge. Similarly, at Luton the plan was cautious about future growth because of fears of over-urbanization. Against that, the report argued that development at Maplin would cause a loss of remoteness and a sacrifice of ecological interest.

In summary, as Peter Shore told the Commons on 18 July 1974, the reduced traffic forecasts to 1990 did not require a Maplin solution. They could be met by varying degrees of expansion at existing airports, without even the need for extra runways. The noise levels would also be much lower than Roskill had expected. And – the clinching factor – the Maplin solution would cost some £650,000,000 in investment, nearly twice as much as the next costliest alternative. So in this statement the government abandoned Maplin.

The announcement was greeted quietly in the media. Though the Essex and Hertfordshire County Councils immediately produced a well-reasoned rebuttal of the arguments in the review, it did not excite the same attention as the Stansted arguments seven years before. Perhaps the public were tired of the whole issue. Or perhaps, in the wake of the great oil crisis the previous winter, people saw the issue in a different light.

At any rate, it gave the government a political climate in which it could move on to the next stage: a comprehensive review of national airport strategy. The persistent lack of such a strategy had been repeatedly criticized by experts[31] and this was a government response. In fact, on the future of the provincial airports the resulting review was somewhat ambiguous.[32] What however it did do was to reinforce the argument in the Maplin review: that the solution of large-scale diversion to provincial airports would be both difficult and expensive. It would need restrictive policies which could delay the need for expansion in the London area by perhaps a year or two. But they would have to be very tough indeed to be effectual. The study suggested that a passenger charge of £4.50 on each London departing passenger would divert only 10 per cent of passengers, while actual constraints could raise this to 30 per cent. But the charges might impose net resource costs of £70,000,000 in the period up to 1990, while the constraints would cost nearly £400,000,000 over the same period.[33]

Beyond that, the first of the two volumes of the review (dealing with the London area airports) essentially deepened the previous analysis in the Maplin review, with the same implicit conclusions. It revised the forecasts of air traffic, again downwards, but since it also assumed that fewer passengers would fly in each aircraft, the net effect on air traffic movements was actually an increase, from 450,000–510,000 movements in the Maplin review to a high figure of 580,000 movements (including cargo) in the consultation document (Table 1). However, this was still within the capacity of the existing airports down to 1990; as before, the constraint would be in terminal capacity. Therefore the document provides a fuller analysis of the 'scenarios' in the Maplin review, by permuting their components; the actual capacity figures however remain the same, as can be seen by comparing Table 8 with Table 6.

In this table, options A–B in effect represent existing commitments, C–J represent the true options, and the last three are inherently unlikely: G involves a second terminal at Luton, which would encounter strong local opposition, H involves a very costly operation and invasion of the green belt, and J involves both together. And it will be seen that on the high demand forecast, the remaining options would give capacity only to 1986–7, a very short time. Further, it is clear from the table that by this point demand would be rising by as much as 5,000,000 passengers a year.[34]

In this, the consultation document mainly repeated the arguments of the Maplin review – which is hardly surprising, since it came from the same authors. The noise problem, it said, should dramatically decrease at all the London airports, as Table 9 indicates.

As before, the main problems with all the scenarios appeared to be ones of planning. But here, too, the document was sanguine. Gatwick lay within a planned major growth area as designated in the South East Strategic Plan; Stansted did not, and this would

Table 8
AIRPORT CAPACITY AND FORECAST TRAFFIC 1975

scenario:	millions of passengers/year					capacity is used up in:	
	Heathrow	Gatwick	Stansted	Luton	total	high forecast	low forecast
A current Heathrow/Gatwick	30	16	1	3	50	1981	1986
B Heathrow 4th terminal	38	16	1	3	58	1983	1988
C expansion of present facilities at Stansted	38	16	4	3	61	1984	1989
D Gatwick 2nd terminal	38	25	4	3	70	1986	1990+
E Gatwick as now, Stansted maximum with existing buildings	38	16	16	3	73	1986	1990+
F Gatwick 2nd terminal, Stansted maximum with existing buildings, Luton maximum with present facilities	38	25	16	5	84	1987	1990+
G Luton 2nd terminal	38	25	16	10	89	1988	1990+
H Heathrow 5th terminal	53	25	16	5	99	1989	1990+
J Gatwick 2nd terminal, Stansted maximum, Luton 2nd terminal, Heathrow 5th terminal	53	25	16	10	104	1990	1990+

Source: GB Department of Trade, *Airport Strategy for Britain.* 1965/6
'1990+' means 1990 or later.

Table 9
POPULATION AFFECTED BY NOISE, LONDON AIRPORTS,
1972 AND 1990

Airport	Air traffic movements	1972 Popn affected (000s) within			Air traffic movements	1990 Popn affected (000s) within		
		35 NNI	45 NNI	55 NNI	000s	35 NNI	45 NNI	55 NNI
Heathrow	257	2,092	373	78	242	227	41	3
					311	289	59	4
Gatwick	73	30	2	1	104	1	1	0
					151	2	1	0
Stansted	4	4	0	0	14	0	0	0
					63	2	0	0
Luton	31	24	5	0	25	2	0	0
					44	4	1	0

Source: GB Department of Trade, *Airport Strategy for Britain* (London 1975/6), 41–4.

'conflict with current strategic and local planning policies'. Nevertheless: 'These policies are not immutable and consideration might be given in the course of the current review of the South East Strategic Plan to whether there could be scope for some reconciliation of possible airport and strategic planning policies both generally in the South East and specifically in this part of the region.'[35] At Luton the expansion would have an impact on employment, but this would depend on the state of the local economy. Only in the case of the Heathrow fifth terminal did the document admit a serious planning conflict.

The two consultation documents were used by government as part of a major exercise to obtain reactions from regional interests, local government and others. But when finally the government announced its resulting policy in February 1978[36] it merely followed the predictable lines laid down in the Maplin review and the consultation documents. The forecasts of future traffic were again reviewed, and the passenger numbers again scaled down (Table 2). In these forecasts, the government expressed scepticism as to whether large-scale diversion of passengers to the provinces was possible or desirable: thus London passengers would remain at roughly 80 per cent of national totals. As in the Maplin review and the consultation documents, the published forecasts stop at 1990: the White Paper says that beyond that growth is expected to continue, but forecasting is very uncertain.

The White Paper also follows the earlier documents in its arguments about noise. It is not as sanguine as the consultation document, because the forecast number of passengers per aircraft has again been scaled down, meaning more movements. Nevertheless, the White Paper expects a great improvement, and says that the government will pursue it by licensing noisy aircraft, especially at night. Similarly, on planning the government is studiously noncommittal. It merely says that to guard against the fear of unlimited growth of London area airports, it will pursue a strategy of placing limits on the number and size of terminals at particular airports.

On this basis the White Paper makes a choice among the earlier scenarios (Table 8). It rather curiously chooses one of the few permutations which was missed: a composite of D and G. Heathrow is to be expanded through a fourth terminal to 38,000,000 passengers: the fifth terminal is abandoned. Gatwick is to be expanded to its maximum possible with one runway and an additional (second) terminal, to take 25,000,000 passengers. Stansted is to extend to 4,000,000 passengers a year, to utilize what are now seriously under-used facilities. And Luton is to be taken to its maximum with a single terminal and a single runway, with a total of 5,000,000 passengers. The total capacity is 72,000,000 passengers a year, which, the White Paper claims, should accommodate the demand through the 1980s. The government promises that all developments at the four airports will be subject to planning procedures. In other words, the British Airports Authority will not be able to get away without an inquiry.

In the longer term, beyond 1990, the White Paper accepts that even more capacity will be needed in the London area. It gives an assurance that Heathrow will not be taken beyond four terminals nor Gatwick beyond a two-terminal, one-runway airport, while Luton will be restricted to the 5,000,000 level. In other words, further expansion at these three airports is ruled out, leaving only Stansted. The choice for the future, therefore, the White Paper finally says, will be between major expansion at Stansted, development of an existing military airfield as a civil airport, and the construction of a new airport. To try to resolve this, the government in August 1978 set up a new Advisory Committee on Airports Policy, significantly chaired by a Department of Trade official and including the CAA, BAA and the airlines as well as local authorities and others.

But, on one point, options were closed. The White Paper repeats the government decision that Maplin is abandoned. The argument is the same as in the Maplin review: the cost. A runway and two terminals at Maplin, sufficient for 18,000,000 passengers a year, would cost £680,000,000 (based on Maplin review estimates, updated to end-1976 prices). Connections to London would have cost about £410,000,000 on the same basis. In comparison the expansion of Gatwick, Stansted and Luton would provide the same capacity for £150,000,000 plus modest costs for better connections to London. There seems to be no doubt that the same argument would apply if after 1990 Maplin were again judged against, say, further expansion at Stansted.

So the big question mark, in 1979 as in 1967, concerns the future of Stansted. The White Paper proposes what seems a fairly modest expansion to 4,000,000 passengers a year down to 1990. But it also quite explicitly states that over time the surplus capacity, amounting in all to 16,000,000 passengers, will be brought into use. And it categorically states that, even with that level of traffic, fewer people would be affected by noise at Stansted than at almost any other airport in Great Britain.[37] It merely says that expansion to 16,000,000 would raise wider issues, including major changes in planning policies for the area. That of course would mean a major change in the Strategic Plan for the South East – on which, significantly, the government answer of late 1978 was delphic concerning airports.

So it is difficult to avoid the conclusion that in the 1978 White

Paper the government has already firmly made up its mind. Stansted will go to at least 16,000,000 passengers with its single runway, and there would then be no logical reason why it should not go up to 25,000,000, the same level as Gatwick will have achieved at the end of the 1980s. Furthermore, that could occur earlier than the White Paper suggests. For oddly, the total capacity suggested then adequate for 1990 (72,000,000 passengers) is well toward the lower end of the 1990 forecast range (65,900,000 to 89,400,000). If the growth of traffic followed the high trajectory, extra capacity would be needed not after 1990 but in 1987, less than ten years after publication of the White Paper. In the resulting panic, almost by definition further expansion of Stansted would be the only practicable option open to the government. And in that case, by any reasonable definition Stansted would become London's third airport: the decision the government abandoned in 1967 and that Roskill rejected as an option in 1968.

LONDON AIRPORT PLANNING: A JUDGEMENT

It is now time to attempt a judgement with the benefit of hindsight. The story of London airport planning in the 1960s and 1970s is an extraordinary record of rapid and radical changes in forecasts of traffic and capacity; of apparently equally extreme changes in major planning considerations, such as noise; of two major reversals of policy, whereby Stansted was first effectively abandoned as London's third airport and was then resurrected. Is it possible to find a rational explanation of this tortuous history?

The most charitable (or, some would say, simple-minded) is that there genuinely were changes in appreciation of the objective future situation on which any plan must be built. A look back at Table 2 shows clearly that during the 1960s forecasts of future traffic were going up; after 1973 they were going sharply down. Further, this revision does correspond to the facts of the then position. Air traffic through London's airports, which was rising at 11 to 12 per cent a year during the period from 1963 to 1973, was rising at less than 3 per cent from 1972 to 1976; Roskill's forecast, of 36,100,000 passengers in the London system in 1975, compared with an actual total of only 28,800,000. Everyone – the Board of Trade and Ministry of Aviation officials of the 1960s, the Roskill Commission at the end of the 1960s – proved equally wrong. There seems no doubt also that they all equally underestimated the future reduction of the noise menace, due to the progressive introduction of the new quieter jets in the 1980s.

The least charitable explanation is to assume that there has all along been a conspiracy of what could be called a London airports lobby. It consists of the people in the airlines, plus the people who are responsible for planning and managing the existing system (earlier the Ministry of Aviation, later the Civil Aviation Authority and the British Airports Authority), plus the government department responsible for airports policy (earlier the Ministry of Aviation, later the Board of Trade and Department of Trade). The evidence is clear that at least since 1950 this group has consistently viewed Stansted as becoming London's logical third airport once the capacities of Heathrow and Gatwick were exhausted. Its logic was that Stansted existed, that the group itself owned it (or had control over it), that it was well sited once the necessary transportation links to London were available, and that it was meanwhile being under-used. The group's strategy was to refuse to plan long ahead or to make a grand design until the airport was urgently needed, and then to rush it through. Around 1960, as we saw, it was doing nothing; then, from 1963 to 1967, it tried to force a quick decision on Stansted. In 1978 it was once again doing nothing. And, according to the pattern, around 1982–4 it will try again to rush through major expansion at Stansted, making it at last London's third airport.

Over the whole of this nearly twenty-year period, this group has kept extremely close control over airport policy in Britain. It lost it just once, for a five-year period between 1968 and 1973, when the real power passed to an independent commission of seven outsiders. It was already winning it back a little over two years after the dissolution of the commission, with the governmental promise of a Maplin review. It won it back completely after publication of the review in July 1974. From then until the White Paper of 1978, its arguments have led inexorably to one conclusion, the same as that before 1968: that Stansted should become London's third airport. The arguments are different, but the conclusion is always the same.

This argument too has plausibility. But the interesting point is the way in which it is reinforced by the earlier 'objective' explanation. Control passed from official hands when it was thought that the problem was so large that it required a completely fresh look and perhaps a radically new solution. The very terms of reference to Roskill, a four-runway airport for the London area, implied a development on a scale never before envisaged save in the 1967 White Paper; it was that, hinting at a development on this scale at Stansted, that had prompted the furore and led to Roskill's appointment. Conversely, the official establishment was able to reassert its conventional solution on the basis that the more sober forecasts of the 1970s made a radical, one-shot, all-or-nothing solution dangerous. It correctly seized the changed psychological mood of the times.

It was also aided, of course, by a split in the opposition. Had the Roskill Commission not divided, then its recommendation would have carried much more weight and the government of the day would have been almost bound to carry it through despite local opposition. But the division, and the resulting emotionally based support of Buchanan's Maplin solution, represented in fact a rejection of Roskill's whole approach. As we saw, that approach was fundamentally economic. It assumed that a rational, balanced judgement could be reached by balancing the advantages and disadvantages of different sites, with as many as possible of these quantified in money terms. Buchanan's approach, based on absolute planning constraints, was a head-on denial of the economic philosophy which he had always distrusted, though Buchanan and his supporters would argue that in the final resort such economic analysis was incapable of producing sound planning judgements. It seems likely that the official establishment could have accepted the Cublington solution provided that political momentum carried it through quickly. But the choice of Maplin, prompted as it was by political pressure, both roused it to total opposition and encouraged it further by demonstrating the fundamental split in the opposite camp.

The official establishment may also have perceived that party politics would probably work in its favour. Generalizations are dangerous in a field where much depends on the personal judgements and prejudices of individual politicians. But broadly, in conditions of major controversy, Conservative politicians seem more concerned to stress the absolute primacy of protecting the rural heritage – as, for instance, in the rigid policies of urban containment that were applied by Ministers like Duncan Sandys and Henry Brooke in the 1950s.[38] They may also tend to support arguments of national prestige, as we have seen in the case of Concorde. Both these led logically to the focus on Maplin as the environmentally superior, nationally prestigious airport-seaport development. Labour politicians, on the other hand, are more inclined to support the channelling of money into social programmes – which makes them suspicious of prestige projects. They are also of course fundamentally less sensitive to pressure from well-heeled rural constituents. Finally, some of them tend to be extremely sympathetic to the economic approach to planning. It is clear that Anthony Crosland was personally influential in getting the Roskill Commission appointed and in ensuring that it took this approach. It is equally clear that he was a critical force in the rejection of Maplin, which he regarded as the negation of this approach. Had the Cublington decision prevailed, then Crosland would have been almost bound to support it; and the arrival of the 1974 Labour government would have merely maintained the previous policy. But as it was, a Labour government became pro-Maplin after 1974, as from 1964 to 1968.

It is arguable, in fact, that the official establishment and the Roskill majority were in effect occupying the same camp – but with a critical difference of detail. Civil servants seldom reveal their personal positions. But in a symposium published in 1974, just before the Maplin review (and significantly edited by

Christopher Foster, a Croslandite), John Heath, who had been Director of the Economic Services Division at the Board of Trade in the critical years 1964 to 1970, gives his verdict on Maplin. It is, he says, one of a series of projects with similar characteristics: long delay between a decision and its final implementation, high uncertainty in technological development or in marketing or in both, and large scale. Heath suggests that Britain has made the blunder of going straight for what was thought to be the ultimate solution, without going through the intermediate stages; in all of which cases (Concorde, the electronic telephone exchange, production-scale nuclear plants) a disastrous mistake resulted.

He concludes: 'I believe that it is our traditional system of decision-making that has let us down in these cases, and that has also landed us with the present controversy over Maplin.'[39] Though Heath had by then left the government service, there seems no doubt that many like-minded people were drawing the same conclusions, especially the government economists who were advising Crosland through the 1974 Maplin review.

But if both the official establishment and the Roskill Commission were united on the 'economizing' approach, how did they come to differ on the resulting recommendation? Some critics would argue that this was because the commission adopted a thoroughly professional and comprehensive cost–benefit approach, while the official attempts from the Maplin review onward were both partial and insufficiently substantiated. But it is clear from the Roskill exercise (Table 4) that surface-access costs will dominate any such exercise – and these might be thought to favour Stansted, which is nearer London than any of Roskill's four sites. The agonizing possibility remains that in rejecting Stansted in favour of Nuthampstead, a site that, on the commission's own admission, proved to have unexpected noise costs, Roskill made the wrong choice. Had it put Stansted on the short list, then Stansted might well have emerged as the favoured site, despite the planning disadvantages which it shared with Nuthampstead.

This relates to another difficult question. In the same symposium edited by Foster, G.H. Peters suggests that the Roskill

Commission asked the wrong question about the timing of the need, and thus got the wrong answer. It found that congestion costs at Heathrow and Gatwick would be greater than the imputed interest charges and operating costs of the new airport by 1980. But it failed to allow for the cost of the disamenities created by the new airport.

But in the longer run, the outcome is less clear. Short-term incrementalism could eventually produce a massively sub-optimal solution. The defenders of Maplin would argue that Heathrow and Gatwick were perfect examples of such incrementalism, and that they had both been found wanting in practice. Like several of the other projects discussed later in this book, the third London airport is a classic example of the problem of how to take a high-risk decision in an uncertain environment, when the big solution could prove vastly superior in planning terms, but with a strong element of uncertainty regarding performance. The problem seems to be that society's judgement of risk seems to be profoundly affected by its feeling of optimism or pessimism about the future. The mood of the late 1970s suggests incrementalism; that of the 1990s could again suggest the grand design. It could be that we are always saddled with the previous generation's value judgements.

CHAPTER 3

London's Motorways

As with London's third airport, so with its motorway system: the most important point about it is that it does not exist. Or, strictly, only small fragments of it exist – some forty miles, out of 350 once planned. These fragments terminate arbitrarily at junctions that lead nowhere. The rest is abandoned, and for the most part even the lines of the motorways are no longer safe-guarded by the planners. London's motorways compete with its third airport for the title of the most costly civil engineering pro-ject ever planned in this country; and both were aborted. They represent classic cases of negative planning disasters. How so much effort and resources came to be invested in their planning, how such a firm political commitment came to be overturned, form a central case study in the pathology of planning.

The core of the story occupies only thirteen years: from the decision to start a major traffic survey and plan for London, in 1961, to the abandonment of the motorway plan by the incoming Labour administration of the Greater London Council, in 1973. But to understand its full dimensions it is necessary to go back to the time of Patrick Abercrombie's great wartime plans for London, in 1943–4, and also, since Abercrombie too drew on previous ideas, some way before that.

THE ABERCROMBIE PLAN AND ITS ANTECEDENTS

Engineers and planners had been grappling with the problem of London traffic at least since the start of the automotive era.[1] Already, in 1905, a royal commission on London traffic had devoted eight bulky volumes to the subject, and had proposed an ambitious system of new arterial highways boldly slicing through London's built-up fabric. Already, too, in 1910 the London Traffic Branch of the Board of Trade had produced a massive plan for new arterial highways just outside the then built-up area, which would relieve existing overloaded radial roads and would provide a new North Circular Road skirting the northern suburbs. And though the royal commission's proposals disappeared for the most part into obscurity, the vast majority of the planned roads of 1910 were actually built between the two world wars. They provide the familiar infrastructure of bypasses in suburban Greater London, and they were ironically completed by the opening of Westway from the White City to Paddington, in 1970. The irony lay not merely in that the road had been sixty years in gestation; it lay more in the fact that the resulting outcry led directly to the abandonment of London's motorway plans three years later.

These new roads of the 1920s and 1930s, however, had two grievous limitations. First, they were built for the most part without any adequate planning of the associated land uses. They were all-purpose roads, with frequent side access; soon, speculative builders ran ribbon developments all along them. Some visionary souls called for a system of *Autobahnen*, on the German model, but a royal commission of 1930 ridiculed the idea that Britain would ever need such a system of 'Motor-Ways'. Secondly, they failed to penetrate into the built-up area of 1918. Thus, while access in the interwar suburbs was at least improved, in inner London it got worse, if anything, as traffic grew. William Robson, writing in 1939 on the government and misgovernment of London, could point out that in its whole history since its creation in 1888, the London County Council – responsible for this inner area – had completed just one major new road in central London, Kingsway; and that had been largely planned some years before by its Victorian predecessor, the Metropolitan Board of Works.

As congestion worsened with the growth of private motoring, the government stirred itself to act. In conjunction with the local authorities of the conurbation, it commissioned an eminent engineer, Sir Charles Bressey, and an equally eminent architect, Sir Edwin Lutyens, to prepare a regional highway plan. Published in 1937, this plan proposed an ambitious series of new boulevards including an embryonic inner circular route round the City and West End, and a major east–west route linked to it formed by the extensions of Eastern and Western Avenues (this last proposal picked up from the 1910 report, and eventually to be implemented by the disastrous Westway project of 1970).[2] It was however an exception. For the Bressey plan was for the most part never implemented; only a few short stretches can be identified in the road plan of Greater London in the late 1970s. Its importance lay more in the fact that it was the immediate precursor of the Abercrombie plans.

Patrick Abercrombie, first holder of the Chair of Planning at the University of Liverpool and then at University College London, was by common consent the most distinguished town planner of Britain in the late 1930s. He played a leading role in the work of the Royal Commission on the Distribution of the Industrial Population, the so-called Barlow Commission, which reported in 1940 with a then revolutionary proposal that after the war the government should seek to curb industrial growth in London as a means to controlling its physical growth. It was logical that the London County Council should ask him to join its own Chief Architect, J.H. Forshaw, in preparing a plan for inner London, and that the government should then ask him to produce a regional plan for the whole area of the conurbation and beyond. Together these two plans of 1943–4 represent the culmination of Abercrombie's planning concepts, and nowhere more than in their treatment of traffic.

In understanding them it is first important to realize that they were based on no detailed surveys. In the middle of petrol-rationed World War Two, that would have been both impossible and irrelevant. But in any case, the modern techniques of the transportation planner, with their jargon words – like generation and attraction, desire lines, trip distribution and assignment, and modal split – simply did not then exist; they were an American invention of the mid-1950s. Abercrombie was content to work with such limited evidence as he had, from pre-war annual Metropolitan Police surveys, of traffic flows along the main roads. But in any case, his interest and concern lay in far more than simply improving traffic flow – though that was certainly an important objective for him.

Abercrombie planned in fact to achieve several objectives simultaneously, and thus to gain the best of all possible worlds for everyone. First, of course, he wanted to improve traffic flow and to reduce or eliminate congestion. This could be achieved only by a new system of free-flowing roads. Secondly, he wanted to reduce the danger and the environmental intrusion that traffic represented whenever it penetrated into living or working areas. This concern Abercrombie shared with his contemporary, the Scotland Yard Assistant Commissioner for Traffic Sir Alker Tripp; and his solution – precincts barred to through traffic – was borrowed from Tripp. Thirdly, he wanted to use road planning, together with open-space planning and the removal of extraneous industry from residential areas, to define new, more homogeneous areas for living or working. Thus the precincts would also be areas of social cohesion; they would be living communities or neighbourhoods. Bringing these elements together, Abercrombie achieved a remarkable synthesis: a concept of a city replanned on organic principles, with cells and arteries, in which each part performed its proper function as a member of the whole urban body. This city would function effectively on three different dimensions: functionally, in terms of efficient movement; communally, in terms of social cohesion and identity; and monumentally, in terms of a strong sense of place.[3]

More particularly, Abercrombie saw the need for a hierarchy of roads both to move traffic effectively and to perform the vital job of reinforcing the organic structure of the city. The topmost level of the hierarchy would be a new system of arterial roads built for through traffic on motorway principles, with limited access and segregation from other traffic. A second level would consist of sub-arterial roads adapted from the existing system, serving as distributors from the arterials and also separating residential and other areas. A third level would consist of the strictly local roads in these precincts, which would connect with the sub-arterials at controlled junctions.

The arterials, moreover, would take a particular form. For Abercrombie wanted them to perform not only a traffic function, but also a vital planning function in giving coherence and identity to the structure of London, a structure he felt had been up to then latent, because the road system needed to define it had been lacking. This must now be remedied. The logical system to provide the structure would be a system of rings and radials, a plan that Abercrombie had advocated for other places and at other times.[4] In this system, the innermost ring, designated by Abercrombie the A ring, would serve as an inner bypass immediately round the central area of the West End; it had antecedents in the Bressey plan. The next ring, the B ring, would run about four miles from the centre, serving to drain the congested inner residential and industrial districts. The next, the C ring, consisted of the recently completed North Circular Road plus a completely new equivalent south of the Thames. This would serve as a bypass for Victorian London as a whole. The next, the D ring, would serve as an outer drain for the suburban areas, near or at the limits of the built-up area. And finally, the E ring was the partly built orbital highway around London, which would henceforth run as a park-way through the green belt that would for ever limit London's physical sprawl. Connecting these to form a rich spider's web, radial roads, for the most part new arterials, would provide a coherent system of high-speed routes and would also help complete the vital process of defining the main organic elements in the planned geography of London.[5]

Incorporating other equally large notions – the green belt itself, the ring of new towns around it, the belt of expanded towns beyond that and the planned migrations that would take more than a million Londoners to new homes outside – Abercrombie's vision was a grand one. The wartime government accepted it in principle; post-war governments produced the necessary legislation to help implement it. The green belt was established and maintained; the new towns were built. But, despite continuing support in principle, the roads became a casualty of the plan.

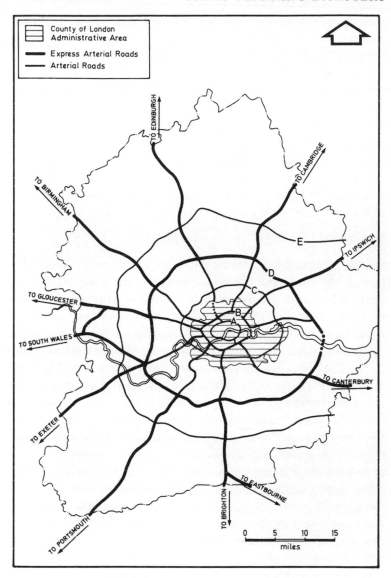

Figure 2: Abercrombie's Roads Plan, 1944.

Shortages of money in the decade after the end of the war in 1945, followed by a concentration of roadbuilding funds on inter-urban motorways from the mid-1950s onwards, left all too little for London. And by the late 1950s, with car ownership rising rapidly in London as elsewhere, traffic congestion came to be seen as a major problem requiring solution. Restraint and control must provide part of the answer, and the first parking meters, introduced experimentally in Soho in 1958, were quickly followed by a rash of controlled zones, one-way streets, clearways and other restrictions. But, beyond that, there was a developing consensus that the problem could not entirely be contained.

THE BIRTH OF THE LONDON TRAFFIC SURVEY

Spectacular peak-hour traffic jams, on a scale never before witnessed by Londoners, thus gave rise to a growing demand for positive action in the form of new roads for London, a demand that was channelled by powerful pressure groups like the British Road Federation and the Roads Campaign Council. At the same time, there was much concern about the inadequacies of London's administrative machinery, particularly for the control and planning of transport, but also more generally. The Greater London conurbation, as officially recognized by the census-takers for statistical purposes and by the Home Office as the concern of the Metropolitan Police, was then administered by over 100 different local authorities, including six county councils in whole or in part, three county boroughs, the City of London, twenty-eight metropolitan boroughs, forty-one municipal boroughs, twenty-nine district councils and a variety of ad hoc bodies. The resulting divisions of responsibility, for measures ranging from one-way streets to roadbuilding, caused delay and muddle. Finally the Ministry of Transport, under its energetic Conservative minister Ernest Marples, was driven to wrest many of the necessary powers over traffic management from the London County Council and the boroughs. But the longer-term planning problems were still unresolved.

In 1957 the government, already conscious of these problems, appointed a Royal Commission into Local Government in Greater London – the Herbert Commission. Its report, published in 1960, was scathing about the procrastination and inefficiency of London government in handling the traffic problem. And there is no doubt that its proposed new structure – with a Greater London Council and a new streamlined system of London boroughs – was largely a response to the perceived need for a single strategic planning authority both for transport planning and for associated land-use planning. The Ministry of Housing and Local Government's evidence, for instance, had defined traffic congestion as London's key problem.[6] Bitterly fought by the Labour opposition in parliament, the resulting London Government Bill was passed into law in 1963. It set 1 April 1965 as the date for the assumption of power by the Greater London Council and the thirty-two new boroughs.

Meanwhile, however, the Ministry of Transport under the ever-impatient Ernest Marples had moved on its own. Anticipating the 1963 Act, or perhaps guarding against its possible non-passage, at the end of 1961 it had already agreed with the old London County Council jointly to set up a London Traffic Survey. Consultants, consisting of a leading British firm of civil engineers and an American organization, would introduce into Britain the new techniques (and also the jargon) of scientific transportation planning. The early 1960s was a period of intense, almost religious fervour for new technology and the fruits it would bring. And, within that paradigm, the new breed of transportation planner fitted perfectly, offering a vision of computerized infallibility that would point the way to a totally motorized, totally mobile future. By 1962, the consultants were ready to conduct the huge sample household surveys, which for the first time would present a comprehensive picture of the way Londoners lived, worked, played and moved about. From this survey would come the models that would provide the predictions of Londoners' future travel needs.

Only one more element was needed to provide the psychological impetus; and once again, with uncanny political flair, Ernest Marples provided it. Shortly after setting up the London Traffic

Survey he appointed a Ministry of Housing and Local Government inspector, Colin Buchanan, to undertake a general study of traffic and planning in towns. Buchanan, then known to the general public only through his handling of an important inquiry into the future of Piccadilly Circus, was picked as the only man who seemed to know anything about the vital relationships between traffic and environmental nuisance. When the report appeared in November 1963, it was an immediate popular bombshell. Buchanan became a household name overnight, and his central planning precept – that environmental quality standards must limit accessibility by car, but that accessibility could be increased by spending money – became almost an article of faith.[7]

In his detailed proposals Buchanan, as he freely admitted, drew heavily on the ideas of Alker Tripp twenty years before. His environmental areas were essentially Tripp's precincts, and his hierarchical road system was also essentially Tripp's. The important point was that, in a political sense, he changed the popular consciousness of the traffic problem. No longer was it seen merely as one of congestion; just like his mentor Abercrombie, Buchanan argued that it was as much a matter of good planning and good environmental standards. The critical point is this: though in theory the Buchanan principles could justify either little spending on roads or a great deal, according to society's preferences for accessibility, in practice, once the standards for environment were set, to buy the existing level of access would cost a great deal indeed. So, as became evident in the years that followed, the Buchanan creed was in practice a demand for massive increase in spending on urban roads. Marples, who was a passionate and effective advocate in his own cause, had once again picked the right person at the right time.

LTS: THE TECHNICAL PLANNING PROCESS

At this time, therefore, and throughout the middle 1960s, there was massive political commitment towards heavy expenditure on urban roads. Public opinion, so far as it could be gauged through the filter of the media, was heavily in favour. London newspapers protested at the creeping thrombosis that threatened their city and enthusiastically applauded the plans for new highways.[8] Their readers, in some cases, were even persuaded to join in with ideas of their own. The importance of this was that, in a benign political climate, the technical experts were left to get on with the job.

They did so speedily. The London Traffic Survey, as it was originally known, conducted its basic household and other surveys in 1962 and published the results in 1964. This picture of London's movement patterns formed Volume One of the original survey; it became Phase One of the London Transportation Study, as the survey later came to be known. Covering an area slightly larger than both the then conurbation and the differently defined Greater London Council area of 1965, it included some 8,800,000 people (over 17 per cent of the total population of Great Britain) with nearly 4,800,000 jobs. Each normal weekday, Londoners made some 11,300,000 trips (these were 'basic trips', sometimes using two or more kinds of transport), of which 90 per cent started or ended at the home, and within which nearly 5,400,000 were trips to and from work. Perhaps most significantly, though in 1962 only 38 per cent of households owned cars, close on 6,300,000 trips a day were made in cars as against just under 6,500,000 by bus and train. The average person in a household made 1.33 trips a day. But while in non-car-owning households he would make only 0.93 trips, in a car-owning household he would make an average of 1.87 trips. Thus, the survey could already argue, as car ownership continued its apparently inexorable climb the impact on traffic would be dramatic.

Precisely how dramatic, Volume Two of the survey showed in 1966. And here, for the first time, technical questions of forecasting became critical. The consultants' method, inherited from countless similar American studies, was to concentrate on road travel and above all travel by car. Walking trips were ignored in the original 1962 survey, and subsequently; now, travel by public transport was relegated to a subsidiary category, and the main efforts were devoted to forecasting the rise in car use. It was assumed that as car ownership rose people would behave roughly as they had been observed to behave in 1962. Thus trip generation rates for car-owning and non-car-owning households were obtained from the 1962 survey, and applied to the forecasts of rising car ownership. Then, the trips were distributed between traffic-planning zones. Lastly, they were assigned to networks on the logical assumption that they would follow the quickest path, in terms of time, from starting-point to finishing-point.

The critical point about this method is contained in a sentence in the summary report on the whole study published in 1969: 'The pattern of travel was calculated using a trip distribution model calibrated from 1962 conditions and using speeds for the primary roads that might reasonably be expected in uncongested conditions and speeds on secondary roads similar to those observed in 1962.'[9] In other words, though traffic grew, congestion was expected to be no worse – a clearly unrealistic assumption. For, as critics have often pointed out, traffic in towns follows a kind of Parkinson's Law: it tends to expand to fill the space available. During peak hours, and during other times in some areas, there will be traffic congestion and this will deter some drivers; they will either use public transport or abandon the journey. But if new roads are built they may bring their cars out, so that new traffic is (in the jargon) generated. There is thus a circular element in traffic forecasting: to some degree, though of course not entirely, the traffic will depend on the roads plan.

In 1966 the experts took an extremely crude approach to this problem, though the fact is tucked away in an appendix to their report.[10] First, they used the computer to forecast total trip generations and attractions, that is, separate forecasts of trips made at each end of the main journey. They were sufficiently close to satisfy the planners that their method was basically sound. But the results were well below what they had expected from their experience in American cities. So then they developed an alternative set of figures, euphemistically called 'control totals'. They were in truth no more than guesses of how they thought Londoners would behave if they had an adequate road system, such as Americans had. Thus trips to shops, or to visit friends, were simply inflated by an arbitrary factor of 25 per cent.

And the result – a total of 16,693,000 trips a day in the year 1981, as against 15,367,000 by the original method – was solemnly presented as the figure that would result if London had a new highway system.[11]

From that point, they went on to distribute the resulting traffic and then to assign it to a network, using their well-developed computer models. For this purpose they had to have a theoretical network, and in fact they chose two. One, the 1981 B network, simply consisted of bits and pieces of new road, to which the GLC and the Ministry of Transport were firmly committed. There was a complete ring around Greater London near the edge, which was Abercrombie's D ring. But inward from this there were just fragments of national motorways like the M1 and M4 and M23, plus a new East Cross Route through the Blackwall Tunnel that the old LCC had planned as part of its reconstruction of the East End. The other, the 1981 A network, was now presented as a first sketch of London's new motorways. It derived heavily from the Abercrombie Plan, as a number of commentators have pointed out;[12] for it reproduced the familiar Abercrombie spider's web of rings and radials, the only substantial difference being the omission of the innermost A ring, which the goverment had abandoned in the 1950s on the grounds of cost. Instead of Abercrombie's five rings, there were now three inside London (later named Ringways One, Two and Three) plus another, the Ministry's planned Orbital Road, in the green belt outside it, and thus outside the plan.

The genesis of this plan was interesting. For it had developed very rapidly after the creation of the GLC's new Highways and Transportation Department under its energetic chief engineer, Peter Stott. One critical element – the so-called Motorway Box, later Ringway One, following roughly the line of Abercrombie's B ring some four miles from the centre – had already been unveiled by the GLC on its first day of authority, 1 April 1965. The rest soon followed. What happened then was that the new authority committed itself immediately in principle to an old set of plans, which had lain in the drawers but were now exhumed.[13] But, as Hart later pointed out, they were now represented purely as a technical solution to a narrow traffic problem, not as a central element in the grand design for London that Abercrombie had conceived.[14]

Even at a technical level, however, some of the results were odd. The 1981 A network contained an integrated system of 444 miles of high-class roads of motorway or near-motorway standard. The 1981 B network contained some 260 miles of this system, but nearly all of it was in the outer suburbs, so that there was no coherent system nearer the centre.[15] Yet the effect on total traffic generation was only to reduce travel from 16,700,000 to 15,900,000 trips a day, or 5 per cent.[16] The flows on parts of the network were equally odd. On the West Cross Route of Ringway One between the Cromwell Road and the river Thames, for instance, the forecast 1981 flow was 339,000 vehicles a day – well in excess of anything ever recorded in Los Angeles or elsewhere, and probably requiring a capacity of some fourteen lanes of traffic.

The traffic planners were very conscious of these problems themselves. In Phase Three, the final stage of their study, they sought to make a much more refined analysis that took them, as they confessed, into difficult research frontier territory.[17] They tested a much greater variety of networks, ranging from a minimal one to a very elaborate one; and they specifically looked at the effect of restraining traffic wherever, on any particular one of these networks, the capacity was too limited to allow traffic to flow freely. They started with new calculations of trip generations and attractions in 1981, and they started by assuming that the quality of the road system would not affect the results. The results are the Phase Three 'No Traffic Restraint' figures in Table 10. As compared with the Phase Two figures, they show slightly fewer trips than the 'Maximum' figures of Phase Two (corresponding to the 1981 A network) but substantially more than the 'Minimum' ones (corresponding to the 1981 B network). Then, however, they incorporated a constraints procedure into their computer models. Where parts of the assumed road network clogged up, some drivers were assumed to be persuadable to transfer to public transport, or abandon the trip. The results now emerged very differently for the two networks, as the figures in the two right-hand columns of Table 10 show. The 'Assumed' network (roughly the same as the 'Maximum' network of Phase Two, and described now as Plan Three) produced slightly fewer trips than before, because even it could not cope with all the forecast demand. (Only an even bigger network, described as Plan Nine, could achieve that.) But the 'Minimum' network, carried over from Phase Two and now christened Plan One, now choked off a very large amount of traffic. Car trips were now reduced by well over 3,000,000; nearly another 1,000,000 transferred to public transport, and the net result was a reduction of over 2,000,000 personal trips per day.[18]

This was a substantial difference. It meant that if only the minimal network were built, the increase in personal trips over the nineteen-year period would be some 23 per cent; if the Plan Three network were constructed, it could be as much as 41 per cent. But as compared with the heady forecasts of Phase Two, both these are somewhat more sober. For Phase Two had forecast an increase in trips by private transport of no less than 118 per cent if the 1981 A network were built, as against only 90 per cent for the assumed network in Phase Three. Perhaps most significantly, though the Phase Two forecasts assume an increase in the percentage of private trips from 46 to 70, the Phase Three forecast for the assumed network calculates an increase to only 62 per cent. The minimal network has only 50 per cent; a very bare increase on the 1962 figure. This was very important; for the GLC used it to argue that, without the bigger network, the level of restraint on private car travel would be intolerable.

The other critical point is that in any case the assumed network, or something very like it, had already been committed by the Greater London Council as a result of the Phase Two studies. This had occurred in 1966, and in November 1967, two years before publication of Phase Three, the Council had already announced its plan for three rings and radials at a cost then estimated at £860,000,000.[19] The plan was thus accepted before full knowledge was available from the studies on which it was supposed to be based, though in the event these provided some degree of justification.

Table 10
LONDON TRANSPORTATION STUDY: FORECASTS OF 1981 TRIPS, PHASES TWO AND THREE*

	Phase One 1962 Actual	Phase Two 1981 No Restraint		Phase Three 1981 No Restraint		Phase Three 1981 Restraint	
		Min.	Max.	Min.	Assumed	Min.	Assumed
Internal car-driver	4.12	8.18	8.98	8.09	8.15	5.20	7.35
Other internal private	1.49	2.98	3.30	2.95	2.99	2.34	3.30
Total internal private	5.61	11.16	12.28	11.04	11.14	7.54	10.65
Internal public	5.72	4.71	4.41	5.46	5.39	6.59	5.71
Unreported public	0.82	0.82	0.82	0.82	0.82	0.82	0.82
Total public	5.54	5.53	5.23	6.28	6.21	7.41	6.53
Total	12.15	16.69	17.51	17.32	17.35	14.95	17.18

Source: Greater London Council, *London Traffic Survey* (London, 1966), 85; Greater London Council, *Movement in London* (London, 1969), 74.

*Table 10 was difficult to produce because the figures are not strictly comparable. First, by Phase Three the planners found that they had earlier lost some public transport trips, estimated at 820,000 a day; these are separately shown. Secondly, the key Phase Three figures exclude car passengers; these have to be factored indirectly to produce the comparison.

Just how great a degree emerged from the economic evaluation made by the Greater London Council at the end of Phase Three. By this point the practical options had been reduced to three: first, the 'Minimal' (Plan One) 150-mile network costing £451,000,000; secondly, the 'Assumed' (Plan Three) 347-mile network costing £1,841,000,000; thirdly, the 'Ultimate' or maximal (Plan Nine) 413-mile network costing £2,276,000,000. (All these three sets of costs are based on 1966 prices and include associated parking costs. The actual motorway land and construction costs are for Plan One, £372,000,000; for Plan Three, £1,658,000,000; and for Plan Nine, £2,063,000,000.[20]) The GLC economists calculated a so-called one-year rate of return for the year 1981, which was a much simpler and also less satisfactory measure than the discounted flow of benefits generally used in evaluating road schemes. It indicated that Plan Three after restraint gave an 8.8 per cent rate of return when compared with Plan One, while Plan Nine gave an 8.7 per cent rate also as compared with Plan One. Plan Three was therefore preferred.

This calculation was the source of fierce controversy in the subsequent public inquiry into the Greater London Development Plan. For one thing, though the costs included the associated costs of parking, they excluded expenditure on the associated secondary network, which the GLC had always calculated, on a rule-of-thumb basis, as 50 per cent of the costs of the primary highway system.[21] For another, it was a one-year rate of return. Thirdly, the consultants who made it warned that the results had to be treated with great caution.[22] Finally, it appeared to be a distinctly poor rate of return compared with the norm generally used by the Treasury for judging such investments, which would be at least 10 per cent. Critics therefore argued with some justification that in comparison with other major public projects, including other roads, there was a weak case for the Plan Three network.

Also tested in Phase Three were two alternative public transport packages. But these were literally bundles of proposals culled from London Transport and British Rail, without any notion of forming a coherent network. Throughout the three phases of the study, indeed, public transport played a strictly

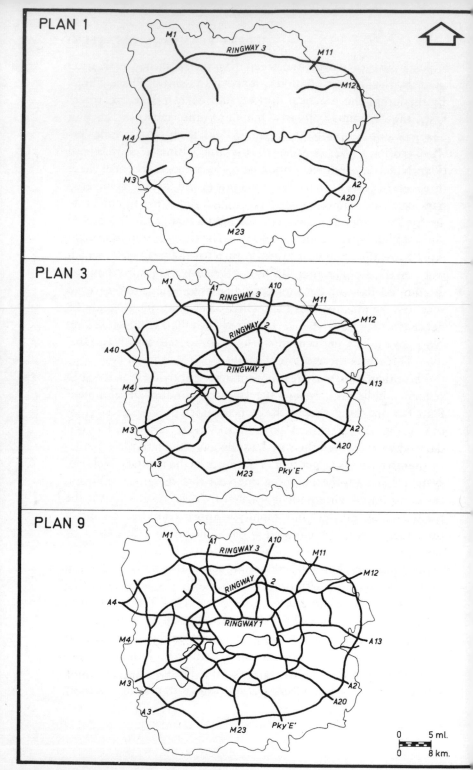

Figure 3: The Three Options in the GLC Transportation Plan.

subsidiary role; it was clearly very much at the back of the transportation planners' minds. For this there were at least three good reasons. The first was that the whole study had arisen as a political response to problems of road traffic. The second was that the techniques inherited from the American studies were simply not well adapted to the needs of an agglomeration where public transport played such an important role. And the third, quite simply, was that the Greater London Council was not particularly interested because until the 1969 Transport (London) Act it had no direct responsibility for public transport at all. Even after that Act came into force in 1970, it meant only that the GLC acquired general policy control over London Transport. The relationship with British Rail was still very tenuous, and it fell a good deal short of the arrangements then being developed in the provincial conurbations, where the Passenger Transport Authorities could arrange to take over British Rail suburban services. Whatever the reason, this lack of interest in public transport was to prove one of the major sources of criticism in the great public debate that followed.

THE GLDP INQUIRY: THE ROADS PLAN AND ITS CRITICS

By this time, the results of the Transportation Study had been incorporated into the Greater London Development Plan, the production of which was indeed one of the GLC's main statutory responsibilities under the London Government Act. It was published in 1969 and the summary results of the study were set out in the volume *Movement in London*.[23] A year later, the public inquiry into the plan opened before a panel headed by Sir Frank Layfield, the notable expert on planning law. It was to rival Roskill on the third London airport as the most protracted planning inquiry in British history.

In its opening evidence, the GLC put the case for the roads in the most forceful terms. Without them, it argued, the result would be '... a continuation of the present conflicts between roads and the environment but over a wider area and of a more intense character in many places.... Overall one must conclude that the London that would be created if there were no investment in roads would be one that would not meet the social and economic objectives of the GLDP.'[24] The main problem, it went on, would be that a policy of no investment would require levels of restraint over traffic that would be neither technically feasible nor socially desirable. Restraint might be possible in and near the centre and at peak hours, but it would not be acceptable over wide areas where people lived – and yet this might be necessary if the roads were not there. The major need, it stressed, was to provide new capacity to satisfy the very large increases in demand for orbital journeys.[25] Two years later, in a modified statement, it repeated its belief that: 'The transport strategy in its entirety must be implemented or else the general strategy for improving the quality of life in London will suffer and the value of the total public and private investment in general renewal and development be diminished.'[26]

But a large number of influential people disagreed. The panel's discussion of strategic transport issues took sixty-three days and involved 460 Proofs of Evidence and support documents; on local transport issues, it took sixty-seven days and read 560 documents.[27] Indeed, of the 28,392 objections to the plan, some three-quarters dealt with transport and especially with roads. A great number of individual local residents' groups, directly concerned at the impact of the plans on their areas, made both collective and individual representations. But the job of collating and synthesizing them into a coherent set of objections was performed by two related groups: the London Motorway Action Group and the London Amenity and Transport Association.[28] This evidence was principally the work of two experts, J. Michael Thomson and Stephen Plowden, who each published books with cogent criticisms of the plan.[29] From all this mass of evidence, certain dominant lines of counter-argument emerged.

The most important was that the American-style approach to transport planning, which the GLC had inherited, was fundamentally misconceived. It concentrated on providing for future increases in demand for the use of roads, instead of first seeking to identify and cure weaknesses in the quality of existing transport services, above all in public transport. It provided for new journeys, mainly of an optional social character, rather than easing present-day journeys to work. Thus it paid all too little systematic attention to the speed and reliability of public transport, the comfort of the ride and the length and the conditions of transfers or waits for services, and it almost ignored the problems of car-less families, who by 1981 would still constitute 45 per cent of all households in inner London.[30] It assumed that public transport should in general pay its way, while providing new road space without any such criterion. And its mathematical predictions ignored the need first to set policy objectives for the whole system.[31]

Secondly, and associatedly, the plan ignored its own impact on travel preferences and patterns. The new motorways, it was argued, would actually generate substantial amounts of traffic that otherwise would not be there: between 70 and 100 per cent more, according to Thomson's estimates.[32] (The corresponding GLC prediction, which can be read from Table 10, was 41 per cent.) This generated traffic would inevitably use secondary and local roads on its way to and from motorways, thus making conditions there worse rather than better. And the diversion of trips from public transport into cars would almost inevitably intensify the vicious circle, already long observed in London, whereby fewer passengers meant poorer service which in turn meant fewer passengers.

Thirdly, and in any event, the critics argued, the plan greatly exaggerated the likely amount of long-distance travel. This was because it projected the travel habits of 1962 car owners, who were mainly middle class, on to the future car owners, who would mainly be working class.[33] The new owners, it was argued, had more limited social frameworks and were far more likely to make short local trips in their own areas – journeys that would seldom require the use of the motorway network. Thus the network was partly irrelevant, and in so far as it was relevant it was likely to be deleterious.

Fourthly, it was said, the plan ignored the considerable indirect costs that the motorways would impose, including accidents to the extra traffic, and environmental intrusion. It was alleged that 1,000,000 people would live within the 200-yard strip that formed the noise shadow of the new roads, 250,000 of them within the shadow of Ringway One.

Lastly, because of these and other factors, it was argued that the system had no economic justification. Thomson in 1969 had already calculated that though Ringway Three gave an adequate return on investment of 14.9 per cent, the corresponding rate on Ringway One was as low as 5.3 per cent, well below any Treasury yardstick for public investment.[34] Later, at the inquiry, the objectors argued that when proper account was taken of factors like depreciation, tax benefits and unperceived congestion costs, the benefits from Plan Three as against Plan One were reduced from £125,000,000 (the GLC's figure) to a mere £19,000,000; indeed, if (as seemed likely) the traffic predictions were too high, the balance might actually be negative.[35]

The objectors did recognize that without the motorways congestion would be fairly widespread and restraint on the use of the private car would be needed. On these points, at least, they were in agreement with the GLC. But they were in total disagreement on two points. The first was that in their view the result of the motorways would be on balance even worse; they saw a system that 'generates large quantities of additional traffic, fails to make much impact on congestion in Inner London and the major suburban centres, and brings relatively modest benefits to road users'.[36] The second was that a general policy of restraint could be effective: it was argued that central London had already shown what could be done without extensive new road construction.[37] The level of restraint need not be onerous; it would be needed only in peak hours and would amount to a modest charge (for instance, on parking) of 20–35p in inner London.

Thirdly, the objectors made a critical relationship (which the GLDP had not) between transport planning policies and land use planning policies. (It was a criticism of other witnesses at the inquiry that the plan had failed to evaluate alternative distributions of living and working.) Land-use planning, in the view of people like Thomson and Plowden and their colleague Mayer Hillman, should seek to provide a maximum range of facilities within easy walking distance, without the need for car travel – and in inner London this should be particularly easy to achieve.

It amounted to a formidable case, based on a fundamentally different philosophy from the one that had animated the whole transport planning process since 1961. And perhaps, though technical argument about forecasts and evaluations were important, in the last resort the argument was really about what kinds of policies would improve the quality of life for the average Londoner. On this there could be no real reconciliation, for the outlooks were too different.

Faced with this clash, the panel finally steered a judicious middle course, and thus, perhaps, tried to reconcile the irreconcilable. Its report specifically rejected the extreme courses of meeting the full demand for roadspace, and of extreme restraint and regulation: 'Since the cost of the first extreme would be prohibitive, and the effect of the second crippling, the policy choice lies in practice somewhere between the two.'[38] It argued instead that planning should be developed within a comprehensive and balanced framework, which should include restraint on the use of the private car and on the routing of commercial vehicles; improvement of the quality of public transport; and improvement of environmental quality. Within that framework, the objective should be to provide as little new roadspace as was strictly necessary.[39]

However, the panel agreed with the GLC on the critical argument that there were limits, political as well as economic, to the possibilities of traffic restraint. Probably, it concluded, the GLC had somewhat underestimated the public tolerance for restraint and the public response to better public transport. Nevertheless, some demands would need to be met. The panel concluded that the minimal network was smaller than the GLC's Plan Three, but larger than the objectors' preference (which was in essence close to Plan One). They recommended that instead of four ringways (three of them within the GLC area, one, the Orbital, outside) there should be only two. Ringways Three and Four should be combined into one, while Ringway Two should be omitted (though the North Circular Road, which was already there, would clearly remain and could be upgraded). Most contentiously of all, therefore, the panel recommended that Ringway One should remain part of the plan, and that many of the main radial routes should be carried through, at motorway standard, to meet it.

The justification for this had to lie partly in economic evaluation. But this was literally impossible, because the GLC had evaluated so few options. The panel recorded a general agreement between the GLC and its critics that the return on Ringway One was low: only some 5.1 per cent. This compared with a Treasury norm of 10 per cent and a Department of the Environment rule of 15 per cent for inter-urban roads. Lacking any evidence to prove or disprove its case, the panel ventured that as part of a reduced system the rate on Ringway One would be higher than this. But the case for Ringway One lay in more than the traffic benefits: it was, the panel argued, an essential element in relieving inner London of heavy commercial traffic, and hence in improving the quality of environment there. This was the case the objectors had strenuously denied. But, the panel countered, it made sense so long as road construction took place within a framework of traffic constraint.[40]

The reduced network would still be considerable, and expensive. It would include some 300 to 350 miles of high-speed road and would cost £2,165,000,000 at 1972 prices, excluding the costs of rehousing (which would be formidable, since the housing take was estimated at 16,600). Additionally there would be a substantial bill for the improvement of the secondary road system, where the panel wanted to see the GLC produce a completely new plan.[41]

THE 1973 ELECTION: POLITICS INTERVENE

The government's reply was remarkably prompt. Simultaneously with the publication of the panel's report in February 1973, the Secretary of State for the Environment (Geoffrey Rippon) issued a statement. The government did this, the statement said, because it thought that '... early decisions of principle will serve to allay public uncertainty and curtail planning blight'.[42]

In general the government simply accepted the panel's main recommendations. Ringway One would remain in the plan, though its phasing would be further discussed. The government reserved its views about a possible modification to the line in South East London. Ringway Two, south of the river, would be struck out. On Ringway Three the government reserved its position until it could see how far the Orbital Road would cope with all the traffic. The government could also not be drawn on the panel's recommendation that the whole network should be completed within twenty years; it would merely try to build as fast as resources allowed. Lastly, the government accepted the panel's recommendation for a new plan for the secondary roads, but wished the proposals in the existing plan to remain as the basis for the highest priority schemes until new proposals were worked out.

Government responses to independent reports are seldom as prompt as this, least of all to plans needing so much money. But there was by now a pressing political case for haste. Already at the 1970 GLC election, some of the key critics of the motorways plans had organized a campaign under the banner of the Homes Before Roads party. They won as many as 100,000 votes but no seats; so they subsequently changed their tactics. They argued that the Labour party should publicly declare its opposition to the plans on the grounds that they were unnecessary, uneconomic and inevitable in their incidence of costs and benefits. After much internal debate, in June 1972 Labour embraced the anti-roads programme in its campaign for the 1973 GLC elections. The Layfield Panel report thus appeared only two months before the polls, at a time when the existing Conservative administration was fighting for its life – and for the life of the motorway proposals.

For by now there has been a remarkable shift of popular opinion, as D.A. Hart chronicles.[43] As late as the 1970 election, both major parties still officially supported the plans, though both were already back-pedalling. The success of the Homes

Before Roads campaign was undoubtedly a warning sign to the politicians. By 1971 David Wilcox, planning correspondent of the *Evening Standard*, could describe 'ringway bashing' as a 'favourite sport'. Most of the press, together with leading academics, the Town and Country Planning Association and the Royal Institute of British Architects, were by now on balance anti-motorway. The well-reported objections at the public inquiry further weakened the GLC case. By September 1972 even the Conservative party was clearly weakening when it produced a cut-price plan that combined sections of Ringways One and Two. For the political momentum was clearly now with the anti-motorway campaigners. In April 1973 Labour regained power at County Hall; on the very morning of the victory, they announced that the motorway plans were abandoned and the safeguarding removed. Hart comments: 'Exactly 30 years after the publication of Abercrombie's *County of London Plan* (1943) and 10 years after the publication of Buchanan's *Traffic in Towns* (1963) the concept of urban order which both documents supported and in a sense which the Primary Road Network symbolized was effectively abandoned.'[44] Labour's victory at County Hall was soon afterwards paralleled across the river. Under the new Secretary of State for the Environment, Anthony Crosland, the government reaction to the Layfield report was sharply reversed. The official argument was that times had changed:

> Since the Inquiry, public concern over the reconciliation of the needs of road traffic and the environmental consequences of large scale road building has grown, and the costs of any extensive motorway network have become altogether unacceptable. The present Council have indeed rejected most of the proposals for new primary roads that were contained in the plan submitted, including the inner ringways.[45]

So the government followed the GLC's lead. Ringway One, apart from those few sections already built or in construction, was deleted, as was Ringway Two, south of the Thames. Only the outer orbital motorway, for the most part outside the GLC boundaries, was committed.

Yet, the statement went on, there was a continuing need for

orbital movement along the general corridors once marked by Ringway One and Ringway Three. The government would discuss with the GLC how to deal with this. Any plan would have to make the best use of existing roads, but some new construction might be needed. What was left on the map instead of the abandoned roads, therefore, was a curious set of numbered points to be connected up by imaginary lines – rather like the children's games that produce a magic drawing. In this case the fairy picture showed the ringways. Perhaps this was a private joke of Crosland or his advisers. Whatever the case, it seemed to be lost on most people.

That was the position in 1975. In 1979, with a Conservative government in Westminster and a Conservative administration in County Hall, the position is again more fluid. The London Conservatives have made it clear that they want to spend a lot of money on roads again. Though they officially deny that the ringways are to reappear, part of Ringway One (the West Cross Route from Shepherds Bush to the river) is in their plan, as is improvement of the North Circular Road and its extension southwards from Wanstead to a new Thames crossing at Barking-Thamesmead. Indeed the proposals are quite consistent with the modified Conservative plan of September 1973, and in June 1974 the government and GLC agreed on a package for East London. But already before the London elections there had been a shift in thinking within the London Labour party; for the industrial decline of east and south London is producing a new set of local pressures actually in favour of major roadbuilding again. Meanwhile, much of Greater London seems to have settled into the state of generalized congestion that the planners had forecast. And in a strange way, perhaps Londoners have simply got used to it.

ANALYSIS OF A NEGATIVE DISASTER

In order to understand better the balance of forces that produced the extraordinary reversal of policy in London in 1973, it is useful to make the three-part analysis created by John Grant in his study of transport planning in three English provincial cities.[46] He found that there were three key groups of actors: the politicians, the community groups and the professionals. The same three key groups certainly can be identified in London, though perhaps a fourth, the opinion-makers and shapers, might profitably be distinguished from the general complex of community activists.

The technicians are perhaps easiest to understand. They are concerned with career maintenance and advancement, which leads them to support interventionist policies based on large injections of public funds. In the case of transport planning the general history and the traditional organization further strengthened and also focused this tendency. The highway engineers in the Ministry of Transport and in the Greater London Council had a specific training and a specific professional competence. Their general philosophy was based on concepts of efficiency in moving people or goods. Flows of either of these commodities should be accommodated by providing channels of the requisite capacity. The notion that there were alternative ways of handling the problem, or other policy considerations, was injected only slowly and painfully. Organizational divisions had much to do with this, for the GLC's remit down to 1970 was effectively restricted to roads, and during this period generous specific grants were available for roadbuilding but not for investment in public transport. Only after the 1967 Transport Act was this changed, and by that time the London Transportation Study was largely fixed.

All this was no doubt exacerbated by the fact that, for the most part, the GLC's new Department of Highways and Transportation – the name itself is significant – had been set up apparently to perform a particular task: to plan and provide a large increase in highway capacity. It should have been no surprise that the professionals were passionately attached to their task. Later, when Transportation was merged with Planning, many saw the move as a takeover by Transportation rather than the reverse. As Hart points out, the central philosophical concept of traditional British planning – that of organic order in a city, in which the transportation system provides just one element – was weakening during the 1960s. The comprehensive mode of planning, represented by this view, was being replaced by a narrower functional concept, in which professionals attacked well-defined problems. And perhaps the most important of these, as it was seen at the time, was the problem of traffic growth.

It was the historic function of the community groups, and in particular their expert spokesmen and related publicists, to point out that in fact the problem was quite ill defined. They attacked the road plans by seeking to show that the engineers had seen only one small aspect of a multi-faceted problem. It was perhaps significant that this anti-establishment group of transport planners was composed not of engineers but of economists and other social scientists. They expressed a view then becoming common, through the influence of the social sciences on the planning schools: that the first essential was to understand and order the problems to be solved.

The reaction of these groups, especially at the grassroots level, was partly an instinctive, emotional one. When the GLC opened Westway in 1970, instead of satisfaction the informed popular reaction was one of environmental outrage at the intrusive elevated structure. The same reaction was happening in cities all over the world, following the first recorded motorway abandonment, that of the Embarcadero Freeway in San Francisco, in 1966. It happened to correspond to a general reaction at the time against massive large-scale development in cities – a reaction expressed in London by the controversies over Piccadilly Circus and Covent Garden. While the catchword of the early 1960s was Comprehensive Development, that of the early 1970s was Small-Scale Rehabilitation. In this new world, motorways had no obvious place.

Partly, therefore, the community reaction was an automatic, dialectical one. Some, who might once have supported the idea of motorway planning at an abstract strategic level, suddenly found that the result threatened their home or their neighbourhood. Others reacted, more generally, to what they saw with their own eyes or on television. For most people, a reaction against motorways, or anything else, first requires something to react against. In many American cities and in some British ones (Birmingham, Leeds) this happened only after a goodly part of the network was actually built. But in London, perhaps because of its middle-class activists and the associated media people, it happened remarkably quickly.

Once it did, the critical question concerns the political route the community activists and their allies chose to follow. During the Layfield inquiry from 1970 to 1972, they chose primarily to follow the route of intervention in the process of technical inquiry. Through highly expert and critical objections to the GLC professionals' forecasts and evaluations, they sought to defeat the professionals on their own territory. In the event, the Layfield Panel compromised on the basis of judgement rather than of strict technical argument, and in doing so, it effectively rejected much of the objectors' case. But by then, they had increasingly switched to an alternative route, through takeover of a critical group of politicians. In this way, they won. The technical-professional planning process was simply overcome by the political planning process.

Perhaps this was inevitable. Faced with arguments that were finally as much about basic values as about techniques of forecasting, the Layfield Panel steered its middle course. But faced with increasing political pressure from a passionate minority, equally the politicians reacted in a political way. In a democratic society, there was probably little else they could do. In London, as in most British cities, local elections are marked by political apathy; a minority turns out to vote. When to this fact is allied the fact that most constituencies tend to be stable politically and only a handful are key marginal ones, the leverage exerted by a small turnover in those key places can be considerable. The most controversial of the motorways, Ringway One, ran through these key constituencies at the border of working-class and middle-class inner London, the classic territory in which the outcome of an urban election will be decided. And so, in 1973, it was.

There was more than pure political opportunism in all this. The Conservatives, at both central and local government levels, tend to have been more unequivocally committed to roadbuilding than Labour for reasons that are intuitively obvious: greater support of (and by) industrial interests, greater support of (and by) middle-class car owners, plus a general commitment to private forms of transport. Conversely Labour politicians are more likely to see roadbuilding as an expensive sport that does relatively little for their working-class constituents, who need better public transport instead. This might suggest that the anomalous fact was the strong Labour support for the roads policy from 1965, when they were actually responsible for initiating it, until the 1973 reversal. Perhaps so. But roadbuilding for the old LCC politicians was seen as an essential element in the comprehensive reconstruction of blitzed and blighted areas, especially in the East End, where their constituencies were. Indeed the East Cross Route of Ringway One, the only secion to be completed, was planned entirely by the old LCC as part of this process, without notable opposition. It was only when the plans threatened middle-class London that they ran into trouble, and it was to capture these areas that Labour reversed its policies.

Cynics might say that the outcome changed very little. What the voters and the media forgot was that by an accident – possibly a deliberate one – of the 1963 London Government Act, most of the planned motorways were not a GLC responsibility but remained a central government one. The only unambiguous GLC motorway was Ringway One, which had been inherited from the old LCC. And in its 1975 statement on the GLDP, the government kept most of its options open. In any case, public expenditure cuts in the mid-1970s meant that there was clearly no money to afford the full motorway programme, so it made sense to concentrate government spending on the outer Orbital Road, which significantly became top national priority, plus reconstruction of the North Circular Road.

In the last resort, though, the history does teach more than this. There was a profound shift of mood among thinking people, in London and other cities, both about the problem and about its solution. One generation, the Abercrombie-Buchanan one, had taken its stand on a planning concept of urban order: Hart's cohesive planning mode. A slightly later generation had narrowed this to a technical problem assessment and a resulting technical solution based on heavy investment: Hart's factored mode. But both these were similar in the important respect that they were hard planning solutions, demanding investment for major urban surgery. And both were in turn faced by a radically alternative planning mode: a demand for a more flexible system in which policies were progressively shaped by changing opinion and above all community concern. Here, in Hart's diffused mode, it was difficult to make large-scale changes; the planning process has a repetitive, often time-consuming character.[47] This is perhaps the most profound change to affect British planning for more than a generation; its impact was felt far more widely than on London's ringways alone. It was felt, for instance, on the third airport scheme.

The strange irony is that all the proponents still claim that their chief concern is with the quality of life of the archetypal average Londoner. Their visions of what make up the good life are very different, and to some extent they represent a *Zeitgeist*. The good future life of the early 1960s consisted in ceaseless mobility in search of an ever widening range of choice in jobs, education, entertainment and social life. The good future life of the early 1970s was seen in almost the reverse kind of life: in a small, place-bounded, face-to-face community. Truly these interpretations recall Blake's alternative visions of the Deity:

> The vision of Christ that thou dost see
> Is my vision's greatest enemy.
> Thine has a great hook nose like thine,
> Mine has a snub nose like to mine.

And almost without doubt, before long a new *Zeitgeist* will produce a new vision – or the revival of an old one.

CHAPTER 4

The Anglo-French Concorde

Daily at 11.15 in the morning and on five days a week at 9.15 in the morning, a distinctive and even anomalous plane lines up on one of the two parallel main runways of London's Heathrow airport, to begin its take-off roll for New York. Passengers in Jumbos and Tristars, in the queue of taxiing planes, stare at it, always with curiosity, often with wonder. For its most anomalous feature is its size. Minute and slim, it is dwarfed by the new generation of giant jets that increasingly dominate the world's airways. It is British Airways' Concorde – one of five in their fleet, and one of the only nine flying in the world.

As it gains height, other people notice the event – not always with curiosity or delight. On Reading University's Whiteknights campus, lectures and seminars pause for what has come to be known as the Concorde stop. For the supersonic plane's howling roar, and the strange reverberations it sets up in its wake, have become its distinctive signal to several hundred thousand people who live or work under its flight path.

This is Concorde flying subsonically. As it achieves its cruising altitude of 55,000 feet – far above more mundane planes – it goes supersonic at 1,350 miles an hour, twice the speed of sound; and at this point it begins to emit its unique supersonic boom. The only people who hear it, in mid-Atlantic, are the crews of occasional freighters or ocean liners. Far away on the other side of the world, there are others – the peasants of Indonesia and the aborigines and sheep farmers of interior Australia – who are as yet spared this sound. They lie under the potential flight path of Concorde between London and Melbourne; the government

87

of India has so far refused to allow the plane supersonic flying rights.

Back in London, a number of people in boardrooms and government offices are equally interested in Concorde's progress. They include the board of the state-owned British Airways, whose Concorde operations made a £17,000,000 loss in 1977, and government officials who are urgently considering a proposal that they should subsidize the plane directly.

For Concorde, in the words of a report by Britain's independent governmental Central Policy Review Staff, is a commercial disaster. Sixteen years after 1962, when it was started on an estimated research and development cost total of £150,000,000 to £170,000,000, and with expectations of selling perhaps 400 planes, only sixteen Concordes have been built and nine have been sold, all to the captive state airlines of Britain and France, the total bill to the two governments coming to some £2,000,000,000. The possibilities of further sales, in late 1978, appear to be dim, and receding. Production at the British Aerospace Filton plant has stopped, and is unlikely to resume.

How the two governments embarked on this technological adventure, what were their expectations of costs and sales and how far these have been nullified, how far the problem of the plane's noise impact was ignored in the crucial decision to go ahead, why it was that the British government failed to withdraw as costs escalated and prospects receded, are questions which have been endlessly debated and incessantly chronicled. There are half a dozen excellent books that tell the Concorde story in detail and with sound criticism. In a sense it is superfluous to tell it again, except for the need to fit it into the general pattern of planning disasters. So, in this case also, the narrative draws freely on previous research, with the aim of isolating the main features of the critical decision processes.

1956–62: TOWARDS COMMITMENT

The story really begins in 1956. In that year the Minister of Supply set up a Supersonic Transport Aircraft Committee, totally composed of air interests (the then Ministry of Supply, Civil Aviation and Transport, plus aircraft manufacturers and engine firms, plus airline corporations), to examine the technical feasibility of a supersonic aircraft and to undertake the basic research needed (at the modest cost of £700,000) before a full design study could be commissioned. Significantly, it had no Treasury representative. Behind this critical initial decision to consider the possibility, two forces can be identified. One was the British aircraft industry, reeling in the wake of the crash of the ill-fated Comet, the world's first jet airliner; in the subsequent success of the Americans in monopolizing the production of first-generation big jets; and the government's cancellation of a supersonic bomber project. The other was the Royal Aircraft Establishment at Farnborough, whose technical prestige in world air development was equally threatened by the Americans' superior military resources. It was Farnborough which urged that the British should now leapfrog the Americans and pioneer the world's first supersonic commercial airliner.

The report of the committee appeared in 1959. Predictably, it argued that the British aircraft industry should start design work on two totally new supersonic airliners: one long-range, capable of flying 150 passengers nonstop between London and New York at mach 1.8 (1,200 m.p.h.), the other a slower, short-haul plane, carrying 100 passengers. The estimated cost of the long-haul version including all research and development up to the completion of a prototype for testing and five other planes, was put at between £78,000,000 and £95,000,000; and it was estimated that there would be a world demand for up to 500 such planes by 1970. This report has never been made public, but *Sunday Times* reporters who claim to have seen it and talked to its authors allege that the figures were simply invented within Farnborough. Though the Cabinet in 1959 rejected a proposal based on this report, nevertheless Aubrey Jones, the Minister of Supply from 1957 to 1959, persisted. And throughout, it appears, the Treasury was prevented from making a detailed appraisal.

There was a perfectly good reason for this, of course: the Treasury, which had had previous experience of speculative aircraft projects, would have fought with all its might. The Treasury representative appearing before the House of Commons Expenditure Committee in 1971, looking back at the whole story since 1945, concluded: 'One remembers cost escalations in the military aircraft field which have been considerable and one must always be sceptical about this ... because these things are very difficult to do, the original estimates that you make for them, and these are not Treasury estimates, tend to be wrong.'[1] There was, he said: '... a history in this field of over-optimism going back a long time ... propositions came forward which were obviously and wildly over-optimistic.'[2] This applied only to aircraft, both civil and military, 'which go beyond the state of the art'.[3] But this pre-eminently included Concorde; the Treasury must have known the prospects then, and equally the proponents of the aircraft knew the Treasury view.

It should have been no surprise, then, that they decided in effect to go behind the Treasury's back. The obvious way to do that was to seek a joint development with some other country, in such a way that the British government would willy-nilly become committed. The obvious partner was France: it had a small but progressive industry, having developed the Mystère and Mirage military planes and the Caravelle short-haul jet; and it had also been interested in supersonic development. The American manufacturers on the other hand were not interested; they were too involved with the first generation of subsonic jets.[4] Later, before a House of Commons Expenditure Committee, Aubrey Jones was disarmingly frank:

It was quite clear to me that were I as Minister to go to the Treasury the money would not be forthcoming. So in June, 1959, I went to France and I took advantage of the then Paris Air Show to suggest to the French that they should co-operate with the British in developing Concorde. It was in this way that I started. In retrospect I have to admit that my Department and I had no knowledge at all and had made no attempt at all to estimate the size of the potential market.[5]

Shortly after that, in September 1959, the Ministry of Supply commissioned feasibility studies from the Bristol Aircraft Company and from Hawker Siddeley, at a cost of about £300,000. Three months later, encouraged by the Aviation Minister Duncan Sandys, Bristol merged with Vickers Armstrong and English Electric Aviation to form the British Aircraft Corporation, which Sandys saw as a vital step in building up a strong British industry to compete with the Americans. Part of this agreement, the government explained shortly afterwards, was that increased government support should be given to civil aircraft projects. Accordingly, in October 1960, BAC were awarded a £350,000 limited design study contract for a 120-passenger aircraft flying at mach 2.2. This was produced in August 1961 and was followed by a revised study in early 1962. Throughout, the committee steering these reports within the Ministry of Aviation was composed wholly of enthusiasts and the Treasury was apparently given as little information as possible.[6] Submitted in October 1962, the twenty-page report and the revised study, described as 'little more than a sketch', proved to be crucial.[7] For, apparently on the basis of it, the British and French governments on 29 November 1962 signed a Supersonic Aircraft Agreement. The costs of research and development were then estimated at £150,000,000 to £170,000,000, to be shared equally, with, astonishingly, no limit, no provision for review and no cancellation clause. A standing committee of officials from the two countries, the Concorde Coordinating Committee, would supervise it. The British companies involved would be BAC, plus Rolls-Royce for the engines; the French companies would be Sud-Aviation and SNECMA.[8]

This agreement became the subject of endless subsequent investigations, most importantly by the House of Commons Sub-Committee on Estimates in the following year. The most important aspect, on which the committee never received a satisfactory reply, was the precise Treasury involvement, or the lack of it. Questioned, Mr Peck, head of the Defence Policy and Materials Directorate at the Treasury, answered:

We had certain figures which suggested that on certain assumptions this project would be economically viable. But in a project of this kind, as I am sure the Committee realize, there are a large number of uncertainties, and he would be a bold man who would say that the Treasury were satisfied that this project was economically 100 per cent viable ... we tended to take a more pessimistic view of the assumptions and possibilities than perhaps did some of those in the Ministry of Aviation, for example.[9]

Faced with this, the committee's chairman had to confess: 'All this talk of not having Treasury authority is something on which I must express a complete lack of understanding.'[10]

Reporting a year later, the Estimates Committee did the best it could. It conceded that the Treasury had taken the initiative in May 1962 in setting up an interdepartmental committee of officials, under Ministry of Aviation chairmanship but with Treasury representation, to ensure that the project was assessed.[11] Further, the subcommittee had been assured that 'Treasury appreciations were available' but, though the official giving evidence would not say precisely what these were, it was obvious that they expressed great scepticism.[12]

It was clear, the committee concluded, that the estimate of £150,000,000 to £170,000,000 was speculative, that it was based on the firms' own figures, and that the Treasury expected it to be exceeded: 'It is therefore evident that Her Majesty's Government entered into a binding commitment with the French government for the development of this project with an imprecise knowledge of the probable cost.'[13] It was further clear that Treasury authorization had not been given to the project, and would indeed have been a formality; that the Treasury played no part in preparing or signing the agreement, and was not represented on the committee set up under the agreement to supervise the project, even though its French counterpart was. Further, the assumption that the aircraft might be able to recover its costs on sales of 150 to 200 aircraft was equally speculative, since there was no assurance that sales of that order would materialize. The committee concluded, in no uncertain terms: 'Your committee cannot understand the failure of the Treasury to make contact with the French Ministry of Finance before the agreement was prepared, their failure to take an active part in the preparation of the Agreement, and their failure to request participation on the Committee of

Officials.'[14] It pointed out that the agreement constituted executive action that committed parliament to an unspecified heavy expenditure on a project on which the returns should be problematical; that the Treasury should be asked to provide an explanation of its failure to fulfil its obligations to the public revenue; and that in future the Treasury should be represented on the joint committee, with a specific formal relationship to the French Ministry of Finance to exercise joint control over the financial programme, which would be subject to specific estimates in the Ministry of Aviation accounts.[15]

Of course, to some extent this ignored the real point. What has become clear much later, through leaks, is that the Treasury had repeatedly tried to kill the project at successive stages from 1957 onward, whenever the Ministry of Supply asked for money for design studies. It fought the Aviation Ministry in the special committee to vet the estimates in the summer of 1962, but lacked aviation expertise of its own and failed to use its own experts fully. The battle was finally fought out over two Cabinet meetings during November 1962, and was won by Julian Amery, Minister for Aviation, on the clinching (but probably false) argument that if the British pulled out then the French would go it alone. Here the Treasury made one last-ditch attempt to intervene, on discovering that there was no break clause, but were persuaded by Amery that this was necessary to hold the French to an agreement.[16] Hence the Treasury's evident embarrassment before the Commons subcommittee.

Of course, behind the Cabinet decision lay two major political considerations, which were closely associated. Some ministers, such as Sandys, were persuaded by the argument that Britain needed a project of this size to maintain a viable and competitive aircraft industry – a point that the industry itself had stressed before the Commons subcommittee in 1963.[17] Since it could not achieve this alone, cooperation with the French was essential. But this had a further and larger attraction: Britain in 1962 desperately needed French support in her bid to enter the Common Market, reflecting Harold Macmillan's decision at the end of 1960 to get into Europe. Technological cooperation seemed the obvious answer to both problems. But with supreme irony, just over a month after the November agreement, on 14 January 1963, President de Gaulle vetoed British entry. As a grand political gesture, the British signature to the agreement proved worthless. But almost immediately, it was to start proving expensive.

COST AND NOISE: THE OPPOSITION GROWS

The agreement certainly did not lack critics from the start. Enoch Powell, a Cabinet minister at the time, later said: 'One hundred and fifty million pounds down, a prospect of breaking even in the long run and an olive branch to the French who might let us into the Common Market after all. . . . You use a truffle hound to find truffles, and a foxhound to find foxes. You use politicians if you want a political result, and businessmen if you want a business result.'[18] And two weeks before the agreement was signed, in a House of Lords debate, a veteran air expert, Lord Brabazon of Tara, succinctly voiced the objections that were afterwards to mount. Quoting the Minister of Aviation as saying 'Space beckons us with a golden finger', he commented acidly: 'My Lords, it beckons us to the three brass balls of the pawnbroker.'[19] The cost, £6,000,000 a plane, against £2,000,000 for a Boeing 707, he correctly predicted, would 'put civil aviation in the red forever' and would fail to attract extra traffic. The time savings were largely illusory since they would be greatly reduced by ground access. Worst of all would be the problem of noise and sonic boom: 'From a political point of view, I cannot imagine a better vote-catching stunt than smashing all the windows of two or three streets in the middle of a cold winter's night; people would then really appreciate the advantage of technology.'[20] He concluded, prophetically: 'We are guessing – we do not know. I do not mind guessing, but you are guessing with the taxpayer's money. You are going to make this machine. Good luck to it! I only regret that when it is finished I shall not have the privilege of saying, because people will not listen to me, "I told you so".'[21]

The judgements of the Commons committee in 1963 attracted

much attention and renewed criticism. So did the Committee of Public Accounts, in 1965, which commented on the escalation of costs that was even then observable: 'Your Committee ... note the Ministry's explanation of the considerable increase in the estimate of cost but they doubt the value of estimates which are so conjectural as to be almost worthless as an indication of the ultimate cost.'[22] It noted that at the time of agreement, the project had not reached the stage at which, for a purely British project, a development contract would have been placed: the project was still in the middle of the design stage, and the design which it was hoped would meet requirements was not available until May 1964. Even at that point, there was no guarantee that the plane would actually be able to fly from London to New York, and the Permanent Secretary of the Ministry of Aviation agreed that for a domestic project Ministers would not even then have reached a decision.[23]

Already by this time, the cost estimates had started their upward climb (Table 11). From then on, the story was one of steady increases. By June 1973, just over ten years after the original agreement was signed on the basis of the £150,000,000 to £170,000,000 estimate, the costs had risen to £1,065,000,000, an increase of six or seven times. As the detailed analysis of a House of Commons committee shows, just over one-third of this could be explained by inflation. Another 20 per cent was due to revision of estimates, in other words, to wrong estimating at the start. But well over one-third was due to 'additional development tasks', meaning the need to redesign the plane as it emerged that the original specification simply would not meet requirements. The most important of these were increased engine thrust and wing area to ensure regular and safe transatlantic crossings; the need to meet noise certification requirements; and, most crucially, the need for major modification in 1968 after the discovery that the machine would not meet payload requirements, involving major alterations to the fuselage, wings and engine nozzles.[24] During 1969–71 the estimate of the British Aircraft Corporation alone rose nearly £100,000,000, from £124,400,000 to £222,700,000; the engine costs similarly rose between 1968 and

Table 11

CONCORDE: ESTIMATED COSTS, 1962–73

All costs in £ million at time made

Date of estimate	Estimated costs	UK cost share	Increase in Costs since last Estimate					
			Total	Changes in economic conditions	Programme slippage	Revision of ests.	Additional development tasks	Other
Nov. 62	150–170	75–85						
July 64	275	140	105	18	–	47	40	–
June 66	450	250	175	34	–	38	103	–
May 69	730	340	280	107	–	57	115	–
May 72	970	480	240	83	26	22	70	39
June 73	1,065	525	95	65	20	10	–	–
Total to 73	Amount		895	307	46	175	328	39
	Per cent		100.0	34.3	5.1	19.6	36.6	4.4

Source: G.B. H.C. Committee Public Accounts (1973), Appendix 2, vii, xii.

1973 from £123,000,000 to £231,000,000.[25] Questioned on the escalation of costs Mr Thornton, Secretary for Aerospace and Shipping at the Department of Trade and Industry, answered with disarming honesty:

Essentially the problem, as I see it, is that you not only had in the Concorde an extremely advanced technological product – that is to say, that one was pushing the state of the art in designing the airframe and engine to the limits at the time when the project was being developed – but you also had the difficulty of the very small margins that we were working with. ... A combination of these very small margins and the degree of the unknown, make the thing as a whole just about the most speculative kind of project one could imagine. Clearly one ought to have multiplied the estimates by some factor, but if I were asked in a similar hypothetical circumstance what factor to multiply by, I really am not sure.[26]

In fact, these two features were really opposite sides of one coin. The problem, Thornton explained, was to design a supersonic airliner that would fly with a commercial payload – and that was an extremely marginal design problem. The total weight of the plane, as originally designed, was 170 tons, of which the structure alone was 70 tons. The fuel took another 90 tons because of the extremely heavy fuel consumption per mile. This left only 10 tons for payload (passengers and baggage). If for any reason a modification were needed, a 1 per cent increase in the weight of the structure meant a 7 per cent loss of payload; half a ton more fuel meant a loss of 5 per cent on payload. So the 'constant attempt' to rectify the structure or the engine performance had a 'totally disastrous' effect on payload and thus on the plane's commercial prospects.[27]

The committee concluded that: 'If estimates previously made have been very substantially wrong, that should at the very least induce some critical scepticism in government in its approach to fresh estimates.'[28] It also noted that: '... throughout the Concorde project the contractual arrangements have had definite defects: in particular, they have lacked adequate incentives to economy and efficiency and have placed the contractors at no risk.'[29] Until 1968, the contracts were placed on a cost-plus basis.

After that, there was a very complex scheme whereby as costs rose the company's profit fell – except that if a company could persuade the department to accept additional expenditure to increase performance, then profits would again increase.[30] The manufacturers thus had a positive incentive to suggest modifications and thus to increase their profits again. Thus, ironically, the committee repeated the criticisms of the manufacturers' profits made by their predecessors in 1967, when they had expressed disappointment with the slow progress on incentive contracts.[31]

By that time, also, there was a widespread protest movement about Concorde's noise and sonic boom problems. Bo Lundberg had been a lonely pioneer in this campaign when he protested against all supersonic aircraft at the Montreal Conference in 1961. From 1967 his cause was taken up in Britain by a schoolteacher, Richard Wiggs, who founded the Anti-Concorde project. Coming at just the time when public opinion was turning against high-technology projects and pollution, it had a great success in the media. Official tests showed that Concorde was very similar in its subsonic noise levels to first generation jets such as the 707 and DC8, though some doubted these figures.[32] What could hardly be doubted was that the sonic boom problem would become critical for long flights over land, which would be necessary for such journeys as Britain to Australia, or North America to South America.[33] For this reason, on its commercial introduction in January 1976, Concorde was not allowed to fly supersonically over Europe.

Yet the noise problem had been fully appreciated when the 1962 decision was taken – and indeed much earlier. There is evidence that it was already worrying the STAC committee soon after it was set up in 1956. By May 1960 Rolls-Royce engineers, who were hoping for the engine contract, had produced a bulky report pointing out a conflict between the aircraft's need for performance, which suggested a conventional turbo-jet engine, and the need for quietness, which suggested a bypass engine. Rolls suggested that the Concorde engines should be designed for 100 PNdB (Perceived Noise Decibels, the best-known standard noise measure), the same standard as the new generation of subsonics. But they were outflanked by the Bristol division of BAC, who sold the idea of 'civilianizing' their exisiting Olympus engine, developed for the abortive TSR-2 bomber, at a cost of £12,000,000. In the event, it was to cost nearly £500,000,000 to develop the Olympus to the point where it could achieve Concorde requirements.[34]

THE FAILURE TO CANCEL

The important point is that the warning lights began to flash early. By 1964 the first major investigation, that of the Commons Expenditure Committee, was finished, and an extremely critical report had resulted. The project had already escalated from £150,000,000–£170,000,000 to £275,000,000 in a mere two years. The problems of noise and sonic boom were well known. The question was to what extent the 1962 agreement, with its lack of escape clauses, constrained any subsequent British government attempting a unilateral withdrawal.

This was just the problem faced by the incoming Labour government in 1964. Labour too were committed to enhancing British technological capacity; but this was one piece of technology they suspected, especially as it appeared part of a package to get Britain into the Common Market, to which many party members (and indeed Ministers) were opposed. There were two obvious candidates: the TSR-2 supersonic bomber, on which the cost had already escalated from the original £90,000,000 to near the final total of £650,000,000; and Concorde. After a review, in October 1964 the Cabinet told the French government that it wanted to 'urgently re-examine' the Concorde project.

But they were then confronted with legal advice that, since the agreement had no provision for withdrawal, the French government could sue in the International Court of Justice for nearly £100,000,000, the amount it had already committed. This would represent a present to the French, who could then continue the project to completion. In addition, there would be the obvious

humiliation before the International Court of a British government shown not to honour a solemn international agreement.[35]
And there was a further factor. Between February and April 1965,
Labour scrapped three prestige military aircraft, the P–1154, the
HS681 and the TSR–2. This meant that the unions in the aircraft
industry were worried about jobs. Anthony Wedgwood Benn,
as MP for Bristol, was clearly sensitive to pressures of this kind.
It was hardly surprising, in all the circumstances, that in January
1965 the Cabinet reversed its previous decision. Concorde, for
the time being, was saved.

About this reversal there was later much confusion. Conservative spokesmen in the Commons claimed that the original agreement had indeed provided for the possibility of a review once
certain parameters of costs had been reached. The Labour
government, they claimed, had allowed this point to go by.[36]
Whatever the case, it appears that in January 1965 the government thought that it had no choice.

There may however have been a choice later. In 1966–7 a new
wave of public criticism assailed the project. The July 1967 report
of the House of Commons Committee on Public Accounts commented that the BAC were in effect allowed to decide how, when
and where to spend government development money, while taking normal profit margins. It was disturbed by the cost-plus and
price-to-be-agreed contracts which contained no incentives for
economy. Over a year before that, BAC had made it clear that
they had no intention of putting any of their own money into
the development or production of the plane. The estimated total
costs had risen to £450,000,000. A new threat to sales had
appeared in the shape of the Boeing Aircraft Corporation's plans,
announced in April 1965, to build a new 747 Jumbo aircraft with
300–400 seats. And the issue of sonic boom began to appear more
and more in the mass media.

It was at this point, apparently, that the government adopted
a policy of regular reviews of the project every six months. In
the words of Anthony Wedgwood Benn, who from 1967 became
Minister of Technology and assumed British responsibility for
the plane, it survived '... on the most elaborate calculations of

money spent, investment to come, likely returns, likely sales and the costs of bringing in foreign currency.'[37] From 1967 to 1979 there never appeared to be a realistic opportunity to terminate the project, although the 1968 redesign resulted in new 1969 estimates which raised the cost spectacularly to £730,000,000. The British share of this increase was met by the new Industrial Reorganisation Corporation, which in effect lent BAC £125,000,000 at commercial rates of interest (but at government risk) together with £25,000,000 from commercial banks with the government acting as guarantor. By this time, significantly, both French and British prototypes were flying, and it seems clear that the government, having sunk so much, decided that there was no alternative but to go on to the end. The end, unfortunately, was in cost terms still some way distant.

THE FAILURE TO SELL

With the prototypes in the air, the critical question now was how far sales would help repay development costs. Amazingly, it appears that down to 1968 there was no firm estimate of sales at all. In that year, the joint committee overseeing the project accepted a BAC report suggesting that even with a ban on supersonic flying overland, minimum sales should total 200–250. This figure apparently was still being used as late as 1972.[38] Yet during these three years two critical changes occurred.

The first, already noted, was Boeing's development of its 747 and the parallel development by American manufacturers of competitive large jets such as the Douglas DC10 and the Lockheed Tristar. The 747 was introduced into regular service in 1970; it brought about a rapid reduction in cost per seat mile on long-haul trips. Thus the 747, not Concorde, proved to be the successor to the 707. At the same time, partly through the costs of the new planes before the older ones were fully amortized, partly through a general reduction in traffic growth and partly through general overprovision coupled with rigid fares policies, airline profits began to drop. Pan Am, which made a profit of $209,000,000 in the four years to 1966, made a $152,000,000 loss in the four years to 1970. On 7 February 1970 it cancelled one of its eight options on Concorde, leading to a loss of confidence on the part of other major world airlines. In 1973 both Pan Am and TWA cancelled all their options – and this was the effective end of the options list.

The calculations made by these airlines are shrouded in commercial secrecy. Estimates suggest that the plane would have cost £10,000,000 to build in 1968; it was revealed as £13,000,000 in 1971,[39] and by 1972 it had risen to perhaps £18,000,000 to £23,000,000, twice the cost of the 747. Further, though the plane's speed makes it half as productive again as the 707, it is also half as much again as costly to fly, and therefore it is up to twice as expensive to fly, per seat mile, as the 747. Because of time constraints on the times businessmen fly the Atlantic, and because of Concorde's need to refuel on flights of above 3,500 miles, its advantage over subsonic planes is greatly reduced.[40] The figures, therefore, told against Concorde, and BAC were left with the argument that if British Airways and Air France bought the plane, then other airlines would buy too.[41] In the event, of course, they did not; the bluff was called. Though airlines had seventy-four options on the plane by 1973, when these were cancelled there were only nine firm orders – from the two national airlines.[42]

There was thus virtually no possibility of repaying the research and development costs. A French official report had suggested that, to achieve this, it might be necessary to sell as many as 300 aircraft, a higher figure than any estimate had suggested was possible. The British government at this time was apparently still hoping for a total sale of between sixty and ninety, to recover between 20 and 30 per cent of the cost.[43] Edwards in 1972 estimated that there would be hidden losses in subsidized sales to the airlines, plus operating losses on Concorde by these airlines themselves, and it was generally thought among outside experts that additionally there were still £200,000,000 or more of development costs that might be saved.[44] But by then the critical question was whether the plane could in future even cover its direct production costs, a point on which a House of Commons committee was expressing scepticism.[45] The £21,000,000 price, which British Airways paid for its five Concordes in 1972, almost certainly can never have paid even the production cost.

In the event, all the calculations proved irrelevant. For the only airlines to order Concorde were the two captive state airlines of British Airways and Air France. To BA's five and AF's four must be added two production aircraft written off after testing. That leaves five planes, never sold after the order book collapsed in 1973. And these seem unlikely ever to find buyers, unless the British government takes them, as well as the existing planes owned by the airlines, and runs them through a Concorde leasing corporation. The British government is under heavy pressure to do that, for British Airways made a £17,000,000 loss on its Concorde operation in 1977. However the bill for Concorde is paid, after all, it is paid by the taxpayer.

The irony is that, almost certainly, the predictions of the most severe critics have proved right. Given the absurd economics of producing planes at a loss, it would have paid the two governments to cancel the project at any stage to save whatever money they could. But given a French insistence on continuing, as the Central Policy Review Staff pointed out in their advice to the government, the costs would have had to be paid in compensation anyway, so there was no point in withdrawing.[46]

THE LESSONS OF CONCORDE

By the time the sixteenth and last Concorde left the Filton works outside Bristol in 1978, the total costs of the project, including the final R and D bill and the production costs, had escalated to some £2,000,000,000. It was one of the costliest commercial blunders – perhaps the costliest – in history. The question is to discover at what point, and in what ways, the critical mistakes were made.

It is easy to say that the most critical error of all was the signature of the 1962 agreement. In many ways this was an astonishing affair. The government reached a binding agreement with another government, with no (or minimal) provision for withdrawal or reconsideration, to develop a totally new kind of airplane without even an elementary notion of its performance specification. Consequently there could be no question of a proper estimate either of costs – which finally escalated over ten times the original estimate for the R and D costs alone – or of sales, which were apparently not even considered until six years later. The Treasury's strong reservations were seemingly ignored in the scramble to sign. The only reasonable explanation is that the British government of the day were tricked. They believed that the agreement, and the evident gamble it involved, was the price they would pay to enter Europe. And in this they were mistaken, for in all probability President de Gaulle had already made up his mind.

This, however, is slightly too simple. The question of the agreement would never have arisen had not a lobby (consisting of the government departments responsible and the aircraft manufacturers themselves) worked consistently, over a six-year period, to prepare the ground. Its method was to set up a committee with a modest budget, to commission design studies with slightly less modest budgets, until a scheme emerged that seemed plausible. In the language of Peter Levin, this is the stage of *espousal* of a project or policy: the stage when, in Civil Service parlance, it is taken on board. From then to government *commitment* is a major step.[47] But, given good tactical timing, such as the fear of missing the European boat in 1962, even a highly unsound, inadequately prepared brief may seem convincing.

Even after 1962, there is the question of whether withdrawal would have been possible or wise. The argument was constantly used that it would involve total loss in compensation without compensating gains. Even then had withdrawal occurred in 1964 against the then estimated cost of the project, it would have been a bargain for the British government. Indeed, the psychological attitude of successive British governments seems to have resembled nothing so much as that of a Las Vegas gambler hoping to cancel out his last loss. Such expectations are almost invariably disappointed – and so it was with Concorde.

The question remains of what would have been a reasonable strategy. The odd fact is that the Zuckermann Committee on the

Management and Control of Research and Development, reporting in 1961, had already provided an answer: a project study should be carried out for each major project before a decision was taken to proceed to a full development contract. This study would examine in detail the scientific and technical problems in developing a system to meet particular requirements, leading to a plan of design, development and costing, including an indication of subsequent production cost. The report of a steering group in 1969 showed that in most cases such project studies had not been done in the detail suggested in the Zuckermann report; that on a number of projects, firms had deliberately submitted over-optimistic estimates, and that the Ministry of Aviation had been reluctant to correct them; but that even if project studies were carried through to the right depth, the estimates in them would still be subject to wide error margins.[48] The group accordingly recommended a two-stage investigation: one, after about 15 per cent of total development cost had been expended over about two years, where there should be a first, well-founded, synthetic estimate of development and production costs; and a second, some time later, with a detailed and refined cost breakdown. This would certainly need a better trained and more experienced staff in the Ministry of Aviation's technical branches, plus a new system of record-keeping for cost purposes.[49]

Certainly, something was known inside government about the problem of cost escalation – and before 1962. The steering committee of 1969 reported an investigation of 1958, not apparently published, by an operational research team which had covered over a hundred projects and which had found an average cost escalation of 2.8 times the original estimate, with extremes up to 5.0 times and more. It had concluded that the main causes, apart from inflation, included changes in operational requirements; lack of proper definition of the research and development task; and incomplete appreciation by the contractor of the full scope of the necessary work.[50] Coupled with the Treasury's 1971 confession that since 1945 civil aircraft development has 'presented a pretty disappointing picture' and that in the early 1960s projects went ahead which were 'obviously and wildly over-optimistic',[51] it seems that some kind of control should already have been possible in 1962. That it was not, must be ascribed to political considerations that finally outweighed economic assessment.

As to broader policies, in 1965 the report of the Committee of Inquiry into the Aircraft Industry laid down a series of important guidelines. Since the UK industry tended to have lower production levels than the Americans, it suggested, the problem was that it found it difficult to recoup its Research and Development costs – and in both countries, R and D costs tended to bear a much higher ratio to net output value than in other manufacturing industries.[52] It found also that the British industry's commercial record had been disappointing, and that it had required a great deal of government support – for at least 30 to 50 per cent of total costs. Though there was a code for some continuing government support, it should be reduced to the level typical for comparable other industries.[53] This suggested not only cooperation with other countries, but also concentration on projects where development costs were reasonable in relation to the expected market. In particular, civil aircraft should be concentrated on projects with a large potential market in relation to costs; though it was impossible to lay down rigid rules, the committee thought that in general these would tend to be medium-short range, small-medium sized, and of simple design. Better market research was needed, to avoid frequent previous over-optimism about sales and about the British size of the market. The Ministry of Aviation's market research department would need to be greatly strengthened. In general manufacturers should be prepared to contribute 50 per cent of the launching costs (though a case like Concorde might be special). And, for major civil aircraft, cooperation with Europe would generally be necessary.[54]

It sounds almost like a recipe for doing everything that Concorde was not. (Indeed it sounds like a recipe for cooperation on the European Airbus, which the British government rejected in 1969 and which has become one of the few outstanding European projects of the 1970s). But, one can say, the Plowden Committee had the benefit of hindsight in relation at least to Concorde's first days. The question must still be whether such statements of good intention are enough.

For the overwhelming impression from the Concorde story is that there did indeed exist some kind of Concorde lobby and that, at least at that time, it united the commercial aircraft manufacturers and the civil servants who would be responsible for giving them contracts. Both of them saw prestige and excitement in the development of a major new project at the margins of technical knowledge. The manufacturers also saw the possibility of big profits – and, given the contractual arrangements they succeeded in making, profits there certainly were. Behind them stood the politicians, obsessed with similar visions of British prestige. For them it was 'supersonic or nothing'. As Geoffrey Rippon, Minister of Aviation under Sandys during 1960, is alleged to have said: 'If we don't do this we might as well give up and knit Union Jacks for tourists.' Finally, there was the glittering prize, or so it seemed, of Common Market entry.

The most astonishing fact in all this, is that no one seems to have been interested in the plane's commercial possibilities. At this time there was virtually no market research knowledge within the relevant ministries. Cost estimates were simply made up. For the fact was that all the interests concerned wanted to build the plane for reasons of prestige, and had no incentive at all to consider mundane marketing matters. The only body that might, the Treasury, was systematically starved of information, for politicians like Rippon believed that their 'narrow book-keeping' approach was misconceived. Significantly, when one leading manufacturer was asked why the industry never considered the alternative of developing a big commercial plane to compete with the Americans' 747, his answer was that it would be 'boring'. And when Farnborough in the early 1960s evaluated the European Airbus, it concluded that there would be no market for this type of plane. This must have been one of the reasons for the British government's disastrous withdrawal from the project.[55]

It was a massive gamble, and it resulted in a massive loss. For, almost certainly, a cool assessment of Concorde's prospects, against the background of the likely development of the 747 and the associated changes in world airline economics, could already have shown in 1960 that the commercial prospects were almost non-existent. But none of this was done.

It would be good to think that governmental decision processes are more rational now. Two examples may prove that perhaps they are. The American SST, Concorde's bigger and faster rival, was also the result of a snap decision for prestige reasons, this time by the Kennedy administration in June 1963, after the Pan Am option on Concorde was announced, despite warnings from an expert committee about the dangers of cost escalation. It too was defended by an embattled administration – the Nixon one – on arguments of prestige and job protection. But it was finally killed by a Senate vote, refusing to provide the necessary appropriations, in March 1971.[56] In Britain, the government in 1978 announced that Rolls-Royce would provide engines for the new Boeing 757 short- and medium-haul plane, successor to the highly successful 727, and that it was seeking re-entry into the European Airbus project. At last, it seemed, Britain was in the business of 'boring', conventional planes that made money. Perhaps, after all, the Concorde experience had its value.

CHAPTER 5

San Francisco's BART System

San Francisco's Bay Area Rapid Transit, or BART, has many admirers, especially among first-time visitors who throng the city's streets during the year-long tourist season. For many of these, the seventy-one-mile BART system is the archetype of everything a modern urban rapid transit system should be, and a model for the great majority of America's large cities that still lack one. These people are impressed by the calm elegance of the stations, each individually designed with mosaic-tiled walls; by the uncannily silent, air-conditioned, carpeted trains; by the automatic train control system that seems effortlessly to accelerate the train to its 80 m.p.h. programmed speed; by the computerized ticketing system which, through a single strip of plastic and without direct human intervention, debits the passenger for each journey until the credit on his ticket is exhausted. For them, BART seems indeed a modern American technological miracle, comparable almost with the feats of Houston's Space Center.

But BART also has many critics, especially among the 4,100,000 residents of the Bay Area. These critics tend to be very well informed and very vocal. They point to the fact that, in 1976, BART carried only 51 per cent of the passengers forecast when the fateful decision was taken to build the system; that the operating loss ($40,000,000 in 1975–6) is so great that every passenger costs the taxpayer more than he contributes in fare revenue; that the system is still plagued by technical faults, which prevent it from exploiting its space-age technology; that the system has almost completely failed to end the typical Californian's long love affair with his car.

Most important of all, the admirers and the critics disagree on the wider lessons to be learned from the BART experience. Other American cities (Washington DC, Atlanta) have committed themselves to schemes in some ways like BART. Others (Los Angeles, Denver) have agonized long over the issue, but have so far failed to agree to rail plans or get them accepted. And many experts, including influential ones in the Department of Transportation in Washington, think that BART is an expensive object lesson to these other cities, showing them what they must avoid.

Whatever the outcome of the debate in these cities, there can be no doubt that in the sense used here BART is a Great Planning Disaster. It is manifestly criticized for its failings and it has conspicuously failed to fulfil the predictions made for it. Had the citizenry of the Bay Area the ability to foresee the true future, there seems little doubt that they would have rejected the whole BART proposal out of hand. But, in the critical decisions between 1959 and 1962, the information on which they acted was seriously deficient.

In this chapter, therefore, we shall follow these critical decisions, seeing them first through the filter of the perceptions of that time, and then through the lens of reality in the late 1970s. We shall see how far this reality diverged from expectations, and how the decision-makers had to react to the consequences. Lastly, we shall try to sum up on the forces that led to the decisions to build the BART system, looking at alternative explanations of the facts in terms of different theories of decision-making.

BART DECISIONS: THE STAGES OF COMMITMENT

The facts of BART history are not in dispute; indeed they are exceedingly public knowledge, since they have been retailed by countless local authors.[1] They start with a 1949 Act of California legislature allowing the creation of a Bay Area Rapid Transit District and a 1951 Act creating a Rapid Transit Commission for this district, with powers to make a preliminary study; this duly reported in favour of a full-scale consultancy study, and in 1953 the legislature approved a loan, to match local funds, for this purpose.

Accordingly, in August 1953 the new commission appointed one of four contenders, the New York engineering firm of Parsons, Brinckerhoff, Hall and Macdonald, to carry out the study and report by 1956. There were four basic questions posed by the commission to the consultants: (1) Is an interurban rapid transit system needed? (2) If so, what areas should it serve and along what routes? (3) What type of facility would best meet the area's needs? (4) Would the cost be justified? The consultants' report, delivered in January 1956, logically tried to answer each of these questions – but in different degrees of detail and precision.

1. Need. Unsurprisingly, perhaps, the consultants concluded that there was a need. But, interestingly, it was defined in terms of the chief problem as the consultants saw it: growing population, and rising car use, leading to increased congestion, which in turn posed a threat to the role of the existing centres and sub-centres of the region as concentrations of employment, commerce and culture. So, from the outset, a principal *raison d'être* of the proposed system was its role in preserving the existing spatial structure of the Bay Area.

2. Routeing. This followed logically from the first. The system, initially 123 miles long, would link existing centres, especially the two major city centres of San Francisco and Oakland, by means of an under-the-bay tunnel.

3. Character. The report did look at a variety of technologies ranging from bus to monorail. But, following tradition (they had acted as consultants for the original New York subway at the start of the century), the consultants reported in favour of supported trains, that is conventional trains running on rails.

4. Cost. Here the consultants were vaguest. They did produce a hard cost estimate of at least $586,000,000 and perhaps $130,000,000 more. And they were quite straightforward that this would mean an annual subsidy of at least $33,000,000 to $38,000,000 that would not be met from revenue. But they did not deal with the justification except in general terms, and their

final conclusion bordered on rhetoric: 'We do not doubt that the Bay Area citizens can afford rapid transit: we question seriously whether they can afford *not* to have it.'[2] The Parsons, Brincker-hoff report thus gave technical endorsement to the proposal, making it seem credible and even respectable; thus it was a vital first stage in winning political support. But from then on, several hurdles had to be negotiated.

First, since public subsidy was demonstrably needed, an acceptable way had to be found of providing it. A study by Stanford Research Institute in March 1956 suggested property taxes, with a higher rate for those areas directly served by the new system, plus sales tax, plus bridge tolls from the existing San Francisco–Oakland bridge.

Secondly, an agency would need to be set up with a commitment to build. The Stanford study suggested that a public agency was appropriate, and in the summer of 1957 the legislature passed an Act dissolving the Rapid Transit Commission and creating a permanent San Francisco Bay Area Rapid Transit District (BARTD), with effect from 11 September 1957. Its remit covered five counties: San Francisco, Marin and San Mateo counties west of the bay, and Alameda and Contra Costa counties to the east; any of these could withdraw and four more distant counties could join if they wished. Most importantly, the district could raise money both by issuing bonds up to 15 per cent of the assessed property value, and by levying property tax; it was also allowed to issue revenue bonds payable only from revenues, and to levy a special tax for general administration, maintenance and operation. This last was immediately used to pay for the general expenses of the new district.

Thirdly, public opinion had to be rallied. The major newspapers of the Bay Area were unreservedly in favour, both in persuading the legislature to set up BARTD, in 1956, and subsequently. But there was opposition from highway interests in the State Senate. Finally, in 1959, the legislature in Sacramento approved a bill providing that as long as voters approved a minimum $500,000,000 bond issue, then some $115,000,000 could be appropriated from Bay Bridge toll reserves to pay for the

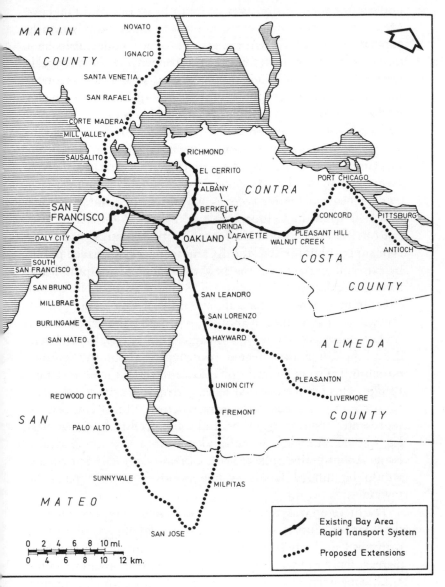

Figure 4: The BART System.

underwater tube section between San Francisco and Oakland. Meanwhile, the first signs of trouble had emerged: the engineering consortium appointed in April 1959 to produce the detailed system design (consisting of Parsons, Brinckerhoff, Quade and Douglas, the new name of the previous consultants, plus Tudor Engineering and the Bechtel corporation) reported in May 1961 that the package would cost $1.3 billion – over $600,000,000 more than originally forecast, and some $400,000,000 more than legislative powers permitted. The response was interesting; in April 1961, after much controversy and manœuvring in Sacramento, the legislature approved a bill allowing a bond issue to be approved on a 60 per cent favourable vote, as against the two-thirds majority that was usual in Californian law. This was critical for two reasons: first, it was thought that the proposal might win 60 per cent support but not two-thirds; and secondly, if it failed to pass by November 1962 then the 1959 arrangement to apply bridge tolls would lapse.

From then, it was a race against time. It was complicated in one way, but simplified in another, when first San Mateo county (in December 1961) and then Marin County (in May 1962) withdrew, the latter after heated controversy about the technical possibility of running trains on a lower level of the Golden Gate Bridge. This left a truncated seventy-five-mile system, estimated to cost $923,200,000 for fixed infrastructure. Of this $132,700,000 represented the transbay tube, to be financed from bridge tolls, leaving the remainder to be funded from a $792,000,000 bond issue. Additionally, rolling stock estimated to cost $71,200,000 would be funded from revenue bonds against a pledge of revenues.

The first step was to win official endorsement of this plan from the Boards of Supervisors (or local councils) of each of the three counties (San Francisco, Alameda and Contra Costa) left in the district. San Francisco readily agreed, Alameda (including Oakland) concurred more reluctantly and Contra Costa approved in July after considerable pressure had been put on an undecided member. Thence, a committee of citizens was formed to 'educate' the citizens to vote for the proposition. Business, especially the major Chambers of Commerce and the Bay Area Council, was enthusiastic; some big corporations helped to pay for public relations, and there was no real opposition. Finally, in early November both the San Francisco daily newspapers, the *Chronicle* and the *Examiner*, gave their endorsement. The proposition passed by 61 per cent on 6 November 1962. Though San Francisco voted nearly 67 per cent in favour, Alameda recorded just over 60 per cent and Contra Costa less than 55 per cent. This proved the perspicacity of those who had secured the change from a two-thirds rule and who had provided that the three counties' votes should be merged. BART was now in business – or nearly so.

In fact almost immediately the district had to fight a major legal action alleging that the bond issue election was invalid and that the contract for engineering services, issued by BART to the consultants immediately after the election, was also invalid. Though the district won, it claimed afterwards that the action had cost between $12,000,000 and $15,000,000 in extra construction costs due to inflation.

BART UNDER CONSTRUCTION: 1962–74

Three weeks after the bond issue, BART hired the Parsons, Brinckerhoff-Tudor-Bechtel consortium as consultants, without asking for alternative bids. The citizens' suit also contested this action, and though the judge found it perfectly legal, it did emerge that the BART directors had virtually no alternative because between them they had little engineering expertise and therefore little ability to hire necessary staff directly. Further, the financial agreement with the consultants, which the judge also found good, gave them no incentive to economize, since it awarded them a fixed percentage of the construction costs.[3]

The crucial decision had already been taken, on the basis of the consultants' report just before the bond issue election, to develop BART on the basis of a very advanced, indeed unknown, technology. The cars would be of lightweight construction; they would be controlled not by drivers but by computerized automatic train control. This involved advancing the existing state of the art in one giant leap – as *Fortune* magazine put it, rather like going directly from the DC–3 to the 747.[4] This would involve the necessity of using a large element of technology that was non-proven. Aerospace engineers, Burck says, have an axiom that if more than 10 per cent of a project is new technology, then there will be problems. BART's proportion was much higher than that; indeed it was almost a 100-per-cent new system.

Since the BART directors were by definition novices in un-explored territory, they handed all this work over to the consultants, who were to manage design and procurement. In turn, the consultants would hire appropriate companies not merely to build equipment, but effectively to design it first. No one was given the job of overseeing what aerospace technologists call systems engineering: anticipating the problems that would arise in putting new technologies together into a system. Further, since the technology was novel, neither BART nor its consultants could provide precise specifications of what they wanted. Instead, they supplied performance specifications: objectives that a system had to meet. Thus the train control system should provide 'automatic and continuous detection of the presence of trains'; cars were to weigh no more than 62,000 pounds and to be able to accelerate at 3 m.p.h. per second. It was left to the manufacturers to design the goods to these specifications. As *Fortune* again put it, while the New York subway authority would specify not just an apple but a Red Delicious, BART just asked for a palatable fruit, leaving it to the grower to define what that might mean.

In practice the consultants found that traditional railroad manufacturers were incapable of meeting specifications of this kind; they had got out of the habit of technical innovation. So they called in aerospace manufacturers to provide the cars and control systems: Rohr for the cars, Westinghouse for the controls. One problem was that Rohr had had next to no experience of the problems of railroad operation. They had to start from scratch.

This had three predictable and associated results. The first, that in practice the new equipment proved to develop all kinds of snags, some of them serious. The second, that it took longer to design, and in particular to be brought into operation, than had been predicted. And the third, that the costs of the operation escalated.

The biggest problems came with the control system. Such systems are used on rapid transit systems elsewhere in the world, for instance on London's Victoria Line, opened in 1968–9. Experienced suppliers did tender for BART, but its consultants opted in October 1967 for a new Westinghouse system, as yet unproven. Once in operation, it was found that it produced 'ghost trains' – reports that track was occupied when in fact it was not. This proved to be caused by overheating of the detector boxes, and was cured by covering them. Much more seriously, a car stopped without power could be lost by the system. For this reason the California Public Utilities Commission, which is responsible for licensing, refused to approve the system, so that BART actually had to open in 1972 with an archaic system of manual block control, more appropriate to George Stephenson's Stockton and Darlington Railway than to the space age. True, the defect could prove dangerous only in very special and rare circumstances. But it proved so nagging that even by November 1976 the system was still not working as originally planned; at that time the original aim of a 90-second and a 45 m.p.h. average speed was abandoned, and maximum speed was cut from 80 to 70 m.p.h.

The lightweight cars proved the other major problem. Even in 1975, three years after the start, 40 per cent were out of action on a typical day; in the first five months of 1977, breakdowns still averaged twenty a day. Failures were legion among the motors, electronic components, brake systems, door controls and air-conditioners. Most of these could not be laid directly at the door of Rohr, the main contractors: they were component failures, exacerbated by the fact that Rohr had little tradition of controlling and coordinating subcontractors.

Mainly because of these control problems, completion of the system was seriously delayed. In the 1962 consultants' report, the system was to have been four-fifths finished by 1 January 1969, and complete on 1 January 1971. In fact service on the East Bay section was started only in September 1972, and on the transbay tube in October 1974. This last delay was due mainly to problems with the automatic train control system, which was particularly crucial on the seven-mile, 80-m.p.h. section under the bay; a complex and extensive back-up system had to be designed to guard against the problem of the lost trains, and even this was not completely satisfactory at the time of opening.

These delays and modifications cost money. During the development of the control system, no less than 114 change orders were issued, leading to an escalation in the cost of the contract from $26,200,000 to $35,800,000. Then, in 1973 BART and Westinghouse had to negotiate a $1,300,000 contract for the back-up control system; further modifications, called for by a Senate panel report of January 1973, would take an estimated $5,000,000 for modification to cars and control systems.[5]

Total costs therefore rose sharply. Already by 1965 BART announced that it would exceed the original estimate, and in July 1966 it issued a revised figure of $941,700,000, which was $150,000,000 more than the 1962 estimate – together with a revised amount for the transbay tube at $179,900,000, which was $41,200,000 up on 1962. The latter was covered fairly painlessly by raising the limit that could be supplied from toll revenues, but the basic system proved more difficult. A 1967 suggestion for an additional bond issue met with opposition, and by April another proposal had emerged: raising the bridge toll, and drawing on state truck taxes. This too failed to pass the legislature, and in July 1967 BART announced a freeze on future construction. During the spring and summer of 1968 a number of other measures to aid BART, through extra tolls, extra taxes and a mixture of both, all failed. Finally, after bitter fighting, the legislature passed a Bill on 27 March 1969, approving a ½c additional sales tax in the three-county district which would service up to $150,000,000 of bond sales.

By January 1971 the total costs of BART had risen to $1,367,200,000, of which general obligation bonds amounted to $792,000,000, sales tax bonds $150,000,000, toll bridge funds $180,000,000 and Federal grants $125,000. The final total, computed after BART began operation over the whole of the seventy-one-mile system in October 1974, was $1.6 billion. And only at that point was it possible to begin to judge the performance of the system in practice.

BART IN OPERATION

Fortunately, BART's progress has been checked by a massive monitoring study: the BART Impact Program, sponsored by the Federal Departments of Transportation and of Housing and Urban Development, and conducted mainly by consultants to the Metropolitan Transportation Commission. Though it will be some years before a final evaluation is possible, by 1976–7 enough evidence was available for a reasonably definitive verdict. And that verdict is highly unfavourable.[6]

The 1962 consultants' report[7] was the document on which the critical decisions to build BART – above all the November 1962 bond election – were taken. It contains predictions of traffic that can be compared with reality, always bearing in mind that BART in 1976 and 1977 was failing to work as originally designed, in matters of both frequency and reliability. M. M. Webber shows that, comparing the 1962 forecast for 1975 with the 1976 reality, traffic was only 51 per cent of forecast: 131,370 passengers on an average weekday, against a forecast 258,496. Further, though the 1962 report expected that 61 per cent of passengers would divert from cars, in fact only 35 per cent actually did so: 44,000 against a forecast 157,000. And, as these people left spare capacity on the highways, so did additional traffic arrive to fill it up. Webber shows conclusively that 'BART has brought about a rise in total transbay travel by both auto and public transit'.[8] In the whole Bay Area, the effect on traffic is so slight as to be undetectable. Because of this, traffic volumes and congestion are still at pre-BART levels and, with increasing car use, can be expected to rise in future. Half BART's transbay riders in fact came from buses, with serious effects on the viability of bus operation.

Overall, the 1962 report forecast that by 1975–6 BART would be producing an operating surplus of $11,000,000. The reality (based on preliminary figures for 1975–6) was a deficit of $40,300,000, and BART was kept going only by a temporary extension of the ½c sales tax, agreed by the legislature as an emergency measure in 1974.[9] In 1976 this was extended until 1978, and in 1977 an act permanently established it.[10] In the year 1977–8 fare revenues were expected to yield less than 35 per cent of operating expenses; in one form or another, the taxpayer was contributing $2 for every $1 raised in fare revenues.

Webber's analysis shows that only 11 per cent of the capital investment and 37 per cent of operating costs (in 1975–6) were paid for by beneficiaries, the capital cost by motorists in the form of bridge tolls (for which they gained more roadspace, a function of the improvement of the double deck San Francisco–Oakland Bridge), the operating costs by fares. The rest of the costs are spread right across the BART three-county district. Since the main sources of revenue are property and sales taxes (both inherently regressive kinds of taxation), Webber and others argue that the main burden falls on the poor, while traffic surveys show that the main beneficiaries, the passengers, are disproportionally from the higher-income brackets. As Webber laconically concludes, 'Clearly, the poor are paying and the rich are riding.'[11]

This is perhaps unsurprising, given that BART was designed from the start to connect white-collar suburban commuters with downtown San Francisco and Oakland. What is perhaps more surprising is that, according to estimates by a group of economists at Berkeley, both buses and cars are cheaper in real costs than BART. The main reason is that even if BART achieves full design efficiency, the Berkeley study indicates that it will still cost more than buses to run – and that it may even cost more to run than a car for each passenger.

These sums are based on the economist's concept of costs. On narrower accountancy criteria, taking account of BART's need to repay its borrowings each year at its favourable 4.14 per cent interest rate, plus the need to cover operating costs, Webber finds that the cost per trip averages $4.48. So, with the average fare at 72c, the subsidy averages no less than $3.76 per journey.[12]

Admittedly, BART's costs were high because the district, as a pioneer, got relatively little Federal aid; systems starting in the 1970s would fare better with Washington. But they also reflect the extraordinarily labour-intensive character of the BART operation, despite the emphasis on automation.

In fact operating costs on BART, as on other transit systems in the Bay Area, were rising far faster than inflation in the mid-1970s. BART's operating costs rose 105 per cent in only two years to 1975, while AC Transit (the area-wide bus agency) saw its costs rise 104 per cent over a five-year period, and MUNI (the local rail-bus system in the city of San Francisco) had an increase of only 46 per cent over the same five-year period. Personnel costs on BART represent 67 per cent of total costs, despite the highly automated character of the operation, against 85–6 per cent on the other two systems.[13] And on all three systems, operating costs have risen while fares have remained roughly constant. Though BART's fares only covered 31.8 per cent of costs in 1975–6, AC did slightly worse and MUNI only slightly better. The predictable result was that all three systems were running deficits by the mid-1970s and that these were expected to worsen by the end of the decade. By 1979–80, indeed, the accumulated five-year deficit for the three systems was expected to be as much as $233,700,000, of which BART alone would contribute $173,400,000. Thus it can be argued that BART not only failed to pay its own way, but also damaged the viability of the existing systems. By failing to divert many car drivers, but instead taking passengers from the buses, it placed the entire public transport system of the Bay Area in jeopardy.[14]

As Webber concludes:

The most notable fact about BART is that it is extraordinarily costly. It has turned out to be far more expensive than anyone expected, and far more costly than is usually understood. High capital costs (about 150 per cent of forecast) plus high operating costs (about 475 per cent of forecast) are being compounded by low patronage (50 per cent of forecast) to make for average costs per ride that are twice as high as the bus and 50 per cent greater than a standard American car. With fares producing only about a third of the agency's out-of-pocket costs, riders are getting a greater transportation bargain than even bus and auto subsidies offer; and yet only half the expected numbers are riding.[15]

A RETROSPECTIVE VIEW: WHAT WENT WRONG?

So, by any reasonable criteria, BART is proving a planning disaster. The question must be where and how the mistakes were made. By going back over the history with a degree of hindsight, it is possible to chart the main lines.

First, BART was posited on its ability to stem the apparently inexorable trend towards the private car. It has manifestly failed to do so, carrying as it does only 2.5 per cent of all trips within its area and 5 per cent of peak trips. The basic reason, Webber stresses, is that it simply does not serve the needs of the Bay Area residents. These people care about door-to-door journey time; BART's planners were obsessed with the time on the BART journey alone. By choosing a rail system, they created a configuration that puts BART out of walking reach for most people. Since they must use buses or cars to feed into BART stations, most consider that they might as well continue with those modes. In a Berkeley study of user attitudes, 59 per cent said that it was impossible to use BART for the work journey, 86 per cent of these saying that this was because it was too far from home or job.[16] Webber concludes: 'It is the door-to-door, no-wait, no-transfer features of the automobile that, by eliminating access time, make private cars so attractive to commuters – not its top speed. BART offers just the opposite set of features to the commuting motorist, sacrificing just those ones he values most.'[17]

The original mistake, therefore, was in perceiving the problem to be solved. It was not seen in the way that the potential passengers – the only people whose views mattered – would see it. Rather, it was seen in terms of the obsessions of the planners, who were in turn viewing it from an operator's point of view. The 1956 consultants' report makes it clear that they thought the line-haul speed was far more important to the commuter than the feeder time; but they had no direct evidence of this, and they were clearly wrong. Subsequent studies, the world over, have proved conclusively that people place a far higher value on waiting and transfer time than on time in motion – even the slow motion of congested traffic.

Allied to this was the failure to grasp that even if successful in diverting car commuters, BART could have little overall impact because too few of these people lived near the projected system. And here, it seems, BART planners made a quite unjustifiable commitment of faith: they assumed that, in some way, the system would work over the longer term to shift the patterns of living and working in the Bay Area. Indeed, the crucial 1956 report specifically claims that BART would encourage the development of large, nucleated, high-intensity business districts in appropriate locations.[18] What this ignored was the fact that Bay Area residents were even then spread over a wide area, and were becoming more widespread all the time. The system could not reach the majority of these people except by transfers from buses or cars – and, as we have just seen, in practice people do not find that worth while.

The system could have worked, in fact, only if Californians had abandoned Californian living patterns and had taken up European ones. And the 1962 report, from the same consultants, seems to be suggesting that indeed this might happen. The major benefits, according to this report, would not be transport ones: they included the preservation of urban centres, the generation of higher property values, prevention of sprawl, better employment conditions and access to social, cultural and recreational facilities.[19] In fact the voters in the subsequent bond election did not find the issues presented in this way;[20] if they had, they might have rejected them. But it may have been very important to other key actors.

The first of these were the original engineering consultants who wrote the early planning reports: they effectively pre-empted the public interest in laying down a 'correct' pattern for the region's development and in asserting that development of rapid transit could help secure this pattern.[21] In doing so the planners ignored the fact that the people of the Bay Area were attached to their cars for good and rational reasons, as they themselves perceived them; the consultants assumed that these patterns could be broken, yet they offered no empirical justification.

It is important to be fair to the consultant-planners. The 1949 California Act, establishing the BART district, had specified a rail-type solution. The Department of Transportation's conclusion, in 1975, was that it was impossible to identify significant numbers of professionals who, at the critical time, during the 1950s and early 1960s, seriously questioned the rail concept. Buses were then losing traffic to cars. A 'saleable' system had to be rail-based. The notion of low-capital-intensive system was unknown. The 1956 consultants' report was received with almost unalloyed enthusiasm by the public, the press, the professional press and the California legislature. During the whole period from 1951 to 1957, no one apparently suggested any serious alternative to the BART concept.[22] Indeed, the very appointment of the consultants probably signified acceptance in advance of the rail idea, since they were known to be pro-rail.[23]

The second group of key actors consisted of those influential people, especially in the San Francisco and Oakland business worlds, who saw real advantage in the new patterns of development that the consultants promised, in particular the enhancement of the major commercial centres. These were influential in the Bay Area Council throughout the 1950s, then in the Blyth-Zellerbach Committee of 1961–2, which was an organization of business leaders with overlapping membership with the Bay Area Council; and in the Citizens for Rapid Transit organization, which was supported by contributions from those business interests (especially banking and construction) that stood to benefit from the bond issue.[24] These links were extraordinarily close, interconnected and persistent (Table 12). Despite this evidence, K.M. Fong, in his thesis on the subject, doubts that at any time there was some kind of conspiracy by these interests to build BART. The business leaders did not overtly represent their companies' interests. Rather, like the consultants and the public, they saw their campaign as being in the general public interest: what was good for Bay Area business was good for the Bay Area. And

BART: ILLUSTRATIVE INTERACTION AMONG KEY ACTORS

Professional Affiliations as Officers, Directors, or Elected Officials

Individual actors	Engineering				Banking					Industry					Research	Public & Gov't.		Labor	BART-related activities					
	Parsons, Brinckerhoff Quade and Douglas	Tudor Engineering	Bechtel Corporation	Kaiser Industries	Bank of America	American Trust	Crocker citizens	Wells Fargo	Blyth, Eastman, Dillon & Co. (then Blyth & Co.)	Bethlehem Steel	Kaiser Industries	Standard Oil of California	Pacific Gas and Electric	Westinghouse	Stanford Research Institute	Board of Supervisors	Chamber of Commerce	Labor unions	Bay Area Council, 1945	Bay Area Rapid Transit Committee, 1949	Bay Area Council Committee on Mass Rail Transit, 1950	Bay Area Rapid Transit Commission, 1951	Bay Area Rapid Transit District, 1957	Citizens for Rapid Transit, 1962
Stephen D. Bechtel Jr.			X												X				X					
William Waste			X				X																	X
Leland Kaiser				X																	X			
Mortimer Fleishhaker						X		X													X			X
Kendric B. Morrish					X	X															X			X
Carl F. Wente					X																			X
Marvin Lewis																X				X			X	
John C. Beckett														X								X	X	
Clair W. MacLeod																						X	X	
Sherwood Swan																					X	X	X	
Arthur J. Dolan, Jr.									X													X	X	
Adrien Falk													X				X				X	X		
Alan K. Browne					X												X		X	X		X		X
Thomas A. Rotell																	X		X			X	X	
H. L. Cummings																		X	X			X		X
Corporate action																								
Funded Bay Area Council			X		X	X			X			X	X				X							
Funded Citizens for Rapid Transit		X	X	X	X	X				X	X	X		X			X							
Received BART Contracts	X	X	X	X					X	X	X		X	X	X			X						

The chart represents an illustrative list only. No effort has been made to be exhaustive.
Source: Metropolitan Transportation Commission (1975), 42.

Fong, like the Department of Transportation, concludes that everyone – planners, political leaders, newspaper writers – shared the same belief in rapid transit: 'It may be unfair to judge the decisions of the 1950s and early 1960s by the preferences of the transportation planners of the 1970s.'[25]

The next key group were the voters – especially at the bond issue election of November 1962. Here, a statistical analysis of the actual vote indicates that opposition was localized – especially from communities, such as those in eastern Contra Costa county, that would get no direct benefit. But it is difficult to isolate reasons for support, which was fairly generalized. Certainly the poor did not perceive the regressive effect upon them. Nor did geographical areas clearly identify their interests pro- or anti-BART. But it must be remembered that the issue was very generally seen as one of traffic congestion; BART was presented as an alternative to forty extra lanes of freeway, and voters may have seen it as a way of getting other cars (not theirs) off the highway.[26]

Later, at the critical and hard-fought 1969 vote on the increase in sales tax, the State legislators became the key actors. But by this time, BART was seen as a *fait accompli*; the only question was how to find the $183,000,000 needed to complete the system, whether by sales tax or by a tax in one form or another on cars. It seems that the sales tax won, despite the dislike of Bay Area leaders, because the opponents of car taxes disliked them even more. They included the highway lobby (for obvious reasons), and also Governor Regan (for reasons of fiscal conservatism, and because he wanted to offer voters the prospect of a new Bay Bridge out of the existing bridge tolls). Certainly, no one then considered questions of equity between income groups or between areas; the sales tax was the product of political expediency in a difficult and complex situation.[27]

Most commentators on BART history, in fact, seem to agree that in practice the decision-making process was highly constrained by a perception of what the decision was about, and that this narrowness of vision was shared by businessmen, media people and voters alike. The technical planning process set no formal goals, looked at no alternatives, and made no formal evaluation until 1961. Obvious alternatives like the use of existing rail tracks on the lower deck of the Bay Bridge (which were taken up in 1958) were considered but dismissed. In any case, no one was then proposing alternatives such as reserved freeway bus lanes. The problem was seen as one of traffic congestion coupled with protest at freeway construction, in which San Francisco led the nation and the world. Mechanisms for public consultation and participation were weak. Although business interests did stand to benefit, no one was really against them. These business leaders, once established on the BART board, were so committed to the idea of rapid transit that, after the bond result, they were willing to give the whole planning job to the consultants – even to the extent of allowing fees as a percentage of costs.[28]

This in turn provides a part-explanation for the apparent willingness of the board to tolerate cost escalation. In fact, BART's record on this score is rather better than that of most comparable major public projects.[29] The escalation that did occur (40 per cent down to 1971) was mainly due to the failure of the original estimates to allow for possible contingencies beyond the typical engineering contract (which was by practice set at 10 per cent), plus an unrealistic construction schedule that failed to allow for the local community opposition that arose in the early 1960s (Berkeley objected to overhead structures, and voted local bonds to underground its section), plus – most important – inflation engendered by the Vietnam war. The original estimates did provide for 3 per cent per annum inflation, but the actual rate during the construction period for the San Francisco Bay Area was 6.5 per cent, a little above the average for twenty major American cities.[30] All these causes are fairly typical for major civil engineering projects in the 1960s and 1970s, especially those where the state of the art is uncertain.[31]

So there is fairly general agreement, among Bay Area experts, over what went wrong. At the critical times when decisions had to be made, in the 1950s and 1960s, almost everyone – techical experts, politicians, media people, the general public – had a certain perception of the problem. It was seen as traffic congestion. Some alternative to the private car was needed, and rail rapid transit was the one seriously considered. Sums were done to show that drivers would divert from their cars and make the system viable. But no one apparently considered whether this was plausible. Similarly, the cost estimates were accepted without even elementary scepticism. The fact was that everyone wanted to believe the predictions, because they seemed to offer a way out of serious present problems. Because of this desire, there was a mass suspension of disbelief, and almost ideological commitment to a new system. Further, because only a completely new technology could perform the needed miracle, the Bay Area committed itself to a vast research and development exercise with all the risks that that entailed. Perhaps, even had the true extent of the uncertainty been known, the voters of the area would not have taken the gamble they did. But no one seemed concerned even to estimate it.

BART'S LESSONS: THE AMERICAN RAPID TRANSIT DEBATE

BART failed, on vital criteria, in a metropolitan area that seems almost ideally suited for an experiment in rail rapid transit. The San Francisco Bay Area has a highly unusual configuration: the urban areas take a 'doughnut' shape around the bay,[32] and mountains rising from the water create another constraint, so that settlement becomes discontinuous inland; all this makes for long hauls under water or through hills – a circumstance uniquely favourable to rail rapid transit. Further, the central business core of San Francisco has proved extraordinarily resilient, with major new high-rise office developments; and the population of the city (admittedly, a minority of the total Bay Area population), displays a positively European preference for medium-density row housing close to the centre, in sharp contrast to the even, low-density sprawl and the decayed centres typical of most large American metropolitan areas in the 1970s.

Despite this, in the late 1960s and 1970s a number of these more typical areas have debated the wisdom of rapid transit investment, and some have committed funds. Others have agonized, but have so far held off. And there is increasing evidence that the BART experience is one of the most important elements in their decisions.

The critical new fact behind these debates has been the Federal entry into mass transit – a neat example of the UR element in planning. A 1964 Urban Mass Transportation Act established a programme of Federal matching grants to marry with local money. Then, in 1968, an Urban Mass Transportation Administration (UMTA) was set up within the Department of Transportation. It was followed by an Urban Mass Transportation Assistance Act in 1970, committing at least $10 billion of Federal money over twelve years. By end-March 1974, UMTA had distributed over $2.5 billion through 394 separate capital grants. All this was far from the circumstances of the early 1960s, when the people of the Bay Area had to carry the whole R and D costs of BART themselves.

Of the total planned capital spending by metropolitan areas over the period 1972–90, amounting to $61.7 billion, no less than 66 per cent ($41 billion) would be for rail rapid transit.[33] And, since the rail plans were concentrated in the nine largest urban areas, these received the lion's share of the funds; $511 per head over the period, as against $230 per head for all other urban areas. This heavy expenditure in turn reflected a concentration of funding on no less than 1,600 miles of new rail lines, most of it rapid transit (that is, urban short-distance rail transport of the BART type). A large part of the total was for five projected systems in cities where there had been no such system before: Washington, Los Angeles, Baltimore, Detroit and Atlanta.[34] And it is in these cities where the BART experience is most relevant.

Washington is one city that has taken the plunge: its Metro system, scheduled to open for the Bicentennial in 1976, actually managed to complete a token stretch of line in that year but a more complete inner-city network by late 1977. Here the story is in many ways similar to BART. A regional plan of 1959 recommended a balanced package including a 248-mile freeway network (most of which was later abandoned), an express bus system and a modest thirty-three-mile rail system, half in subway, to be developed by a special-purpose Federal agency. Congress in 1960 accordingly created the National Capital Transportation Agency, which duly set out to study rail transit and in 1962 reported to the President in favour of an eighty-three-mile, $796,000,000 system. It was significant that neither the 1959 nor the 1962 reports had any formal consideration of planning goals, save for the vague objective of 'improving transportation'; and that the 1962 plan produced no fully quantified analysis of alternatives. But in 1963 the NCTA lost responsibility for freeway construction, and henceforth pursued a single-minded goal of building transit. Its 1962 plan was rejected by Congress a year later, but in 1965 its more modest twenty-five-mile, $431,000,000 scheme was approved; accordingly, in 1966 President Johnson replaced it by a three-state Washington Metropolitan Area Transit Authority (WMATA) committed to building transit. In turn this authority returned with a plan for the ninety-eight-mile system, and in November 1968, six years after the BART vote in San Francisco, Washington voters approved the necessary bond issue by 71.4 per cent. Construction accordingly began in December 1969.

Since then, however, Metro has become the centre of BART-style controversy – and for similar reasons. Costs have escalated, from an original estimate of $2,500,000 to $8,000,000, due to delays in construction plus the effect of inflation; as with BART, the 10 per cent contingency allowance for costs proved hopelessly optimistic. Additionally, inner-area residents have become increasingly suspicious that the completed system will serve suburban commuters at their expense. So the issue, in the mid-1970s, was whether to complete the system, or to cut out extensions serving thirty-six stations, thus losing 26 per cent of forecast passengers and 35 per cent of forecast revenue, as well as running the risk of legal actions from those areas which would lose service. The only way out of this dilemma would be somehow to obtain extra Federal funding retrospectively – or to divert highway funds, a move that would arouse opposition from the State of Virginia, which is one of the three parties on WMATA.[35]

Professor Henry Bain is one of those who criticize Metro, and call for a cutback, quoting the lesson of BART. He writes:

Five million dollars is too much to spend on *anything* unless it will do some very wonderful things for people. There is something about our decision-making process that causes us to spend millions on studies and plans, and billions on projects and programs, without ever looking squarely at some basic facts that seem to call for some quite different courses of action.[36]

Bain points out that Metro's financial performance is posited on one million passengers a day – eight times the level BART is achieving. The problems, in practice, will be the same. Population is too sparse around the suburban stations to pick up enough clients. Once in their cars, people will continue to drive them to their destination if they can. Even if some transfer to Metro, Bain urges, the same phenomenon will occur as in San Francisco: by an Iron Law of congestion, traffic will expand to fill the available space.

Bain does however conceive that there are some favourable indications for Metro, not present for BART. Washington has an exceptionally large and spread-out central business district, in which traffic congestion is rife for long hours of the day. (San Francisco's CBD (Central Business District), in contrast, is very compact; many trips are on foot.) It can also provide quite successfully for the low-income residents who live in the inner area, only about a hundred square miles in extent, around the central area. Bain's argument is that the system ought to stop here, and that the suburban counties should connect by commuter buses. In 1978 the issue was not resolved, but the system was proving to be strike-ridden and unreliable as well as expensive.

Atlanta, Georgia, is another city that has taken the fateful step. The citizens of its region voted in 1971 to accept a sixty-mile, $1.3 billion system together with improvements in bus systems, some involving reserved busways. Here, as in San Francisco, local business interests have strongly backed the plan, feeling that it will cement Atlanta's role as one of the United States' strongest regional growth centres. And here too the consultants are Parsons, Brinckerhoff, Tudor, Bechtel. But the system, on which construction started in 1975, has already escalated in cost from $1.3 billion (in 1971) to $2 billion, because of the delays in construction (partly occasioned by Federal insistence on an Environmental Impact Analysis). The Metropolitan Atlanta Regional Transit Authority (MARTA) has already received $200,000,000 in capital grants plus a $600,000,000 discretionary capital fund, amounting in total to some 10 per cent of presently committed funds; but this, together with 20 per cent local funding, would pay for only 13.7 miles of the system. Meanwhile MARTA is saddled with the obligation to run the existing Atlanta Transit System which runs at an increasing operational deficit. Thus, currently, transit planning in Atlanta is on the horns of a dilemma. Either it must claim more money from Washington or the State government, or it must rely more on a regressive sales tax. If none of these work, then fares will rise, denying the basis on which the 1971 proposal won broad popular acceptance. As the Office of Technology Assessment concluded in 1976, 'If UMTA policy holds, and if funds are not available on the State or local level, the Atlanta transit system will look far different from the way it was originally envisioned.'[37]

This hints at a tougher line on the part of UMTA. Indeed, in 1976 the Authority turned down the proposal for a very ambitious scheme in Denver, Colorado. This would have been a personal rapid transit system in which passengers rode small cars to their desired destination, with the aid of sophisticated computer technology. A prototype was tested at Morgantown, West Virginia, where it served the scattered campus of the local state university; it was at first plagued by technical defects but is now being expanded. Another system is operating at the giant Dallas–Fort Worth airport in Texas, serving an area that when fully developed will be larger than New York City; neither is this yet functioning as a proper personal rapid transit system, and there are doubts about the feasibility of developing the necessary technology – which was undoubtedly one of the reasons for the UMTA rejection of the Denver proposal in favour of a more modest bus-based scheme.[38]

This decision may have been symbolic. For Denver is one of a number of large metropolitan areas of the American west which have experienced their major growth since 1945, that is, in the age of mass car ownership, and which in consequence have developed on a decentralized, sprawling pattern. Phoenix in Arizona, Salt Lake City in Utah, San Diego in California are other examples. But the ultimate example is of course provided by the 10,000,000 mass of humanity in the 10,000-square-mile Southern California megalopolis based on Los Angeles. And it is here that the greatest rapid transit controversy has swung back and forth.

Los Angeles is known worldwide as the freeway metropolis, though its 400-mile system is now challenged by other major American urban areas. What is less known is that it once had the longest rapid transit system in the world: the Pacific Electric Railway, which at its peak in the 1920s boasted 1,114 track miles, 4,000 cars and more than 106,000,000 passengers a year. That system was allowed to decay from the 1920s onward, as car ownership rose, because in practice no one was prepared to save it.[39] But this was not for want of studies and plans. In 1925, 1933, 1939, 1945, 1947–8 and 1959–60 there were published reports for ambitious improvements to the existing system and/or the construction of new subways. But all foundered, and the last Pacific Electric train ran at the end of the 1950s.

The 1959–60 group of reports, by the consultants Coverdale and Colpitts, recommended a priority development of four radial lines serving the city centre; but the detailed financial analyses suggested that they could not be expected to pay except at an unrealistically low interest rate. Then, in 1968 a further consultant's report advocated an eighty-nine-mile, five-line system as the first stage of a 300-mile network. As in the previous plan, indeed as in virtually all previous plans, these would cross the central business district. But the voters of the area rejected this plan in a November 1968 bond issue.

This in no way deterred the rapid transit advocates. By 1971 the City of Los Angeles Department of City Planning was proposing a similar system. Then, in 1973, the Southern California Rapid Transit District (SCRTD), which had also been responsible for the 1968 report, proposed a $7 billion system requiring Federal help plus a major bond issue: $148,000,000 in 1975, rising to $300,000,000 a year in 1999 would be needed to service it. Of the $7 billion, no less than $6.6 billion would be required for rapid transit: 116 miles of 'fixed guideway' (i.e. rail) along six heavily trafficked corridors. Busways, proposed for two other corridors, would cost a little over $250,000,000. By the end of the twelve-year construction period, in 1986, the entire system could be running at a $287,000,000 a year deficit, which would be met by a bond issue plus a ¾ per cent sales tax plus highway funds.

The next year, however, it proved that this plan was insufficiently ambitious. A new plan, unveiled by SCRTD after consultations with local government, suggested building an ultimate network of 242 miles of transit, of which the initial 145 miles alone would have cost some $8–10 billion: as a Los Angeles planner succinctly put it, the biggest public works project in the history of mankind.[40] But in fact it was really just another version of plans that had been circulating in 1968, and earlier.

The immediate funding problem was to raise a ½c sales tax to start operations, though the 1974 report made it clear that more ambitious support would be needed soon after 1981.[41] The proposal went to the polls in November 1974, with heavy support – from four out of five county supervisors, from Mayor Thomas Bradley, from the *Los Angeles Times* and major radio stations, from the League of Women Voters, the Chamber of Commerce, the Auto Club of Southern California, and even the Sierra Club. Yet again, as in 1968, it failed by 56.7 to 43.3 per cent. Los Angeles city voted 54 per cent in favour, the working-class suburb of Compton voted 71 per cent yes, and even the citizens of Beverly Hills (who can hardly have expected to use the system intensively) voted 61 per cent. But the proposition was lost on the blue-collar votes of areas far from the proposed routes.

Marcuse and others argue that they were right. The proposed system would attract only 6 to 8 per cent of all trips, and many of these would come from the bus system; only 3.5 per cent were expected to switch from their cars. (Today, Los Angeles has a far lower proportion of public transport users than San Francisco, Washington, Boston, Chicago, Philadelphia or New York.) Because population is actually declining along the corridors as further dispersal takes place, by 1973 already no corridor met the critical criterion, of 20,000 peak-hour frequency, necessary to justify rail transit. The system would create an enormous tax burden, which would chiefly fall on the poor; but these people would get few benefits, since most of them lived far from the routes, and their jobs were outside the central area. (In fact the great majority of all citizens could not directly benefit.) Some low-income jobs would be lost. Researchers have calculated that the present pattern of taxation greatly benefits the car driver in Los Angeles at the expense of the bus passenger.[42] But if this is so, the new rapid transit would make the inequity worse; so Marcuse and others argue.[43] In fact, Marcuse claimed, the capital cost was sufficient to buy every family in the city a Honda Civic.[44]

Faced with this rebuff, the rapid transit interests refused to lie down. In 1975 they returned with the idea of a single 'starter line', fifty-three miles in length, costing $4,527 billion for capital and operating costs down to 1994. It would require the sales tax, already defeated in the 1974 vote. Meanwhile, until it could be agreed, the emphasis would be on the so-called Diamond lanes (reserved bus lanes) on the existing freeways.[45] By 1979 one of the Diamond lanes, along the Santa Monica freeway, had been abandoned; and a 'starter line' along Wilshire was again being considered.

So for the moment the matter rests, though doubtless not for long. The Los Angeles saga is an amazing illustration of an attempt to sell rail rapid transit to an area that has demonstrated it does not want it. One reason, the Office of Technology Assessment make clear, is that the SCRTD is enthusiastic about rapid transit and depends for its support on areas whose demand for equal treatment are by definition bound to lead to over-ambitious plans. Because the district has no representation from Los Angeles city, it may be ignoring the real needs of city residents, which are mainly for short-distance travel. (Oddly, for those who think of Los Angeles as the city of car-based mobility, the average journey to work is short, with 50 per cent going less than six and a half miles.) The legislative mandate, plus a commitment to a BART-type system, made SCRTD uneasy with the job of evaluating a full range of modes, though the Federal UMTA was encouraging it to do so. Similarly, the district argued for a 145-mile system leading to a 240-mile one, even though its own studies indicated that only about sixty miles were absolutely good for rail. The scale of the resulting budget undoubtedly alarmed many voters and killed the proposition at the 1974 vote.[46]

SOME LESSONS

The lessons of BART are at one level fairly clear, at another level less so.

At the first level, it is easy to use the benefit of hindsight. Rapid transit for the Bay Area became likely, even probable, as early as 1949 – as soon as the legislature set up first one body, then another, committed to the idea of exploring the need for rapid transit and then presenting the case to the public. To some extent, the exercise from then on was one of public relations. (Exactly the same has happened in Washington and Los Angeles, save that in the latter city, remarkably, the voters have resisted the case.)

Secondly, there was a considerable political force working in favour of BART, and of similar schemes elsewhere. But it would be much too facile to call it a conspiracy of downtown business interests, grinding their own axes. Many people, who wanted to be thought independent, also came to identify the future of the central business district with that of the larger urban mass. The role of that centre, and of people who travelled to it, came to be distorted out of all proportion; the interests of the great majority of residents and workers, who have other needs, were pushed into the background. This was only possible because of some distortion in mass perceptions. It was probably triggered by general frustration at traffic congestion and at the side-effects of mass car use. Rail transit appeared a miraculous and a virtuous answer, and no one stopped to ask rigorously how far it would really provide a cure.

Thirdly, and associatedly, there was a general suspension of disbelief about costs and technical problems. It was assumed that the highly optimistic timescale of the consultants could readily be followed; that there would be no technical snags delaying the project; that the rate of inflation would be gentle. No one, apparently, was tempted to act the joker and question some of these naïve beliefs.

Fourthly, and perhaps most oddly, there was a belief that the advent of a new technology would change established behaviour patterns: that Californian suburbanites, long wedded to their cars, would desert them for what they would perceive as a new form of transportation, quite unlike older, traditional kinds of public transport. Even more oddly, over time it would cause them to abandon their preference for low-density detached housing and to live more densely around transit stations. For this there was no empirical justification from behavioural studies. Again, it seems to represent some form of political wish-fulfilment.

But, it can be argued, it is unfair to use the benefit of hindsight. The people who made these decisions were time-bound and culture-bound. They reacted to events as they saw them, which they could not quite cope with: to the fact of rising car ownership, to the smog menace, to the apparent threat of endless freeway construction. The range of possible solutions seemed very small: traditional buses clearly were proving unattractive, and only a high-technology, capital-intensive solution seemed to offer much hope. Small wonder, then, that there was some naïvety in the response.

That is fair, but it does point lessons for the future. It does suggest some approximate ways in which we can guard against the same mistakes in the future. (Indeed, there is evidence that in the United States and elsewhere, the very scale of government involvement is bringing with it a much more systematic and hard-headed approach to project evaluation.) Clearly, such an approach would contain at least three main elements: the nature of the problem should be analysed much more critically; a systematic attempt should be made to identify the widest possible range of solutions; and estimates of timing and costing deserve a particularly sceptical look on the basis of accumulated past experience. We shall return to these principles, and treat them in more detail, at the end of this book.

CHAPTER 6

Sydney's Opera House

Sydney's new Opera House belongs to a select group of buildings that become immediate popular symbols. It *is* Sydney, just as Big Ben is London, the Arc de Triomphe is Paris and the Empire State Building is New York City. It could thus be argued that it put the city on some sort of mental map of great world cities. Furthermore, though residents and visitors disagree on its aesthetic merits, no one would question that it is a highly memorable building. Whether seen by day in the crisp Sydney sunlight, or at night against the reflected lights in the great harbour, its unusual sailing-ship form is a sight that no one forgets. And, despite the disagreement, there are many, both professional architects and lay critics, who think it one of the twentieth century's great buildings.

Yet, even if the Sydney Opera House is a great architectural triumph, it is without doubt a planning disaster. It sets some kind of world record, against strong competition from other projects in this book and elsewhere, for time delay in completion and for cost escalation. Originally estimated in 1957 to cost just over $A7,000,000 and to be completed by January 1963, it was in fact finished in October 1973 at a cost of $A102,000,000. In the meantime its total internal design had to be changed in order to avoid even greater delays and cost increases, so that it does not even function as the major opera house that was its principal *raison d'être*. The story is an extraordinary one involving classic ingredients of inadequate cost estimates, major problems of engineering design and inadequate technical control. It has been well documented in Australian sources, on which this account freely draws.

THE BEGINNINGS: COMPETITION AND COMMITMENT

Bennelong Point is Australia's Plymouth Rock. It was one of the two points enclosing Sydney Cove, where Captain Phillip landed in 1788. (The other forms one end of the Harbour Bridge, Sydney's other symbol.) It was small wonder that imaginative individuals saw it as a logical place to put a unique cultural monument. One of these was Eugene Goossens, director of the New South Wales Conservatorium of Music and resident conductor of the Sydney Symphony Orchestra, who campaigned from 1947 onwards for an opera house and concert hall worthy of a great metropolitan city. The other was John Joseph Cahill, in the 1950s Labour Prime Minister of New South Wales, who saw this as a political opportunity for a great imaginative gesture.

So, in November 1954, a committee was set up to consider how to build an opera house. It recommended, and the government of New South Wales accepted, that for such a prestigious building an international competition would be appropriate. In September 1955 the government announced the terms. There was to be a large hall, housing between 3,000 and 3,500 people, for grand opera, symphony concerts, choral works, ballet and large meetings; and a smaller hall, seating 1,200, for drama, intimate opera, chamber music, smaller concerts and recitals. The international jury consisted of Eero Saarinen, from the United States, Leslie Martin from Great Britain and Henry Ashworth and Cobden Parkes from Australia.

In January 1957 Cahill announced that out of 233 entries the jury of assessors had chosen that of a relatively unknown thirty-eight-year-old Danish architect, Jørn Utzon, who had submitted a highly unusual design consisting of two sets of interlocking concrete shells, or half-domes, placed side by side. The assessors commented:

The drawings submitted for this scheme are simple to the point of being diagrammatic. Nevertheless, as we have returned again and again to the study of these drawings, we are convinced that they present a concept of an opera house which is capable of becoming one of the great buildings of the world. We consider this scheme to

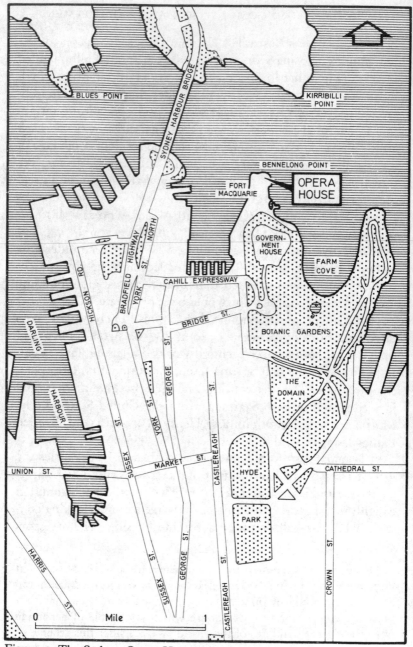

Figure 5: The Sydney Opera House.

be the most original and creative submission. Because of its originality, it is clearly a controversial design. We are, however, absolutely convinced about its merits.[1]

The statement that the drawings were 'diagrammatic' was almost an understatement. In the words of Ove Arup, who became structural engineer for the scheme:

It certainly required great courage to back a scheme like this which contained hardly any details or any evidence of its structural feasibility. Had the panel of Assessors included an engineer it might have meant the loss of one of the great buildings of the world – but I suspect it was reassured by the then prevailing faith amongst architects of the omnipotence of shells.[2]

Equally elementary was the consideration of cost. The assessors' report stated that they had required cost estimates to be made of all the schemes placed in their final list, and that Utzon's was actually the most economic. Arup's subsequent comment was: 'This estimate of three and a half million [pounds], prepared, I believe, by some unfortunate Quantity Surveyors under duress in a few hours, was of course hopelessly out.'[3]

So, remarkably, the competition was won on the basis of an expert judgement by a jury that lacked hard evidence either of the structural soundness of the design or of its eventual cost. It was said that Eero Saarinen, then at the height of his prestige, persuaded his fellow jurors to go for an adventurous solution. Whatever the case, they certainly left the state of New South Wales with a major problem of decision-making in uncertainty.

But at this time, some politicians at least were inclined to be adventurous. It is suggested that Cahill well knew that the original estimate, which translates to $A7,000,000 (Table 13), was hopelessly over-optimistic. But he used it to push the project through a rather apathetic Labour party caucus, which in 1958 accepted it by a narrow margin of twenty-four votes to seventeen.[4] One reason was the need for an exciting project to put to the electorate at the forthcoming March 1959 election, where Cahill was fighting for his political life against strong Country party

Table 13

SYDNEY OPERA HOUSE: COST AND TIME ESTIMATES

Date of estimate	Estimated cost $A million	Estimated completion date
January 1957	7.20	January 1963
January 1959	9.76	
October 1961	17.94	
August 1962	25.00	Early 1965
June 1964	34.80	March 1967
August 1965	49.40	
September 1968	85.00	End-1972
November 1971	93.00	
March 1972	99.50	
May 1974	102.00*	October 1973*

* Actual figures

Sources: M. Baume, *The Sydney Opera House Affair* (Melbourne, 1967); J. Yeomans, *The Other Taj Mahal: What Happened to the Sydney Opera House* (Camberwell, Vic., 1973), and *Sydney Morning Herald*, various dates, 1969–74.

opposition. A revised estimate of $A9,800,000 was made by a firm of surveyors, again on the basis of such information as Utzon had, and was used by Cahill to press on with a start, despite the advice of Utzon and the engineers. So a contract was actually let for the foundations in January 1959, before the structure and roof were designed. In 1960 the New South Wales parliament passed the Sydney Opera House Act, allowing the revised estimate of $A9,760,000 (with a 10 per cent contingency) to be raised from state lotteries, without the need for tax funds – an important part of the scheme that Cahill had sold to his own party in 1958 and to the electorate in 1959.[5] Thus, by a snap commitment, the government and people of New South Wales embarked on the enterprise. Ironically in this same year, 1960, Cahill died.

1960–6: THE QUEST FOR STRUCTURAL SOLUTIONS

When work started in 1959 on the foundations, there were still two fundamental technical problems to be solved. The lesser (though still substantial) was the movement of stage scenery. Utzon's design put the two auditoria side by side, greatly simplifying problems of pedestrian and vehicle circulation on a restricted site, but at the expense of leaving no wing space for the big sets inseparable from grand opera. Utzon solved this by hiding towers within the wings of his domes, which could be used for vertical movement of scenery. This problem was given to a specialist engineering firm.

The bigger problem by far was how to support the shells so as to make them strong enough to withstand high winds. It arose because of the unusual shape of the shells, which, as one Australian author put it, resemble 'an elephant standing on its two front legs'.[6] This was obviously a job for a structural engineer, and logically the advisory committee set up in 1957 to supervise the design of the building decided to bring in the firm of Ove Arup, the most experienced in Europe for this kind of work. Thus it came about that the real structure of the building, to be provided in Stages I and II of construction – the foundations, the sails and the podium – were in the hands of Arup, while Utzon was restricted to cladding and paving in Stage III. Arup were furthermore made directly responsible to the government of New South Wales. Since Utzon had had no previous experience of supervising anything bigger than a medium-sized housing project, it was obviously felt necessary to bring in Arup in effect as co-principals, with separate subcontracts to specialist consultants in acoustics, electrical engineering, mechanical engineering, heating and ventilating, air-conditioning and lighting. And this itself made it uncertain whether the sub-consultants' fees could be recovered from the budget available from the government to the main consultant.[7]

As the design work proceeded, more and more complications appeared. Enormous quantities of work had to be modified or scrapped. The Arup firm alone spent a total of 370,000 man-hours on the job down to 1965.[8] The root of the problem was the persistent difficulty in getting an adequate solution for the shells, plus the interrelationship of all the subcontractors. As Ove Arup himself put it:

... most of the alterations which have occurred on this job – and they are numerous – are due to the cropping up of new design considerations owing to Clients' wishes, unforeseen difficulties and especially the work of other specialists on heating, theatre techniques or acoustics, etc. impinging on the structure or *vice-versa*. The interdependence of all these 'trades' makes it impossible for any of them to go forward with a clear brief – the briefs for each have to be gradually developed through a process of trial and error. This is the central difficulty. It wouldn't be so difficult if one were only looking for a technical solution, but every possible solution has architectural or aesthetic repercussions, and all the easy ones are probably taboo on that score. Sometimes the only really satisfactory answer is to start all over again from the beginning, incorporating the new requirement.[9]

Sometimes, indeed, just that did happen. Stage I of the work, for the foundations and the concrete box over it, was contracted in February 1959 for completion by February 1961 with the notion that the whole building would be ready by January 1963, though Utzon, apparently, never agreed these dates. This first contract was started on approximate bills of quantities and without benefit of Utzon's drawings, which were supposed to be ready a few months later but were in fact much delayed. So sizeable mistakes were made, and a large part of the foundations built in 1961 had to be demolished in 1963 because the design of the shells had been changed. Stage I was eventually completed nearly two years behind schedule, at double its original estimated cost of $A2,800,000.[10]

The roof design was finally ready in 1962, after five years' work by Arup, and the Stage II contract for it was let in October of that year to an Australian contractor (Hornibrook Pty Ltd) on a cost-plus basis. It was not finished until 1967. Arup was responsible for scheduling this contract in association with the contractors and the quantity surveyor. During this period relations between Utzon and Arup deteriorated to the point when, in 1963, there was no longer any on-site communication. Utzon objected to receiving advice from Arup, and apparently became convinced that Arup was trying to take his responsibilities for Stage III (cladding and paving) from him. The argument came to a head over the design for cladding the ceiling, where Utzon wanted pre-finished plywood components which Arup thought impractical. Eventually, asked for a report by the Minister, Arup sent a statement to this effect in January 1966.[11]

The problem was exacerbated throughout this long period by the fact that the executive committee, a part-time body, lacked the necessary resources to evaluate the designs in detail and to provide the proper client role that such a major project needed. From the 1960 Act onward, they played a merely advisory role to the government, which was the legal client. But they still gave the vital advice about release of payments, and from 1963 onwards this precipitated a crisis. In March 1962 Utzon told the executive committee that he expected to complete the detailed Stage III drawings by March 1963. But two and a half years after that date there was still no sign of them.

1966–73 : POST-UTZON

Meanwhile, in May 1965, the long-running Labour government in New South Wales had been toppled by a Liberal-Country party coalition headed by Robin Adkin. In the election, the escalating cost and delayed completion of the Opera House had naturally become a major controversy. At this time the government took the power over payments from the executive committee and transferred it to the Minister of Public Works, Davis Hughes, who had been the original Stage I engineer. It was this that precipitated the final showdown with Utzon. At the end of February 1966, goaded by Arup's roof report, he resigned on the issue of non-payment by the state government of fees for engineering work by his staff. Ten days later, he was offered the compromise post of design architect – but in a hierarchy headed by the New South Wales government Chief Architect E.H. Farmer, and including also Peter Hall,* D.S. Livermore and Lionel Todd.[12] He naturally refused and disappeared from the scene, inevitably triggering further controversy. His critics claimed that he had sought to design the perfect opera house, regardless of cost, time or any other consideration; his defenders alleged that he had been frustrated by the lack of adequate briefs and by the refusal of the government to provide testing facilities for his designs.[13]

Whatever the case, the new architects immediately found themselves in the middle of a new controversy. It appeared that in direct contravention of a brief to design the Opera House for a concert capacity of 2,800, Utzon had told his acoustic consultant, Professor Cremer, to work for a total of 2,600. In June 1966, the Australian Broadcasting Corporation Symphony Orchestra, who were to be principal users, laid down their conditions for the hall. It was to have a capacity of 2,800, plus a reverberation time longer than Utzon had designed for, plus a rehearsal room three times the size of the one Utzon had designed, plus a host of detailed requirements which the new architectural team found simply impossible to satisfy. After six months of wrestling with the problem, they emerged with a drastic solution. Having consulted seating and management experts, they recommended a complete reversal of Utzon's original design. The main hall, with the original capacity of 2,800, would be reserved for concerts only; the scenery space, thus saved, would be used for a rehearsal and broadcast room, and for an enlarged small theatre to act as a cinema and a chamber music hall. The smaller auditorium would then become the opera house, with a capacity of 1,500. Since the original design had provided only 1,904 seats in the big auditorium for opera, the total redesign provided for a big increase in capacity:

Big auditorium	1,904 to 2,800
Small auditorium	1,150 to 1,500
Small theatre	350 to 6/700
Total	3,554 to 6,550

* A leading Australian architect; no relation to the Director of Britain's National Theatre or to the author of this book.

This was an economic solution; and it would satisfy the concert interests, since the necessary reverberation times could be met. But it would mean scrapping most of the elaborate stage machinery to move the stage sets vertically in the big auditorium, already installed at a cost of $A2,700,000. And it would mean that the Opera House could never fulfil its original purpose of housing full-scale grand opera by companies such as La Scala of Milan, since the stage sets could never be fitted in. The result was a furious controversy between the concert lobby, represented by the ABC, and the opera interest, represented by the Elizabethan Theatre Trust and the Opera House Trust, with the Australian architects falling in on the concert side. Finally, in March 1967, the Cabinet of New South Wales accepted the proposal of the Minister of Public Works that the modification should go ahead.[14] Not until a year after this was a detailed brief ready, with consequent slight alterations in capacity. The redesign meant removal of the proscenium arch and the great steel stage tower.[15]

It was at this point, as Table 13 shows, that the major cost escalation occurred. Now costing $A85,000,000, more than ten times the original estimate, the building was re-scheduled for completion at the end of 1972. In March 1969 the New South Wales legislature accordingly passed an Act providing for further lotteries to yield the $A85,000,000 total. But by March 1972 it was revealed that the cost had risen to $A99,500,000, of which no less than $A11,200,000 represented unpredictable price rises in the building industry.

The Sydney Opera House was actually opened on 20 October 1973. Half a year later, in May 1974, the Minister of Public Works announced the final bill: $A102,000,000. All but $A9,300,000 had been raised from lotteries; this remainder was owed to the State Treasurer as bridging finance, to be repaid over twelve months from further lotteries. The building had actually opened without car-parking facilities, estimated to cost a further $A7,000,000 as long before as 1969; the government attitude on that, somewhat understandably, was to wait and see.

The Opera House proved not only expensive to build, but also expensive to run. In 1974, its first full year of opening, its costs were running at $A6,000,000 a year, of which more than half represented salaries; as one politician said, Utzon had designed a very labour-intensive building. Only one-third of this came from revenue; the remaining $A4,000,000 had to be found from government subsidy, raised by continuing the lottery. But since inflation of wage costs was very rapid in Australia, the threat was of a $A7,500,000 bill in 1975 and of an increase in Opera House rents to $A7,000 a week plus a share of ticket revenues. This, it was suggested, might cause ticket prices to be raised above $A10 per performance, prompting sales resistance and even causing the Australian Opera to retire in search of a cheaper building. Thus, ironically, the threat existed that the Opera House would prove too expensive for the main purpose for which it was originally designed. But part of the problem, undoubtedly, was the redesign which had given the Opera House in its final form only 1,400 seats, making it the smallest opera house in the world (except for specialist ones, like Glyndebourne).

One counter-argument was that it did not matter much. The Opera House had actually cost the taxpayer of New South Wales very little to build, because of the lottery device that had proved so popular. The possibility always existed that most of the running cost could also be paid this way. Thus, the average Australian's gambling fever could pay for the minority Australian's culture. But it remained to be seen how far that argument could run with populist politicians.

A RETROSPECTIVE VERDICT

It has sometimes seemed that there were as many views on the Sydney Opera House as there were Australians. Certainly, hardly any public project can have had more words of controversy written about it. But certain key points of agreement do perhaps emerge.

The Opera House set some kind of record in cost escalation. In this, certain key factors proved critical. The government of the day was committed to a prestige project for political reasons.

Cost was almost a secondary consideration. Thus the jury of assessors was encouraged to look at designs on their merits. Though the jury did do a costing exercise, it was elementary, certainly in view of the originality and complexity of the design. Such a design was by definition extremely difficult, if not impossible, to cost in advance. Normal contingency allowances were almost bound to be inappropriate, even wildly so. Arup's comment is perhaps the best verdict:

... the thing we wanted built was Utzon's Opera House, not some botch up of it. And that Opera House costs that amount of money – approximately – and would from the beginning have cost that amount of money, only nobody knew it then ... if these facts had been known to begin with, the Opera House would probably never have been built. And the fact that it wasn't known, and that clients and public were completely misled by the first so-called estimate, was one of the unusual circumstances that made this miracle possible.[16]

This is perhaps slightly disingenuous. Those most concerned to get the Opera House certainly understood how delicate was the political balance at its start. As Arup himself admits, '... it was explained to me that if a *fait accompli* were not established whilst Mr Cahill was Premier the job would probably not go forward at all. And nobody knew for certain whether Mr Cahill and his party would be re-elected in March '59.'[17]

So the Stage I works were let deliberately in order to establish a commitment on which the Country party, if elected, could not readily renege. It has been suggested that at this point Cahill must have been doubtful that the estimate was at all realistic. It was later estimated by David Hughes that the premature start added $A12,000,000 in stop-go procedures and demolition of wrong structures. But probably it saved the Opera House – for, had there been time for a more sober assessment, the political commitment might have evaporated.

The next point is the personalities of the chief professionals. Utzon was a perfectionist who, understandably, regarded this as his master work; he evidently refused to compromise for the sake of time or cost. Since he was inexperienced, the responsibility was split equally between him and Arup, leading to personality clashes, over technical details, that were eventually to lead to Utzon's departure. The point of difference, which finally escalated into the resignation controversy, concerned payment of fees. Utzon refused to deliver any drawings until he was paid; the government finally refused to pay until it saw the drawings. When the Stage III drawings finally appeared in May 1966, four months after Utzon's departure, the new architectural team found that none of them dimensioned a room, identified a material or described a building component. Behind this was a complete lack of knowledge of user requirements, including such vital technical standards as acoustics, equipment and catering, which could lead the principal prospective user, after nine years of design work, to reject the planned accommodation as unsuitable.[18]

Part of the explanation for this could have simply been long lines of communication. Utzon first visited Sydney six months after the competition result was announced. Thereafter he worked in Denmark, with occasional visits to Arup in London and to the site in Sydney, until 1963 when he moved to Sydney. The main engineering design work was done from Arup's London office where much of the expertise was necessarily concentrated. There may therefore have been a failure to maintain regular contact with the clients, whose requirements in a building of this kind were very exacting. All this was exacerbated by the executive committee's part-time role and by their consequent lack of detailed supervision, as witnessed by the fact that they did not even know of Utzon's deviation from the seating plan.

Where to place final blame, if blame in such a case is appropriate at all, will depend to some degree on personal predilections. Conspiracy theory is certainly appropriate for the role of some of the politicians. But a conspiracy was possible only because of the basic uncertainties over costs and timing which were inseparable from such a project. If the government and people of New South Wales had wanted an opera house with firmer cost limits, they should have accepted a simpler and entirely more conventional design. But they surrendered that job in effect to the experts, and they clearly felt they had to respect the resulting verdict. And given that, they had to go along, at least for a minimal number of years, with the working methods of the architect, including his constant search for perfection and his unwillingness to delegate details.

The final point might be phrased in Melvin Webber's questions, originally asked about San Francisco's BART system. Who pays? Who benefits? Who decides? In the case of Sydney Opera House, the gamblers paid. A minority of people, mainly but not exclusively in the upper income bracket of Sydney society, gained directly, though it might be claimed that there was a psychic income, as the economists put it, to all the people of Sydney and to the visitors who see it. Those who decided, ironically, were politicians, and behind them the electorate, who voted for an elitist project in a highly populist society. The irony is that the decision taken in 1958–9 might have been rejected with hindsight in 1965–6 but, just possibly, reaffirmed with further hindsight in 1979.

CHAPTER 7

Two Near-Disasters: California's New Campuses and Britain's National Library

It is useful, perhaps, to end this section of the book with two case studies of decision processes that for a considerable period looked like planning disasters, until they quite suddenly re-appeared in a different light, as relative planning successes. One study, of the new campuses planned and built in the 1960s for the California universities and colleges of higher education, tells a story of a set of institutions that found themselves the centre of national controversy, and that for some time seemed almost to be fighting for their lives. Yet by the late 1970s, it appears that they have weathered these storms, and that despite dire criticisms the forecasts on which the investments were based have proved broadly correct. The other study, of the planning of a new British national library, concerns an intense controversy on a relatively narrow issue: that of the correct location of the new facility within central London. It shows how government stuck tenaciously to its original decision in the face of mounting criticism – but how then, once it reversed its decision, the forces that had opposed the change to all intents and purposes collapsed.

The studies thus offer some positive light to counteract the sombre impression of the preceding chapters. But perhaps the most interesting point is that they show how, sometimes, planning successes can be snatched from the jaws of planning disasters. For, when this book was originally planned, both of them were on the disaster list.

CALIFORNIA'S NEW CAMPUSES

The new campus programme of the state of California is an example of a planning gamble that might readily have become a planning disaster – and indeed was criticized as a potential disaster in the late 1960s. But in practice, at the end of the original planning period in 1975, it appeared that the new campuses had fulfilled the role envisaged by their planners, and so were a qualified success. In this brief study we need to look first at the assumptions of the plan-makers; then at the course of events, which at one time threatened to upset them; finally at the actual record against the forecasts on which the plan was based.

The Master Plan and its Antecedents: 1957–60

The campus programme was part of a much bigger blueprint for higher education in California, published in 1960 but necessarily embodying parts of earlier plans.[1] But this plan can be understood only against the background of an explosive growth in California's population in the post-war period, and particularly in the school-age population. Between 1957–8 and 1974–5, the Liaison Committee responsible for the Master Plan calculated that graduates from California's high schools would rise 175 per cent, from 123,800 to 341,400. And, if demands were fully met, this would lead to extraordinary pressure on all sectors of Californian higher education. The University of California would have a projected 227 per cent increase in freshman enrolment; the State College system 330 per cent; and the Junior College system 135 per cent. And there would be increases of a similar order at graduate level.[2]

Behind these forecasts lay facts of both fertility and migration, and of the relationship between these two. Births in California had risen 210 per cent between 1940 and 1959, the product of a rising national birth-rate compounded by heavy in-migration of young adults.[3] The babies born in 1960 would become the freshmen of 1978. So, up to 1975 at least, the most important element in the forecasts was already known. The only complication factor was the future rate of migration into the state of adults with children. But it seemed safe to assume that this would continue at roughly the rate of the 1945–60 period.

Faced with this quantitative challenge, the Liaison Committee laid down some principles. The most important was how the demand should be channelled into the three main segments of public higher education in California. First of these was the University of California founded at Berkeley in 1868, which by 1955 was a federation of two general campuses and four special campuses with altogether close on 50,000 students. Second was the State College system, developed from 1857 onwards to train teachers, but broadening into a wider curriculum after 1935; the system had doubled in enrolment from 1948 to 1959, though with admission standards that were often more flexible than those of the University. Third were the Junior Colleges, developed from 1907 onwards to provide a one- or two-year continuation of school education, and subsequently emulated by many other states. These three segments were clearly competing for the same body of students, and the students in turn were competing for entry; the University and State Colleges were both worried by the Junior College plan to develop three- and four-year programmes. So the Liaison Committee was faced with the need simultaneously to fix admission standards, to develop a plan for resulting numbers in the three segments, and to determine a building programme.[4]

They solved the problem by a tough and far-reaching set of proposals. There was to be a clear differentiation of roles between the segments, and each would then be able to strive for excellence within its allotted sphere. The Junior Colleges were to continue to be restricted to a two-year programme (that is, up to the fourteenth grade, or twenty-plus), but they could develop collegiate courses for students who could then transfer to the other segments. The State College system was to concentrate on liberal arts and professional courses plus teacher education, through bachelor's and master's programmes; a PhD programme might be developed jointly with the University. The University should have the same functions, with the sole authority for doctoral work, except by agreement with State Colleges; it was to be the primary state academic body for research. The University would recruit from the top 12 per cent of California high school graduates, the State Colleges from the top one-third. By 1975, 50,000 entering students would be diverted from these two segments to the Junior Colleges; to cope with the extra load, the Junior Colleges should have extra state aid, and should fully cover the state. For the future, there should be a California Coordinating Council for Higher Education, covering all three sectors, to review budgets, to interpret the functional differentiation and to plan growth.[5]

But the report also recognized the need for major expansion of the University and State College systems. Even under the diversion plan, enrolments in the University of California were expected to rise by 135 per cent overall, and in the State Colleges by 208 per cent. Here the committee noted that three years earlier they had looked at the development of the University, and had concluded that to expand any campus beyond 25,000 students would tax facilities so severely that the resulting adjustments would be equal to the creation of a new campus – which would be the preferable solution. It had found then that Berkeley and Los Angeles campuses would both exceed these numbers by 1970, so that there was a need to relieve them by new campuses close by – in the Berkeley case by a campus in the Santa Clara valley area south of San José, and in the Los Angeles case by a campus in the south east of Greater Los Angeles as well as by expansion of the specialist La Jolla campus (near San Diego at the southern tip of the state) into a general campus.[6]

The 1960 report modified these principles in detail and extended them. University campuses should have maximum numbers of 27,500 (the then levels of Berkeley and UCLA), State Colleges of 20,000 (12,000 outside major metropolitan centres) and Junior Colleges of 6,000. There should be new University campuses at La Jolla, in south east Los Angeles and in the Santa Clara valley area, to be started not later than 1962, with planned 1975 enrolment of 7,500 at La Jolla, 12,500 at south east Los Angeles, and 10,000 in the Santa Clara valley area; in 1965 and perhaps in 1970 there should be a further review of the case for

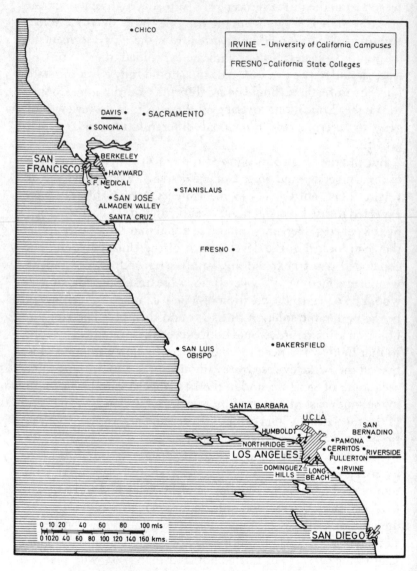

Figure 6: The California Public Sector University Campuses.

new facilities in the Los Angeles area and in the San Joaquin Valley. Similarly, new State Colleges should be started by 1965 in the area near Los Angeles international airport and in the San Bernardino–Riverside area near the eastern end of Greater Los Angeles; and there should be consideration in 1965 and 1970 of the case for further campuses in the San Francisco Bay Area (two) and in the Los Angeles, Ventura County and Bakersfield areas. However, apart from the immediate starts, new University and State College campuses should not be established until there were adequate local Junior Colleges; and the new campuses should concentrate on non-freshmen programmes until there were junior college opportunities for the freshman year.

Thus the Master Plan, which was accepted by the California legislature, devised a clear fifteen-year blueprint for the development of public higher education in the state. Both the University and State College systems were to expand through new campuses, but only on the basis that substantial numbers of more junior potential students should be siphoned off to the Junior Colleges. Thus their growth would be limited to the role in which they alone could properly function. The implications for numbers are set out in detail in Table 14 for the whole of California higher education.

The Master Plan was fully in line with the University's own ideas. Between 1957 and 1959 the University Regents had already formally redesignated the former specialized campuses* at Davis, Santa Barbara, Riverside and San Diego into general campuses, and had determined to establish two new campuses – one in the Greater Los Angeles area, the other in Santa Clara valley–North Central Coast area. By 1964 Berkeley already had 27,400 students and Los Angeles 23,700, so the case for new campuses was strong.[7]

The targets for the expanded and new campuses, published

---

* Davis was first developed as a University farm in 1905 but developed general programmes in the 1950s. Santa Barbara, a former State College, started as an undergraduate college in 1944. Riverside started as a citrus experimental station in 1907 and also generalized in the 1950s. San Diego began in 1912 round a marine research station.

Table 14
CALIFORNIA HIGHER EDUCATION (STATE SECTOR)
PROJECTED V. ACTUAL STUDENTS: SUMMARY

		1960	1965	1970	1975/6
Total	Projected	224,750	338,100	535,500	593,400
	Actual	203,064	363,457	552,669	630,839
University of California	Projected	50,400	66,250	89,150	118,750
	Actual	46,801	75,743	103,193	119,646
State University/ State Colleges	Projected	58,600	98,950	145,200	180,650
	Actual	56,480	98,940	166,876	183,077
Community (Junior) Colleges	Projected	115,750	172,900	230,000	294,000
	Actual	99,783	188,874	282,600	328,116

Growth Rates per cent

		60–5	65–70	70–5(6)
Total	Projected	+ 50.4	+ 58.4	+ 10.8
	Actual	+ 79.0	+ 52.1	+ 14.1
University of California	Projected	+ 31.4	+ 34.6	+ 33.2
	Actual	+ 61.8	+ 36.2	+ 15.9
State University/ State Colleges	Projected	+ 68.9	+ 46.7	+ 24.4
	Actual	+ 75.0	+ 68.8	+ 9.7
Community (Junior) Colleges	Projected	+ 49.4	+ 33.0	+ 28.0
	Actual	+ 89.1	+ 49.6	+ 16.1

Sources:
1. California Department of Finance 1960a
2. California Department of Finance 1960b–1977

by the University in 1965, are set out in Table 15. Berkeley and
Los Angeles would be held at their 27,500 ceilings. Of the former
special campuses, Santa Barbara and Davis would have grown
by 1975 to just short of their ultimate 15,000 targets; Riverside
would have reached its final 10,000 target; and San Diego would
have grown modestly to 7,400, little over one-quarter of the way
to its ultimate figure of 27,500. This last figure was also adopted
as the target for the new campuses, but here also only a small
part of the planned expansion would be achieved by 1975.

By this time, the precise locations for the two new campuses

Table 15

UNIVERSITY OF CALIFORNIA. PROJECTED V. ACTUAL STUDENTS:
SUMMARY

		1965	1970	1975/6
Total*	Projected	—	95,250	113,550
	Actual	78,441	103,193	108,522
Berkeley	Projected	—	27,500	27,500
	Actual	27,500	26,326	26,240
Los Angeles	Projected	—	27,500	27,500
	Actual	26,020	24,564	26,771
Davis	Projected	—	10,700	13,775
	Actual	8,384	12,173	14,592
Santa Barbara	Projected	—	11,175	13,925
	Actual	9,887	13,186	13,992
San Diego	Projected	—	4,500	7,425
	Actual	1,350	5,174	8,772
Irvine	Projected	—	3,850	8,075
	Actual	1,000	5,433	7,966
Santa Cruz	Projected	—	2,900	5,350
	Actual	600	3,587	5,462
Riverside	Projected	—	7,125	10,000
	Actual	3,800	5,602	7,966

* Excluding San Francisco Medical School
Sources:
1. California Department of Finance 1960a
2. California Department of Finance 1960b–1977

had been chosen. In the north, a consultant's report of 1959 had already narrowed the choice down to four locations and by 1960 the Regents restricted this to two: the Almadén Valley, seven miles south of San José, which was the better site in terms of accessibility to population, and the Cowell ranch just west of Santa Cruz, which had the advantage of a superb natural location amid redwood forests. In 1961 the Regents decided in favour of the Cowell ranch, and by 1963 there was already a plan based on development of between fifteen and twenty separate residential colleges here.[8] In the south east Los Angeles–Orange County area, consultants considered twenty-three sites and recommended in favour of the Irvine ranch, a vast open area being planned as a private enterprise new town; the Regents endorsed this recommendation in 1959 and approved a one-thousand-acre site a year later. This was donated by the Irvine company, who saw a unique opportunity for the growth of the new university and the new city to take place in parallel.[9] Both the Santa Cruz and the Irvine campuses admitted their first students in autumn 1965, as had originally been proposed in the Master Plan.[10]

Meanwhile the State Colleges – reorganized in 1963, following a Master Plan recommendation, into a single system with a Board of Trustees similar to the University's Regents – were also expanding rapidly. And this brought the Board of Trustees into conflict with another new body which resulted from the Master Plan: the Coordinating Council for Higher Education. In 1967 the Trustees approved sites for new campuses at San Mateo and Contra Costa in the San Francisco Bay Area and at Ventura in the Greater Los Angeles area; and, between 1968 and 1972, these were bought for development. But twice the Coordinating Council recommended that construction should not proceed, on the ground that the nineteen existing campuses could accommodate the forecast demand until at least the late 1990s – a recommendation that was strongly challenged. This argument had roots in the feeling of many State College academics and administrators that they were regarded as second-class institutions in matters of class loads, salaries, sabbaticals, research support and travel funds, which was heightened by the University's opposition to the proposal that some or all of the colleges should be raised to university status.[11] In 1972, however, fourteen of the colleges were elevated to the status of State Universities.

Change in the 1960s: the system in crisis
This single incident was, however, a mere indication of fundamental changes in expectations. By 1970 both the present and the future of California higher education looked very different from the picture of 1960. While in 1960 the keynote was optimism

and expansion, by 1970 it was deep pessimism and the possibility of continuing cutback.

One reason for this, which had begun to appear at the end of the 1960s, was demographic. The birth-rate fell throughout the 1960s and 1970s. By the mid-70s the official projection showed the eighteen-to-twenty-four age group still rising through the 1970s, but thence falling through the 1980s and only reaching the 1980 level again in the late 1990s. Already, the numbers aged fifteen to eighteen were almost static in the early 1970s and were predicted to decline from 1976; behind that, the expected rise in births in the late 1960s, a product of the 'baby boom' of the late 1940s, proved short-lived. Additionally, net migration into the state by the early 1970s was only one-tenth of the levels of the mid-1960s. Enrolments in all segments of higher education could thus be expected to decline from 1980 (Fig. 7) unless there was a quite dramatic increase in the propensity of this and older groups to consume higher education.[12]

Simultaneously, the whole system was experiencing fiscal crisis. Costs rose throughout the 1950s and 1960s. Universities, used to the principle of asking for as much as possible and spending it immediately, failed to anticipate the long-term problems of ageing plant with no provision for renewing it, the high cost of graduate programmes and the inevitable incremental creep as staff moved up salary scales. Federal funding to American universities as a whole fell dramatically from about 15 per cent in 1963–4 to 2 per cent in 1967–8. State governments also were reluctant to pay out extra money, for a variety of reasons, not least of them political antipathy to student radicalism. In the four academic years between 1966–7 and 1969–70, the University of California's operating budget revenues were cut by an average of 8.5 per cent a year in comparison with the funds needed to support a projected increase of enrolment of 20 per cent. And in 1970 Governor Reagan succeeded in cutting the request by no less than 12 per cent, keeping the budget at the same level in money terms as the previous year, despite a 6 per cent increase in the consumer price level and a 5 per cent increase in expected employment; while the legislature undertook the

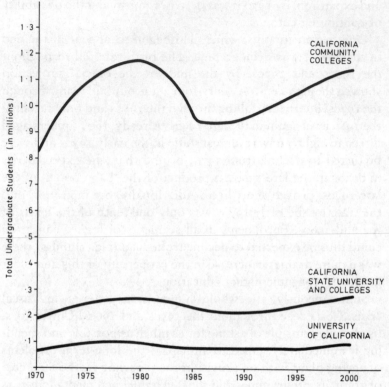

Figure 7: California – Actual and Projected Student Numbers 1974.
(Source: California Postsecondary Education Commission, 1974).

unprecedented step of denying University and State College employees the 5 per cent cost-of-living adjustment paid to all other state employees, for 'disciplinary' reasons. The result, according to the calculations of Earl Cheit, is that by 1971 Berkeley fell into the category of 'institutions in financial difficulty': schools that were forced to make cuts affecting essential programmes or the quality of programmes. By this time the student: faculty ratio was rising; one research institute was shut, while seven others were operating without regular budgets; and many new courses were postponed. For the future, considering both Berkeley and the State College at San Diego, Cheit concluded that during the 1970s they could hardly expect income to rise more than about 4.4 per cent a year, leaving them with a gap below their minimum need for about 6 per cent growth.[13]

Behind all this lay a sorry story. In 1963, towards the end of a golden age for the University of California, its president Clark Kerr had written his famous essay on the Multiversity: a series of communities and activities with a common name, common government, and above all common purposes. The basic reality, wrote Kerr, was that universities controlled new knowledge, and that this was now the most important factor in economic and social growth, and possibly the most important single element in culture. So the university was becoming a vital adjunct to government: the Federal government alone poured $1.5 billion into American universities in 1960 – almost exclusively into the three areas of defence, science and technology, and health, and heavily concentrated in a few institutions on the east and west coasts, notably Kerr's own university.[14] Yet only four years later Kerr was summarily dismissed by his Board of Regents under pressure from one of them, Governor Ronald Reagan; and by 1971 Cheit, a Professor of Business Administration at Berkeley, could complain that universities and colleges had lost the vital public purpose that alone could guarantee them Federal and state support.[15]

Such a sudden decline in prestige seems at first sight inconceivable. But the intervening period saw the start and the escalation of the Vietnam war, the tradition of student protest that began with the Free Speech movement on the Berkeley campus in 1964 and ended with the violence and bombings of 1970, and a remarkable resulting polarization of Californian – and American – society between radicals and conservatives. This story is well charted both in contemporary annals and in academic interpretative commentaries.

The Berkeley Free Speech movement of 1964–5 had no precedent in campus history. Initiated by a small group of activists, it linked campus and non-campus issues in a then confusing way, and used new techniques of disruption. When the university authorities tried to react, they provided further confirmation of the thesis that they were part of a repressive society.[16] But it is difficult to isolate any particular feature in the Berkeley of 1964 that was sufficiently different from the past to provide an explanation for the birth of the movement at that time and in that place; universities had been big and bureaucratic for a long time, they had been serving 'national needs' without protest, and later experience indicated that different administrative styles had little relevance.[17] Nor, at this point, was the Vietnam war an issue: the first reactions were recorded in August 1965, four months after the collapse of the Free Speech movement.[18]

But the aftermath was that the campus became a key issue in the 1966 election for governor between Edmund 'Pat' Brown and Ronald Reagan. Kerr had already threatened to resign his presidency at the height of the Free Speech movement crisis in March 1965 and this made him a vulnerable figure. After Reagan's election in November 1966, with nearly a million majority over Brown, he established his key themes as government economy and law and order over both of which a struggle with Kerr was certain. Almost immediately, on 20 January 1967, the Board of Regents under Reagan's chairmanship voted 14–8 to dismiss Kerr with immediate effect; they quoted reasons for his handling of the 1964 troubles and his 1965 resignation announcement. The Berkeley Senate immediately condemned the 'reckless and precipitate dismissal' and eight years of warfare began.

Eleven days after Kerr's departure, Reagan submitted a budget that cut appropriations to all State departments by 10 per cent but to the University by 29 per cent and the State College system by 28 per cent. The aim was to force them to introduce tuition charges for California students, a move resisted by the Regents at meetings in February and August. Next year's budget, though it marked an increase over 1967 for both institutions, was nevertheless $31,000,000 less than the University's request and $25,000,000 less than the State Colleges'. And in November, after Reagan had headed the State College Board of Trustees in ordering San Francisco State College to reopen during troubles, President Smith resigned. By November, Reagan was publicly saying that police would ring the California campuses if necessary.

Looking back at these events in 1970, the President's Commission on Campus Unrest identified several key factors. A new youth culture – profoundly idealistic, non-materialistic and committed to the idea of the autonomous individual – came to clash with the idea of a university as a staging-post into the meritocratic world; and the clash came to have its own dynamics, as a spiral of thought and action produced activists frustrated by their apparent inability to affect events.[19] Radicals created a rhetorical climate in which the university itself was identified as an agent of repression.[20] Students could accept this argument since they felt themselves to be attending compulsorily, their upbringing did not prepare them for large organizations, and they could not identify with many of the university roles. Thus a 'youth city' developed, in opposition to the university establishment.[21] The Regents, drawn from other walks of life, had little knowledge of, or sympathy for, university procedures, and thus tended to take unrealistic decisions.[22]

After the election of President Richard Nixon in 1968, the struggle acquired a more specific political dimension. The Vietnam war escalated, and on 29 April–1 May 1970 Nixon ordered American troops into Cambodia, prompting the protests and shootings at Kent State University in Ohio. Clark Kerr, by then chairman of the Carnegie Commission on Higher Education, reported by October 1970 that the campus reaction to Nixon's decision had been unprecedented in the history of American higher education. Out of replies from 2,551 universities and colleges, 57 per cent reported organized dissent and 21 per cent reported that normal activity was shut down. The strongest reactions had been in the north east and on the Pacific coast.[23] And, almost simultaneously, the President's own commission warned of an unparalleled campus crisis that could 'threaten the very survival of the nation' since it represented a crisis of understanding as deeply divisive as at any time since the Civil War. The commission appealed to the President to end the war – a request that led to immediate rejection of the report by Vice President Spiro Agnew.[24]

Though contemporary interpretations differ, there are strong common threads. What was occurring was a bitter political difference between different generations, different individual philosophies and different political persuasions. On the one hand was a group, largely middle-aged, that upheld principles of patriotism, an American mission to intervene to save other nations from communism, and internal law and order. On the other was a somewhat inchoate movement, or set of movements, based on the individual's right to self-determination and on a profound antagonism toward large-scale bureaucratic institutions, whether called the American State, the American Army or the American University. Between these, Clark Kerr's sanguine view of the modern American university – as a key element serving, yet ultimately controlling, the purposes of a fundamentally liberal and beneficent state – was ground nearly to dust.

The impact on university planning

Yet life went on. Even in the worst years of 1968–70 universities, even in California, kept open, taught students, and did research most of the time. After 1972 came the end of the war, Watergate and Nixon's removal. The year 1974 saw a Democratic Governor in California, 1976 a Democratic President in Washington. But in the process, a change had occurred in the way decision-makers saw the future of the California campuses.

In 1970, before the end of the time of troubles, the California legislature set up a joint committee to produce the first Master Plan since 1960. The Coordinating Council, working in parallel through its own select committee, produced guidelines for the plan in 1972. It recommended little change – at least for the immediate next years – in the basic 1960 principles of open admission of qualified students, the tripartite structure, and even admission requirements. It did conclude that, despite a falling birth-rate, demand for places would stay unprecedentedly high through the 1970s. But, since high school graduates would begin to decline in number, caution was needed to avoid overprovision of traditional facilities.[25] Taking its cue from this report, in 1973 the Master Plan itself reaffirmed the principles of open admission, of the different roles for the three segments, and of the basic admission standards for each segment. But it did recommend creation of a fourth segment, called the California Cooperative University, clearly modelled on Britain's Open University. This, designed to provide 'alternative delivery systems', could clearly take pressure off the existing three segments – if pressure after all existed. Otherwise the Master Plan was silent about numbers, either of students or of campuses. But it did recommend an end to Master Plans. Instead, a new Postsecondary Education Commission (replacing the Coordinating Council) should prepare five-year plans, regularly updated.[26]

In practice the Postsecondary Education Commission followed policy lines that had already been set by its predecessor. For already in 1969 the Coordinating Council had doubted the need for new campuses, preferring more intensive use of existing plant in evenings or during vacations, plus further development of existing campuses, plus direction of students to underdeveloped campuses.[27] In 1970 it had accordingly rejected a proposal for a new San Mateo State College, though it did approve a new Community College.[28] In 1971 it had noted with approval that the Legislature had sanctioned evening operation of campuses where economic and feasible.[29] And in 1972 it advised governing boards to be very cautious in developing new graduate or professional programmes, in view of the likely levelling-off in the 1980s.[30] So it was hardly surprising that already, by late 1974, the new Postsecondary Education Commission was declaring its strong conviction that total demand for places would fall in the 1980s and 1990s (Table 14) and that no new campuses either in the University or in the State University/State College system would be needed until well in the 1990s, if then.[31]

Thus, from 1969 onwards, campus planning was dominated by extreme caution. The main reason for this was the hard facts of demography; but undoubtedly the bleak story of finance came into it, and reinforcing that the loss of the University administrators' self-confidence.

The question finally must be: had the planners of 1960 been able to foretell these remarkable changes of outlook and fortune, would they have produced the same expansion plan? A.G. Coons in 1968 was already noting that the development of the new campuses was proving far from easy. In the academic year 1967–8, after eight years of planning, the two new campuses plus San Diego totalled only 7,556 students. Similarly Sonoma and Stanislaus State Colleges, with 1,730 and 1,090 students respectively in 1968–9, were clearly destined for slow growth. Coons concluded: 'The University under President Clark Kerr, too early and too rapidly, but primarily to occupy the high ground and to close out State College competition possibilities, embraced the doctrine that each campus, old and new, should be a general campus.'[32] The result, he argued, was the possibility, and even probability, of duplication, high initial cost, and high unit costs per student. In this he was perhaps gripped by the feelings of resentment that so often affected members of the State College system. But he could point to some evidence, for the Master Plan had quoted average costs per student that were systematically higher for the University than for the State Colleges, but were also higher for smaller than for larger campuses in both systems.[33]

The fact, however, is that the authors of the Master Plan were convinced that very big campuses also brought increasing costs, though they quoted no hard evidence. Therefore there was surely a case for expanding some other campuses to deal with a necessary overspill from Berkeley and Los Angeles and the bigger State College campuses. The only question is whether the necessary growth could have been more concentrated in a smaller number of campuses – with a greater proportion of existing rather than new ones.

Santa Cruz, Irvine and the new State College campuses may therefore have been costlier to the California taxpayer than expansion at Davis, Santa Barbara or Riverside. But there is not much hard evidence. Probably the most problematic aspects of the whole plan are the smaller State Colleges such as Bakersfield (3,055 students in 1976), Dominguez Hills (6,696), San Bernardino (4,065), Sonoma (5,677) and Stanislaus (3,183). Significantly, these were the five centres that had not received promotion to university status by that time. It was small wonder that the Coordinating Committee and its successor were resisting the call for yet more campuses.

But at the end, the striking point is that despite all vicissitudes the forecasts of the Master Plan have been remarkably fulfilled. Table 14 shows clearly that not only were actual student numbers close to those forecast for the major segments; they were also remarkably close for individual campuses of the University of California, with only Riverside falling behind. This demonstrates that with buoyant demand in a competitive system, the most favoured institutions will succeed in meeting targets, even after a decade as troubled as 1965–75.

Put another way, the University of California faced mounting political pressure during the 1960s and early 1970s. It was transformed by events from an institution enjoying prestige and favoured treatment into a state whipping-boy. Yet even so, the effect was marginal. True, resources were cut back; the development of new programmes was restricted; salaries fell behind those in comparable major universities elsewhere on the North American continent. Yet the university survived, and its inbuilt reputation allowed it to weather the storms. Further, because of the rising demand both from in-state and from out-of-state students, it continued to be able to pick the best of a large pool of candidates. Relatively, in relation to the rest of the Californian higher education system and in relation to other prestigious universities, it was probably little worse off in 1975 than in 1960 – however much its faculty members might argue otherwise.

Much the same story could be told elsewhere on the North American continent, and in Europe, over this period. For in some ways the Californian story was a microcosm of higher educational history in the western world. In the United Kingdom, for instance, the government after 1965 created a parallel new kind of higher education – the polytechnics – to rival the universities. Resources were diverted away from the universities to the polytechnics, in order to allow the latter to take the lion's share of the growth of student demand. And then, after the mid-1970s, the so-called binary system developed in effect into a trinary system. For, with drastically falling demand for teachers as a result of the decline in birth-rate, and the consequent threat to the programmes of the colleges of education, many of them developed new general degree programmes, sometimes in association with the polytechnics, sometimes independently. Significantly, the end result was very close to the Californian one: a university system that provided education all the way to the PhD, a polytechnic system that broadly extended to the Master's level, and a college of education system that taught only to the Bachelor's level. The difference was only in the level of demand. For in the late 1970s recession, while demand for university places in Britain remained far in excess of overall supply, elsewhere places remained unfilled and the Department of Education was being forced to reduce its forward estimates of the scale of higher education in the 1990s.

All this merely suggests that in any expanding system of education, so long as potential students perceive differences in standards and prestige, whether these are real or imaginary or some of both, the most prestigious institutions in the system can survive attack and even a relative cut in resources. So long as they can maintain their basic programmes at roughly the same scale and level as before, indeed, the rising demand will create even more intense competition for places, making them ever more prestigious in relative terms. It is an amusing irony on which politicians aiming (whether for motives of pure revenge, or for highest motives of egalitarianism) at reduction of the universities' power and influence should surely ponder.

BRITAIN'S NATIONAL LIBRARY

The second story has few points in common with the first, save that it too is concerned (indirectly) with education and it too became a subject of intense political controversy. What it does illustrate is the extraordinary time-span that is sometimes needed to resolve even a very narrow issue of an apparently technical character – at any rate, where deeply entrenched interests and institutions are involved.

The British Museum Reading Room is perhaps the most famous library in the world. In size, its stock of 6,000,000 volumes is easily exceeded by the Library of Congress in Washington DC or by the Lenin Library in Moscow. But only it became part of

European cultural history, as a succession of celebrated refugees from persecution on the European mainland – most notably Karl Marx, who worked here in exile for some thirty years on *Das Kapital* – joined British scholars in the pursuit of research. Arguably, in terms of Britain's contribution to modern culture in literature, the humanities, and the social sciences, it was the country's best investment – particularly since, as first copyright library, it acquired its British book stock automatically and without charge. It has certainly proved a powerful aid to Britain in allowing London to remain an international centre of writing and publishing, long after the Americans might have been expected to seize pre-eminence. And the great domed reading room, with its famous echo and its constant share of notable eccentrics, has become a part of national and international legend.

But even by World War Two, when a bomb gutted the Reading Room and caused its temporary closure, the system was bursting at the seams. Created in the reign of George II in 1753, the Museum almost from the first contained the collection (the King's Library) that later developed into the first national library. The Reading Room itself was finished in 1857, at just about the time when Marx began to work in the museum. Additional reading space was provided in 1914 when the museum opened a major extension. Then, in 1926, the great majority of the bulky newspaper collection had to be moved out to Colindale, twelve miles away on the edge of London. Confined on a tight island site, with the book-stacks wrapped around the corners of the circular reading room, the system could not cope with the rising tide of books and journals. After World War Two, the upsurge of published works meant providing a mile and a half of extra bookshelves a year.

Already, in the middle of World War Two, the great County of London plan by Abercrombie and Forshaw (earlier noted in this book as the source of London's road plans) proposed a dramatic solution. Bloomsbury, the area around the museum, was to be turned into a national education and research precinct. Much of it was to be redeveloped by the University of London immediately to the north of the museum – a process that had already started in the 1930s, when the London underground station architect, Charles Holden, had produced his controversial skyscraper plan for the area. This process would continue with the redevelopment of much of the famous heritage of Bloomsbury's Georgian garden squares. And to match it, to the south – between the museum's main front on Great Russell Street and the main traffic artery of New Oxford Street – the museum itself was to extend, through a process of massive redevelopment. The whole area would then become a precinct – one of Abercrombie's central planning options – by the exclusion of through traffic, which would be channelled on the bounding main roads of Tottenham Court Road, Euston Road, Southampton Row and New Oxford Street.[34]

The Abercrombie-Forshaw plan, coming as it did just when the tide of war was turning and when national thought was starting to concentrate on post-war reconstruction, received immediate acclaim. It seemed to provide a grand blueprint for keeping the best of the character of the old London, while subtly reshaping it to give it an order that it had never before possessed. In any case, the middle of a war, with large parts of Bloomsbury destroyed by German bombs, was hardly the time to argue over details. After the war, and the 1947 Town and Country Planning Act, the team of official planners in the new London County Council planning department in County Hall sought to give statutory expression to Abercrombie's ideas. Their County of London Development Plan, published in 1951, provided for the wholesale redevelopment of the rectangular area of seven acres in front of the museum (bounded by Great Russell Street, Bloomsbury Square, Bloomsbury Way–New Oxford Street, and Coptic Street) for the extension of the museum and the creation of new library space.[35] And in the same year, the Civil Estimates for the first time included a sum of £2,000,000 for the necessary acquisition of land. Only £50,000 of it was needed in that financial year 1951–2 but, as The Times pointed out, 'it draws public attention to an important, though still fairly distant, project that has had too little notice'.[36]

That was not to remain true for long. For at the 1952 inquiry

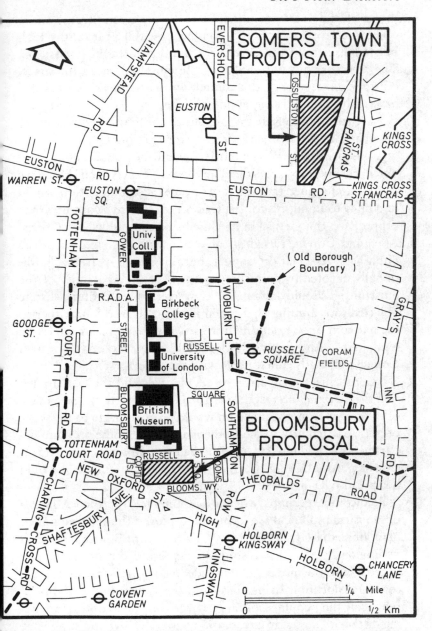

Figure 8: The Two Alternative Sites for the New British Library.

into the London Development Plan, there were no less than fifty objections from owners and occupiers as well as from the Holborn Chamber of Commerce, which coordinated the opposition. The objectors did not challenge the museum's need for space, but they did challenge the contention that it must be provided here, next to the existing buildings. They argued that alternative sites – two at South Kensington, one on the South Bank (recently designated by government as the site for a national science centre) and one nearby in Bloomsbury – would be equally good, and much cheaper to acquire. The British Travel and Holidays Association argued that the loss of hotel accommodation would be a blow to London's tourist trade, and claimed Board of Trade support for the view. Philip Unwin, of the publishers George Allen and Unwin, raised an objection with the support of the Publishers' Association, saying that this whole quarter – traditionally devoted to publishing because of the proximity of the museum – should retain its character. The Bedford Estate objected too, arguing that when it had conveyed land either to the museum or to London University the character of the estate had altered. And finally the local authority, Holborn Borough Council, formally allied itself with the objectors.

Against this, the museum representatives and the LCC argued that the national interest outweighed local objections. Severance of the library from the museum would do great harm to the work of both, particularly to the study of antiquities. The museum departments would have to acquire their own libraries, an extravagant step. And though the disturbance was recognized, it would be spread over many years.

Predictably, perhaps, after a long interval, the then Minister of Housing and Local Government approved the redevelopment plan. Immediately, in April 1955, the Holborn Borough Council unanimously passed a resolution deploring the decision, and urged him to postpone the plan indefinitely on the ground of the serious dislocation to business and the virtual impossibility of rehousing the people, estimated at between 1,000 and 1,500, living on the site. Later, in a resolution passed in July and supported by both major parties, they called for an independent public inquiry. At this point it was alleged by the local Chamber of Commerce that Sir David Eccles, the then Minister of Works (the Minister directly responsible for the development of the museum), had instructed the LCC to pick one of three sites adjacent to the museum, thus closing options for the Minister of Housing and making the public inquiry, in their words, a public farce.[37] *The Times* was moved to an editorial comment:

The whole working of the museum is closely dependent upon its contiguity to the library; and of adjacent sites none is so suitable for the National Library as that now earmarked. This does seem a matter upon which, with all proper consideration for those affected, the interest of a great national institution must come first.[38]

Again predictably, the Minister took *The Times*'s advice. But, the Minister of Works assured the local MP Mrs Lena Jeger, the redevelopment would not start for at least ten years and the second stage would not start until 1975 or later.[39]

There, for a time, matters rested. But Holborn Council, aided in the Commons by Mrs Jeger, were not satisfied. In 1961 they were again calling for a further inquiry and announcing that they would fight the plan tooth and nail. They believed that the needs of the library could be met on a much smaller two-and-a-half-acre site.[40] But a little later, in 1962, they reluctantly agreed to the development.

By this time, the point of decision was approaching. For, as the new Director and Principal Librarian of the museum, Sir Frank Francis, reminded a librarians' conference in 1962, the 1955 decision had a twelve-year time-limit on it. Soon enough the government responded. In August 1962 (significantly, perhaps, in the holiday season) it announced that Professor Sir Leslie Martin and Colin A. St John Wilson were appointed architectural consultants for the development of the site and the design of the building. Martin had earlier acted as consultant to London University for the redevelopment of their part of the precinct. Then, in November, the government published a British Museum Bill allowing, *inter alia*, the national library collections to be split up on different sites. Not only would this allow the development of the new library on the Bloomsbury site, at a cost of £10,000,000, it would also permit the development of a new National Science Reference Library on the South Bank at a cost of £1,000,000, following a decision by the government in April, and allowing unification of collections then scattered between the Patent Office in Holborn and Whiteley's store in Bayswater. This complex too would be administered by the museum. It was hoped, the government announced at the Bill's second reading in December, that a start would be made on the South Bank project in 1963, for completion in 1966; and on the Bloomsbury site in 1965.[41]

The Bill duly became law; and in 1964, in the middle of the general election campaign, the Martin-Wilson plan was unveiled with provisional approval from the Minister of Works, Geoffrey Rippon. It treated the site as an entity with buildings grouped around open courts and with extensive underground car parking and servicing; a small part of the site was reserved for housing and shops. The Minister by this time thought that acquisition would be completed to allow building to start in the early 1970s, extending over ten years. After the election, with Jennie Lee as Minister for the Arts bent on a major extension of museum facilities, prospects at first seemed even brighter.

But soon a new political factor of great importance emerged – and that somewhat ironically. On 1 April 1965 the reorganization of London government took effect, with a new Greater London Council and twenty-eight London boroughs. The former borough of Holborn was merged with St Pancras and Hampstead to become the new London Borough of Camden. And the irony was that though Labour had bitterly opposed the London reorganization, Camden became a Labour borough and immediately took over Holborn's implacable opposition to the scheme. The difference was that as a very powerful Labour local authority, allied to an energetic local MP in the person of Mrs Jeger, Camden was in a strong position to put leverage on the new Labour government.

It took just over two years. On 26 October 1967, in simultaneous statements in the Commons and Lords, the government announced that after formal objections from Camden they would not proceed with the Bloomsbury proposal. Few decisions can ever have excited such instant obloquy from the British establishment. The Trustees of the British Museum, who included Lord Radcliffe, Lord Eccles, Lord Annan, Sir Kenneth (now Lord) Clark and the Archbishop of Canterbury, announced immediately that they were 'outraged' by the content of the statement by Mr Patrick Gordon Walker, the Secretary of State for Education and Science, and also by the way it had been made without consultation. *The Times*, in a leader, supported the Trustees, pointing out that the plan had been part of policy since 1952 and that the Ministry of Public Buildings and Works had already acquired three-fifths of the site at a cost of about £2,000,000. The word 'outrage', in the view of *The Times*, was not too strong a one. It ended: 'The folly of this decision will make people who care for learning almost despair of the present Administration.'[42] And four days later the Chairman of the Trustees, Lord Radcliffe, wrote to *The Times* to confirm that he had never been consulted on the matter at all. He stated merely that he had met the then Secretary for Education, Mr Crosland, to make the point that the Trustees should be allowed to make representations on Camden's objection, which they later did. He concluded:

... it would not have occurred to me, in the context of this case, in which the Trustees are responsible by Statute for the conduct of the Museum, that their views would be set aside and a long settled plan abandoned without even a discussion as to the reasons for the rejection and an honest attempt to work out an alternative, if there is one, for what we all know to be so urgent and so important. Nothing of this has been done.

Evidently my expectations have been falsified: but in view of the rapidly deteriorating standards of public administration which are now presented to us I am probably old fashioned.[43]

The sense of outrage was clear. The Trustees regarded themselves as in some way a part of government. But the government had regarded them as just another group of people wanting to develop a site. Further, the government had set aside a decision long ago made after a public inquiry, at a late stage in the planning process. From the other side, Camden would argue that their predecessors had been objecting to the plan for years, without much response.

Meanwhile, as Lord Radcliffe pointed out to *The Times* in another letter, the position was even further confused since in June the Greater London Council had closed the option of building the National Science Library on the South Bank. The Trustees had gone along with the South Bank scheme, though it was not their choosing, because at least it promised a quick solution to the problem of housing a collection that was divided between two inadequate premises, one in Chancery Lane and one in Bayswater. But now there was no plan at all either for the Museum Reading Room or for the science collections. He ended: 'It is the Trustees' belief that only a comprehensive and unified national library can adequately meet the needs of scholars and the public. What the Department of Education and Science believes I have not the faintest idea.'[44]

Subsequently a petition, signed by seventy-six representatives of British universities, presidents of learned bodies and societies, authors, librarians and publishers (including no less than ten Vice-Chancellors), went to the Prime Minister asking the government to change its mind. It repeated the argument that the abandoned plan was the only one that adequately met the needs of the library and museum. It was speedily if politely rejected. The resulting debate in the Lords, on 14 December, was a stormy one but the government still did not give way – despite threats from Lords Radcliffe and Eccles that if the government persisted in its folly the Trustees would have to be dismissed. Out of the wreckage of the proposal, the government's October announcement had produced one positive new idea. This was, in the words of the Secretary of State, '... that the present pattern of national library services is a patchwork which has developed piecemeal over the years under different institutions.'[45]

Accordingly he proposed to set up a small independent committee to look at the functions of the British Museum Library, the National Central Library, the National Lending Library for Science and Technology and the Science Museum Library, to see whether in the interests of efficiency and economy such facilities should be brought into a unified framework. There was widespread scepticism about this proposal, since the names of those on the committee were not immediately announced. However, in the December debate Lord Longford told the Lords that it would be chaired by Dr F.S. Dainton, the Vice-Chancellor of Nottingham University, and it would include academic, publishing and business people. There was still a suspicion that the committee would be precluded from recommending the Bloomsbury site if they thought it right, despite government assurances.[46]

Early the next year the government, and the committee, found that they were facing a formidable advocate of the Bloomsbury site. For Lord Eccles, who had ended the Lords debate by claiming that 'We are now governing our country with words that mean nothing,' was appointed as Chairman of the Museum Trustees in succession to Lord Radcliffe. He immediately told the press that the work of the Dainton Committee was unnecessary but that nevertheless, now it was there, the Trustees would make full use of it. He was still optimistic that an objective assessment would bring them back to the original plans. He still hoped for a parliamentary Bill on which the government and trustees would agree.

But, meanwhile, the Trustees and the government were both looking to the Dainton Committee. When its report appeared in 1969, it recommended a fundamental structural change but tactically avoided the issue of controversy. It called for a new National Reference Library, in a new building, administered by a completely new body separate from the British Museum. Four museum departments – Printed Books, Manuscripts, Oriental Printed Books and Manuscripts, and Prints and Drawings – should become a National Reference Library. A National Reference Library for Science and Invention should take over the central science and patent collections, as part of the National Library Organization. It need not be next to the National Reference Library but should be in central London. But then, on the critical point of location, the committee steered a delicate course through the minefield. The Bloomsbury site was best for staff and visitors, and for creation of a national library service; but if for 'other reasons' the library must be separated from the museums then a site in central London, near to Bloomsbury and Aldwych, was essential.[47]

What was perhaps most interesting about the Dainton report was not this conclusion but the detailed evidence that could support it – or fail to do so. For earlier the report had shown that the overwhelming majority of readers did not need to be near the antiquities and that the total number inconvenienced by a split would be small. In April 1969, only 6 per cent of Reading Room users intended to visit other departments, and only 3 per cent thought this essential; only four staff members in April visited the library. However, students and staff of the University of London were by far the biggest single group of users; and two-thirds of these were from the Bloomsbury-Aldwych area. The real truth seemed to be that a site in this area was well-nigh essential, but that the controversial site was not.[48]

Still, the conclusion was apparently enough to swing the government, since by this time Camden Council had fallen to the Tories. In a White Paper of April 1970 the government announced that they accepted the main Dainton recommendation for a national libraries authority, and that the whole complex of libraries, including the new national science library, should after all be built on the Bloomsbury site. It was a remarkable volte-face, welcomed enthusiastically by Lord Eccles. And it was small surprise when, after the 1970 election, the new Conservative government announced implementation of the decision with a £36,000,000 scheme to create a new national library complex, called the British Library and incorporating the British Museum Library, the National Central Library, the National Reference Library of Science and Invention (to be renamed the Science Reference Library) and the British National Bibliography, all to be housed on the Bloomsbury Site. (Another part of the new organization, the National Lending Library, would continue to be housed at Boston Spa near Wetherby in Yorkshire.) Colin St John Wilson was to be architect for the whole complex.[49]

The new complex, the White Paper said, was a 'desperate need' for the British Museum and the Science collections, for both were bursting at the seams. Recent investigation had shown that both could be put on to the Bloomsbury site while still preserving all the most important listed buildings, especially St George's Church and the west side of Bloomsbury Square. The whole would involve an annual cost averaging less than £3,000,000 a year over some thirteen years, with work starting as soon as possible – perhaps even before the new National Library came into being. The White Paper concluded: 'If Parliament approves the programme outlined the result will be the creation of a national library system without rival. It will also provide in the centre of London the most significant complex of museums and library resources in Europe.'[50]

Significantly, the Minister for the Arts in the new Conservative administration, who introduced the White Paper, was Lord Eccles. It seemed a great personal triumph, and the conclusion of one man's long dream. When early in 1972 Parliament gave the British Library Bill its unqualified approval, with only a murmur of regret for the loss of the Bloomsbury quarter, it seemed assured.

But, as always in this extraordinary saga, it was not assured for long. At the end of 1971, in an obscure news item, it was announced that the GLC and Camden had agreed that the Bloomsbury site was no longer suitable and that they should investigate an alternative at King's Cross. Just over a year later, in May 1973, the new British library building was deferred for a year in the first of many government spending cuts. Meanwhile, the rumble of opposition was heard again, and the opponents by now were concentrating on the King's Cross site as a viable alternative. And by December 1973 – as Lord Eccles re-entered the battle in yet another incarnation, as Chairman of the new British Library Authority – the estimated cost had risen to £130,000,000, more than three times the cost quoted in March 1972. The opposition, naturally, was arguing that the King's Cross site would be cheaper; by January 1974 Camden Council were joining them, in a booklet arguing that the Bloomsbury development would be an unjustifiable extravagance as well as a social and environmental disaster. By this point, just as in the old Holborn days, both parties in Camden were united in opposition together with Mrs Lena Jeger. Either King's Cross or Covent Garden, from which the old vegetable and fruit market was due to move that summer, would be a viable alternative in Camden's view.[51]

The King's Cross site was the really new factor. It was the old Somers Town goods yard, located immediately west of St Pancras station and rendered derelict by containerization and the end of the coal trade. Its advantage, apart from the fact that it displaced no businesses or residents, was its superb accessibility. It was within ten minutes' walk of three major main-line stations (St Pancras, King's Cross and Euston); it was directly served by four underground lines (Northern, Piccadilly, Metropolitan/Circle and Victoria) and by many bus routes. And, above all, it was indubitably right on the edge of the Bloomsbury-Aldwych area, with excellent connections to all parts of it. On every count, save direct contact with the rest of the museum, it was equal, or even superior, to the Bloomsbury site.

In December, the incoming Labour government once again made a volte-face. In the face of continued opposition, it announced that the library complex would be built after all on the King's Cross site. Significantly, the statement – by the new Minister for the Arts, Hugh Jenkins – came as a parliamentary reply to a question from the indefatigable Mrs Jeger. The British Library Board predictably reiterated its view that the Bloomsbury site was the most convenient and that siting the library next to the museum would bring 'incalculable benefits'. But, compared with 1967, the reaction was strangely muted – possibly because the government was giving a clear commitment, even to start on the first stage of the development in 1979–80 provided economic conditions allowed.

Intensive consultations then followed between the government, the British Library Board and the GLC and Camden. In August 1975, agreement was reached. Again replying to Mrs Jeger, Hugh Jenkins announced that the government were satisfied that the Somers Town site could provide for the library's need. Negotiations would now take place with the owners, British Rail and the National Freight Corporation, to buy the site. And detailed design would start with a view to building a substantial first phase in 1979–80. The British Library Board accepted the decision with regret but with a brave face, hoping that '. . . at last the long story of plans and counter-plans has been ended in an agreement that will be carried out with the least possible delay.'[52] And Mrs Jeger, needless to say, was delighted.

In March 1978 Shirley Williams, Secretary for Education and Science, told the Commons that the first stage of construction would start the next year. The building would take about ten years and would cost an estimated £74,000,000 at mid-1977 prices. It would house the Science Reference Library. Assuming that the second and third stages were approved by future governments, the total project would not be completed until the end of the century, at an estimated cost of £164,000,000. The ten-acre site would eventually provide three times the combined facilities of the Reading Room and the Science Libraries, with space for 3,500 readers, 2,500 staff and 25,000,000 books. The design, unveiled in March 1978 by Colin St John Wilson, was a highly imaginative one with red brick and massive overhanging slate roofs, providing an apt foil to the neighbouring Gothic fantasy of St Pancras Station. It won immediate plaudits from architects and laymen alike.

Thus, at the end of a saga extending over thirty years, it seemed, miraculously, that everyone was satisfied – though not to the same degree. The conservationists had saved their corner of Bloomsbury. The residents would live in peace. The bookshops and curio shops would continue to delight visitors to the museum, who were growing in number year by year. The users of the libraries would get a superb complex of buildings, maximally accessible from all parts of London and from much of Britain. Even the National Library Board was consoled by the offer of a virtually immediate start to the complex for which everyone had waited so long.

Some of the lessons from this story are evident, some less so. One is that the nature of the forces changed when the new institutional structure came into being, as doubtless the government anticipated in 1967. Though Lord Eccles remained the common link between the old Museum Trustees and the new National Library Board, he was heading a quite different body with a quite different remit. Its first loyalty and responsibility was to a unified library complex on a convenient site, not to a unified museum complex on the Bloomsbury site. Thus, by changing the structure, government changed the critical parameters of the decision. Another lesson is that values shifted in the late 1960s and early 1970s. In the great Covent Garden fiasco on a closely adjacent site, the government and the GLC had retreated from a massive redevelopment plan after concerted local opposition. Neither was any longer in a mood for another similar battle. A third lesson is that technological changes, unforeseen in the early 1960s, had released a site that was in many ways ideal for the library complex considered as a unity. This may illustrate that in critical decisions, it may sometimes pay to wait for the unexpected. In any case, the remarkable fact is that the whole protracted saga made for very little delay. In the mid-1950s, the projected starting date for the main work was 1975 or later. In the late 1970s, it is 1979 – though ironically the Reading Room, which was supposed to represent the most urgent problem, is still left to make do on its present site into the late 1990s.

PART TWO
ANALYSIS

CHAPTER 8

Approaching the Problem

In various ways, our case studies have all concerned one of the central problems of the modern world: the way societies plan the output of public (or collective) goods. It is important because in most if not all advanced industrial countries, these goods account for a large and steadily increasing proportion of the total output of goods and services. Schools and colleges and universities, roads and airports and docks, armies and navies and air forces, hospitals and clinics, old people's homes and welfare cheques, now help to swell a public-spending bill that in recent years, in a number of European countries, has topped the magic mark of 50 per cent. One reason for this rise (a reason we shall want to explore in detail later) is the possibility that their producers tend to make more of them than people would demand in a true economic market. But a more basic, and perhaps more plausible, reason is that, as the level of *per capita* income rises, many people want to spend much of their additional real incomes on goods that can perhaps only be produced, or perhaps can be more advantageously produced, by collective action.[1]

PUBLIC GOODS AND THEIR SUPPLY

Concerning the term public – or collective – goods, there is confusion: some economists restrict the term to goods that can be produced only in a collective way, others widen it to include goods that are commonly produced in this way either from necessity or from choice. Throughout, I shall be using this latter, wider sense: public goods are all those goods and services which the public are willing to pay for but which the private sector is not motivated to provide.[2]

More precisely, public goods can include three broad categories. First, there are collective goods in the strict sense: goods and services that cannot be marketed because no one can be excluded from their consumption. This 'free rider' problem applies to many areas of government provision: defence, public health, law and order, town planning. Secondly there are goods and services that must be provided publicly because of various market imperfections such as poor information, monopoly power and the high costs of transactions in the market. Thus we provide public education because, even in a world where everyone was equally free to buy education, better educated parents would make so much better bargains for their children that the result would be socially inequitable (and probably inimical to economic development). Similarly, we provide water and electricity through public monopolies because of a feeling that unfettered private monopolies would exploit their power. And we do not charge road users on a pay-as-you-go basis because (at least so far) it has not appeared technically feasible to do so without causing intolerable urban congestion. Thirdly, there are goods and services provided because of a concern with the general quality of the social or physical environment: into this last category come higher education, museums, an employment service, government support to scientific and technical research, and public broadcasting.[3]

Notice that, though the first of these three groups must be provided collectively, the other two might be (and in some societies, at some times, have been) provided privately; the dividing line between private and public goods is fluid. We shall find this important; many critics allege that the inefficiencies of public planning arise in part from the fact that it tries to do too much. If Concorde or the Sydney Opera House had been evaluated by private entrepreneurs, these critics say, they would never have come into existence; the sum of human welfare would thereby be the greater. We need not accept that last value judgement, but the statement of fact will need close examination.

At any rate, it is prima facie plausible. In the market, the entre-preneur who makes a misjudgement faces losses and eventually bankruptcy; but he constantly gets information from customers about their preferences. In supplying collective goods, public entrepreneurs face no such penalty; but, more important, they have no such stream of relevant information. As we shall see, if people are simply asked whether they would like more of a service, then in the absence of a price system they will surely say yes; and the public sector is likely to try to meet their needs, since it faces no disincentive in doing so.[4] Faced with over-supply of a service they lack the market consumer's option to 'exit'; they can merely 'voice' their disapproval, in Hirschman's distinction.[5]

Much of the following chapters will be devoted to spelling out the implications of this problem. But we can surely list some straightaway. First, there are no clear economic criteria for the supply of public goods and for their distribution to individuals and groups, because of the impossibility so far of devising adequate operational collective decision rules. Secondly, the eco-nomic problem is massively complicated by the fact that it is diffi-cult adequately to tax negative externalities, or subsidize positive ones. Thirdly, producers of these services tend inevitably to be monopolists with a very high degree of control over what is pro-duced and at what price. Fourthly, some consumers are rather well organized and they may collude with producers to obtain a production level greater than the economic optimum. And lastly, voting proves a notoriously inferior mechanism for deter-mining the quantities and prices of collective goods.[6]

POSITIVE AND NORMATIVE ANALYSIS

An obvious way of starting to approach these problems (some would say too obvious to be helpful, but they miss the point) is by distinguishing *positive* statements from *normative* state-ments: statements about what *is* from statements about what *ought to be*.[7] If we do this, we find that most normative state-ments predicate some ideally rational mode of policy-making or decision-making that may or may not be followed in this imperfect present world. Most start from economics and from the philosophical basis of that science, which is nineteenth-century utilitarianism. This is true, for instance, of most of the scientific or 'systems' approaches to planning, developed by operations researchers in the 1950s and 1960s. Such an approach proceeds in a series of logical steps. The present environment is scanned to isolate main problems. A hierarchy of goals and objectives is set up, and is edited to manageable proportions. An inventory of available resources is established. Alternative ways of meeting the objectives are hypothesized and then evaluated in terms of some common metric of costs and benefits, generally associated with the achievement of the objectives. Usually, some calculation is made of probabilities of different courses of action; the preferred course is the one that maximizes the net expectation (probability multiplied by utility). The choice is translated into managerial action and implemented. The implementation is constantly monitored and, if unexpected outcomes are discovered, appropriate modifications are introduced.[8]

Positive analyses, too, may start from a rational viewpoint. In other words, they may assume that actors in a decision all work according to normatively rational rules, to the best of their abilities. Classical and neo-classical economic theory, which is simultaneously positive and normative, is a good example of rationally based analysis – and so are its latter-day derivatives, such as systems theory. The problem is that, very soon, it will become obvious that some behaviour of actors cannot be explained in this way. First, the rational model requires perfect information, which is often lacking. It is generally impossible, for instance, to assess objective probabilities for outcomes; the best that can be done is to ask decision-makers for their subjective assessments.[9] Secondly, it assumes that all the actors hold the same values – which, in a complex decision, is highly unlikely. As will soon be clear, values and consequent preferences are very often in conflict. Thirdly, and stemming from this last, actors may well perceive that a gain to one group may mean a loss to their own group; the greatest good of the greatest number, in these circumstances, may prove an unhelpful guide. Fourthly, while some objectives are readily quantifiable, others are not. Arising from this, fifthly, there is no common agreement on an objective function which can be valued on a single scale, such as money values.[10] Sixthly, the rational model parameters of the decision remain fixed during the decision period, yet fluidity is a central feature of the real world. In practice, actors have different perceptions of and prejudices about the world they see. They have very different values, depending in part on their individual histories but also on their group or class affiliations including their loyalties to the institutions that employ them. And they must grapple with a changing environment where the factors in their decisions never stay still long enough to keep the decision stable.[11]

In consequence, rational positive analysts have developed alternative models to explain observed facts. The *incremental model*, set out by Dahl and Lindblom, assumes that decision-makers consider only incremental alternatives at any one time, together with a limited number of alternative means. Solutions will be considered only if they are realistic, or in other words appropriate to the available means. There is no clearly defined problem, no one decision; problems are never 'solved'. Such 'wicked problems' which lack definitive formulations or tests or one-shot solutions are special to planning.[12] But it can be argued that this, too, is over-simplistic: it ignores the fact that social change and innovation comes about through incorporation of new social values. Consequently, it has been claimed, the right mode of analysis is a kind of *mixed scanning*, which distinguishes fundamental *contextual* decisions from *individual item* decisions. Contextual decisions are made through a fundamental exploration of the main alternatives in the light of goals and objectives of the individual actor; at this stage, details are properly omitted. Then, piecemeal incremental decisions are made within the context of the fundamental ones.[13] Etzioni concludes:

> Democracies must accept a relatively high degree of incrementalism (though not as high as that of developing nations) because of their greater need to gain support for new decisions from many and conflicting sub-societies, a need that reduces their capacity to follow a long-run plan.... Democracies tend first to build a consensus and then to

proceed, often accomplishing less than was necessary later than was necessary.[14]

From such a model comes a concept of planning '... as a *process* of preparing a set of decisions for action in the future directed at achieving goals by optimal means and learning from the outcome about possible new sets of decisions and new goals to be achieved.[15] Thus, positive analysis is used in developing normative solutions.

At the end of this book we shall return to normative theory. But, before doing this, we need to go further in discovering how positive theory has approached these problems. For in helping to understand how the world is, it may provide a better theory of how the world might be. In particular, we need to look at alternatives to the economist–rational model of explanation.

ALTERNATIVE EXPLANATIONS: ALLISON'S THREE MODELS

In his classic study of decision-making during the Cuban missile crisis of 1962, Graham Allison looks at the same piece of historical reality in three ways, each of which approaches a different level of reality.[16] His model 1, the *rational actor paradigm*, corresponds closely to the rational model we have just considered. It assumes that action results from choice by a unitary object, called a nation or a government. Such a rational actor has a single set of goals (his utility function), a single set of options and a single set of consequences of alternatives. The actor reaches a static solution through analysing his goals and objectives, setting out his options, calculating benefits and costs of each, and reaching a choice that gives maximal excess of benefits. But Allison shows convincingly that, applied to the American-Russian confrontation at that time, the model 1 paradigm fails to account for a great deal of observed behaviour.

So Allison tries another approach. Model 2, the *organizational process paradigm*, assumes that most decision-making behaviour results from established routines within organizations. Here, the actors do not form a unity, but rather a constellation of individuals in organizations, with government leaders at the top. Problems are factored into sub-problems and are then acted upon by individuals with constrained powers. Organizations, developing a collective view, develop stable perceptions and procedures; their reactions thereby become predictable. Goals are dominated by the need to maintain the health of the organization and to avoid threats to it. Problems are tackled one by one as they arise, using standard procedures; uncertainty is avoided as much as possible. If unexpected problems are faced, the search for an answer will be biased by tradition and by the training of the actors. Dramatic changes will occur only in an organizational crisis involving personnel changes, or perhaps collapse of the entire organization. If any attempt is made from the centre to get a better integrated process, it will be found almost impossible to maintain the necessary continuing process of monitoring and control. Thus government is an established conglomerate of organizations, each with goals and programmes; change will be marginal and incremental, and long-range planning will be disregarded; solutions will not be adopted, indeed they may not be considered, if they depart from existing programmes or demand cooperation with other rival organizations.

Yet even this approach, Allison argues, still fails to catch the whole reality. Therefore he uses another mode of analysis: model 3, the *governmental (bureaucratic) politics paradigm*, assumes that decision-making by government is a political resultant from conflict, compromise and confusion among individuals whose behaviour must be understood in terms of game-playing. The players in these games each have positions; they may be chiefs, or their immediate staff, or Indians, or *ad hoc* players on the fringe (such as legislators and press). They have parochial perceptions and interests, especially organizational ones (a throwback to model 2). Their interests are represented as stakes, on which they may take stands; these stands are forced by deadlines, set by routines, by crises or by political actions. Each player will affect results depending on his power, which in turn will stem from a combination of bargaining advantages, skill and will in using them, or his perceptions of these things. Power must

be invested wisely, otherwise the result will be a loss of reputation, and hence a loss of power. The game will be played through
action channels, which government lays down for action of specific issue. The rules will be set by the constitution, by statutes,
by regulations, even by culture; they may range from the very
clear to the very hazy. Action then becomes a political resultant;
politics is the mechanism of choice, and each player struggles for
outcomes that advance his perception of his national, organizational, group or personal interests. The roles of players vary
according to action channels; thus chiefs make decisions but Indians must implement them (and may fail to do so); Indians also
frame most problems and propose most solutions. Solutions are
reached by immediate responses to problems; deadlines impose
quick decisions and a false air of confidence in them. Perceptions
and expectations differ; communication is often poor; and decisions can be obtained through vagueness, with different actors
understanding different meanings.

Allison's three models are distilled from many different insights
in sociology, psychology and political science. Using them as a
starting point, we can now look more critically at some of these
elements of rational-positive theory.

Economists' explanations and sociologists' explanations

A critical starting point is a fact already noted: the rational mode
of analysis or explanation, Allison's model 1, rests fundamentally
on philosophical premises that are basic to economics. Indeed
the central methods (assessment of uncertainty and comparison
of utility) are economic techniques. In contrast, model 2 draws
on insights from sociology and social psychology. Model 3,
clearly, also draws on psychology, but at its interface with political science.

Here we can notice a fundamental difference: between what
Daniel Bell and Mancur Olson call the economizing and sociologizing modes.[17] In the economizing mode, the focus is always on
the individual; his satisfaction (or utility) is the unit in which
costs and benefits are reckoned. In the sociologizing mode, the
focus is on the individual in society. The economic ideal is Pareto

optimality (of which more later) in resource allocation, so as to get the most efficient use of scarce resources. In contrast, the classical (or Parsonian) sociological ideal is to integrate society so that it forms a community with common norms and values and group associations and affiliations; in such a society, formalized groupings (including pressure groups) are particularly valuable. For Olson, these two models are normatively in conflict: an economically oriented society will have great dynamism but little social stability (as in many developing nations today), while a (Parsonian) sociologically-oriented country will have great stability but little economic growth (as, perhaps, Britain today). The choice between the two modes, Olson stresses, has to be made by the political system. We shall want to look again at this distinction in chapter 13, where we return to normative models.

But, just now, it provides a useful insight into our positive models. Sociologists of the Parsonian school stress mutual adjustment; but in contrast, sociologists of a Marxist or neo-Marxist kind stress conflict between groups. Thus Ralf Dahrendorf's model shows us that a society is exposed to change, with ubiquitous and permanent social conflict, and with constraint of some groups by others; there will always be a dominant and a dominated quasi-group, and these two groups will organize themselves into groups with manifest interests, which will then fight over the preservation or removal of the status quo.[18] Similarly, John Rex questions the assumption that society is organized around common values; instead, he argues, social systems have built-in conflict situations, in which the parties will have unequal power giving a ruling and a subject class, struggling for legitimacy.[19]

We can say that Parsonian sociology has been the basis for one kind of alternative model, with both positive and normative aspects, but that conflict sociology has surely been the foundation for radically different alternatives. In the rational-economic model, by way of contrast, there is no conflict between one individual and another; there is competition, but in the end it serves the greatest good of the greatest number. Producers compete to make profits, consumers compete to get bargains; they mutually adjust their supply and demand levels until the market is cleared. In contrast, sociological theory sees bureaucracy as serving its own ends. And a whole group of social psychologists-turned-organizational analysts, especially at the Carnegie-Mellon school in Pittsburgh, has developed a general theory of conflict resolution within organizations. It was this group which first suggested that organizations work by reducing general goals to sub-goals, to which individuals and groups could then become attached. Out of this came the behavioural theory of the firm; it treats the firm as a conflict-solving organization, constantly dividing and reforming itself into coalitions which form for particular problems or particular times with temporary organizational goals.[20] Clearly the Carnegie-Mellon theorists have influenced both Allison's second and third models.

Models of game-playing behaviour, on the other hand, draw on theory developed by economists, but use it in a quite different sense from the rational-economic models, allying it to experimental work on the assessment of risk. Thus the stress is again on the individual rather than the organization; but now, there is no assumption that the outcome of the activity will be necessarily optimal in any way. In fact, the theory of games in its original form is quite incapable of application to these kinds of problem, since (as we shall see) it cannot yet be extended to cover games with many players where the outcome may be better or worse for the whole group of players (n-person, non-zero sum games). But, as Bower suggests, it may be used in non-rigorous formulations to describe a variety of complicated decision processes in conditions of uncertainty.[21]

The conclusion might as well be stated in advance: none of these methods, in itself, will provide a touchstone to adequate understanding. But perhaps each of them can contribute something to an eclectic theory, still to be developed. To advance that aim is the central object of this book.

A TENTATIVE POSITIVE THEORY

It may be tentatively stated thus. Decisions arise from a complex process of interactions among actors. All these people think themselves rational, and are trying to behave rationally for much of the time; but their conceptions of the rational differ. They have different goals, and different ways of achieving these goals. Some of them, particularly senior professionals and bureaucrats, have been trained according to rational modes and will try particularly hard to apply these in decision-making. Others, in particular politicians, will tend to follow more intuitive, adaptive, piece-meal methods. The most important definable groups are the *community*, or more particularly those members of the community who play an active role in various formal or informal organiza-tions that try to intervene in the decision-making process; the elected *politicians*, who must promise certain policies to the elec-torate in order to gain re-election and who will be subject in office to pressures of events; and the professional and administrative *bureaucracy* which must administer policy but which invariably also plays a large role in shaping it. Each of these broad groups splits into *sub-groups* (different citizens' groups, often with con-tradictory purposes; political parties, and sub-groups within parties; divisions of bureaucracies, such as ministries or bureaux within ministries); any of these sub-groups is likely to have interests that in part coincide with the wider group, in part diverge. These sub-groups, and the wider groups, are to some extent bound by established perceptions and procedures. Members of groups or sub-groups, and even individuals, engage in strategic behaviour to gain what they perceive as their objec-tives. Their power stems from a variety of sources, including legal and institutional authority, reputation, skill in bargaining and acuteness of perception. They are bound by rules of the game, which may be extremely rigid (laws, established procedures) or fluid (custom) in different societies. No outcome is ever decisive, since it can be reversed or can wither away due to non-imple-mentation. Thus the process of decision-making is not discrete, but is part of an ongoing complex of interrelated acts; and non-decisions may be as important as decisions.

Much of any such eclectic body of theory must derive from the United States, for that is where most of the work has been done. But in applying it to other countries, especially to Britain, from which many of our case studies are drawn, caution may be needed. As Kenneth Newton has pointed out, in comparison to the United States Britain is more centralized, with a stronger national context; the role of bureaucracy and of political parties is certainly greater, and the role of voluntary organizations possibly so; a vital role is played by pressure groups, most of which are middle-class but at least one of which (the trade unions) is not.[22] We need to reinterpret the theory in terms of different formal political structures.

CHAPTER 9

The Actors: (1) The Community

In theory the people are sovereign; in practice, in most so-called democracies, they are at best semi-sovereign,[1] since their power is circumscribed by the positions of other actors in the policy-making and decision-taking process. They are, at least partly, in conflict with these other actors. To understand this process, it is useful to borrow concepts from the conflict school of sociology, which we have already briefly surveyed in the previous chapter.

INTEREST GROUPS AS CLASSES: DAHRENDORF'S ANALYSIS

For this purpose, the father of sociological conflict theory is not highly relevant: Marx's proletariat and bourgeoisie are not the contenders in most of the battles we have been studying. Individuals and groups might care to label themselves thus; but it would hardly be helpful, indeed it could be positively confusing, for understanding what is at issue. We need a more fluid and flexible theory of conflict, and we can find it in Dahrendorf. For Dahrendorf, as we have already seen, change and conflict are permanent and ubiquitous features of social life. And these conflicts take place between social classes. But we should not understand classes in the old Marxian sense: a social class, for Dahrendorf, is any group that has common interests, and that exists in a society where one group exercises authority over others. (Dahrendorf calls such societies *imperatively co-ordinated associations*). Some classes, or groups, are not yet conscious of their common interests; Dahrendorf calls these *quasi-groups*. Some have become conscious, and therefore organized; Dahrendorf calls these *interest groups*. Both quasi-groups and interest groups are social classes, and *by definition* they will come into conflict.

In this process, people (as the phrase goes) can wear different hats: the civil servant who defends a motorway plan during his working day may attack a local airport proposal in the evening. But conflict can be prevented, or weakened, by various organizational devices or conditions: these may be technical in character (communication, patterned recruitment). And psychological conditions, which are quite independent of social structure, may help in this process. Class conflict will be less intense if, in some way, different kinds of conflict can be split off and kept separate; conversely, the more conflicts can be grouped and aggregated, the more intense will the conflict pattern be. So in Dahrendorf's words:

> If, in a given society, there are fifty associations, we should expect to find a hundred classes, or conflict groups in the sense of the present study.... In fact, of course, this extreme scattering of conflicts and conflict groups is rarely the case. Empirical evidence shows that different conflicts may be, and often are, superimposed in given historical societies, so that the multitude of possible conflict fronts is reduced to a few dominant conflicts.[2]

Thus, in any controversy over a planning decision, by definition there are already two classes in Dahrendorf's sense. One critical question then to be asked is: will this conflict elide with another, to form a kind of meta-conflict? For in that way, we have the ingredients for intense confrontation. The repeated battles over motorways, between the Department of the Environment and the conservationist lobby, become a case in point.

How then will classes form? How will conflicts develop? J.S. Coleman lists five kinds of event-provoking controversy.[3] First, the issue must touch on an important aspect of life, directly affecting the welfare of individuals. Jobs, housing, education are obvious examples. But even these, and still more other issues, may have a different intensity for different groups at different times.

Environmental planning, the main subject of our case studies, is a particularly good example: there is strong evidence that it is an income-elastic public good, so that richer people (or groups, or whole societies) want more of it than poorer ones. Here, however, the second point is particularly relevant: the issue must affect different community members in different ways. The most extreme example is where some members will gain and others lose (as for instance with alternative lines of a motorway); less extreme is the case where all gain, but some gain much more than others. Thirdly, the issue must be susceptible to public action. Fourthly, the event may be generated either inside the community concerned or by some outside agency. And lastly, the issue may affect a number of different areas. Here, Coleman suggests that some nominal issues may be merely pegs on which to hand individual or group hostilities. Some conflicts may be over substantive issues (such as economic ones); but others may reflect different cultural values or beliefs. Some of our case studies – the London motorways, for instance – finally extended to basic questions of life styles in a big metropolis.

THE COST OF INTERVENTION

Another way of looking at this question comes from Buchanan and Tullock's analysis of the *costs of intervention*. In this analysis, any individual who takes any form of action can be expected to impose external costs on the rest of the community – the classic economic problem of negative externalities arising from the fact that the individual considers only his own costs and benefits. So the community will impose certain conditions on the numbers of people necessary to make a binding decision, such as the well-known majority principle. As the number of individuals involved in such a decision increases, so the external costs to the rest of the community will fall; if the community requires unanimous decisions about everything, then there are zero external costs. Why then does not every community insist on unanimity? Simply because, in any society with conflicts, the costs of reaching agreement will be too high. Thus, as the numbers required to reach agreement rise from one to the whole community, one set of costs (external costs) falls while the other set (bargaining costs) rises. The individual, and thus the community, will seek the lowest combination of these two costs, and this will fall somewhere between the two extremes; exactly where is a question we shall want to examine further, when we come to analyse political activity in Chapter 11.

Meanwhile, we can say that these are preconditions: whether, or when, they turn into actual conflict will depend on particular conditions at particular times. A few activities may gain support; there may be a general climate of suspicion; in particular, the administration may become isolated from the wider community, which may allow an opposition group to activate the passive majority.[4] From then on, according to Coleman, conflicts tend to develop a dynamism of their own. First, specific issues may be turned into general ones (the process of grouping and aggregating, in Dahrendorf's model). New and different issues may arise, unrelated to the original ones; partly this may be accidental, partly it may be a device on the part of the opposition to mobilize new forces. (In the case of the Maplin airport proposal, the environmental impact of the surface links to London became such a new issue.) Generally these issues are of a one-sided character, allowing response only in one direction. Next, disagreements may turn into personal antagonisms. New leaders may emerge from the background, often without leadership experience (the Homes before Roads movement in London). The established organizations of the community are drawn into the conflict, despite pressures (both internal and external) to remain neutral. Word-of-mouth communication will supplement or even replace the media, which come to be regarded as manipulated and hidebound.[5]

Overall, in Coleman's conclusion, some kinds of community are more likely to generate conflict than others. There will tend to be less conflict in communities where many people identify with the local community, and this even applies where, as often happens in such places, there is a large number of local organized groups. Generally, lower socio-economic groups participate less in conflict but are more difficult to restrain when they do. Interlocking mechanisms among different groups also help contain controversy; in places where these are lacking, for instance commuter suburbs, people with similar interests form separate and isolated groups, so that conflict is externalized up to the level of the entire community.[6] The division between middle-class residents, who approved the third London airport at Thurleigh, and the trades unionists who supported it, provides a good example.

STAGES IN POLITICAL CHANGE

Supposing then that, in a community, a conflict exists: some groups desire change, others oppose it. What then must be the strategy of those who desire change? Bachrach and Baratz, in their study of political power, show that they must win at three separate stages; their opponents need triumph at only one of these stages to block the change. The first is *issue-recognition*. Here there are formidable barriers to change. The values or myths of the dominant groups may simply fail to admit new issues. It takes time to generate what D.A. Schon[7] calls an 'idea in good currency'. Or they may claim them to be illegitimate because they clash with community values or with one prime value, such as individual freedom. Thirdly, there are procedural and organizational devices that may block the road to the decision-making area. As Gordon Tullock stressed, most new ideas may prove unpopular; for minority ideas, it may be necessary to adopt a long-range and indirect strategy of 'spreading the gospel' with only a low chance of success. In these circumstances the best bet may be to try to move the received majority view progressively closer to the minority view.[8] The triumph of the technological approach in the early and mid-1960s, and its request by the environmental gospel in the late 1960s and early 1970s, is a classic example, which affected the outcome of several of our case studies.

Suppose though that this first hurdle is cleared; the next is the process of decision-making. By definition, this concerns small groups in the political or bureaucratic arenas. They have particular perceptions of the relevant factors and conditions (which we shall be examining in detail in later chapters). Their information may be far from complete. Their contribution will be constrained by their formal role, by informal social rules, by personality. All this presents profound barriers to change, as we already noticed in looking at Allison's bureaucratic model for analysing the Cuban missile crisis.

But thirdly, and equally underlined by Allison's analysis, once a decision is made it needs to be implemented. It is at this point that bureaucratic discretion really comes into its own; it allows officials to circumvent the intentions of politicians. Thus change may be widely desired, it may be agreed; but nothing is done – until perhaps, new evidence can be found to support a return to the status quo.[9] The reversal of the Maplin airport decision is a case in point.

The same point is put in a slightly different way by Cozzens in analysing 'slippage', defined as '... types of powerlessness experienced by client and user groups at different stages of a policy process'. One cause is mobilization of bias, or the prevention of latent issues from emerging; this is clearly equivalent to the first hurdle in the Bachrach-Baratz model. Secondly, there is explicit political failure, through inability of a group to form a winning coalition. (The anti-motorway campaigners in London, and the anti-BART group in San Francisco, failed here.) It may arise through mobilization of bias, or through lack of resources, which may be cut off at some other (higher) level. Thirdly, the instrument of change may be unsuitable for the bureaucratic structure of the implementers. But also, there may be inadequate incentives or controls for the private actors whose cooperation is required. Lastly, and more generally, there may be incentive and control problems across the whole structure of different levels of government, whereby some levels set ground rules or objectives or incentives for others.[10]

STRATEGIES FOR POLITICAL ACTION

Can groups hope to understand better how to act as levers of change? Can researchers help them? Robert Dahl sets out four alternative strategies for political activists. First, they might organize their own separate political party. Secondly, and less drastically, they might form a new coalition party together with another group having similar overlapping (though not identical) aims. Thirdly, they may act as a pressure group on one or another of two major political parties (as the Homes before Roads movement did in the London motorway controversy).

Fourthly, they may enter into one of the parties and become a major element in a party coalition (as the London anti-roads campaigners later did). Dahl goes on to suggest appropriate rules. Suppose for instance that the goals of the group are broad and are acceptable to both political parties; that members are few yet highly homogeneous. Then the right course would be to form an independent party which could try to win concessions from the two major parties. If the goals are broad but unacceptable to the two parties, if the members are many yet highly diverse, then the right course is to try to form a new coalition. If the goals are narrow but acceptable to the two parties, if members are few but have little common character, a pressure group is indicated. But if the goals are broad and are acceptable to one party, with a numerous and diverse group membership, a coalition with an existing party may prove the right solution.[11] In our case studies we have seen how often a narrow issue (anti-motorway or anti-airport) became broadened into a general (pro-environmental) issue, so that the optimal strategy shifted.

These political strategies will need more intensive analysis, which we shall be making in Chapter 11. But, meanwhile, it is important that political action alone is only part of the strategy. It is important also that activists understand the inner structure, values and powers of the bureaucracy. They also need to take account of the operations of the political elite, which includes not only key politicians and bureaucrats but also private decision-makers with access to communication channels.[12] Above all, perhaps, they need to understand these communication channels and those individuals, or groups, that have control over them. Very little is known, as yet, about the forces that control the opinions of key controllers of the mass media: the economics of the media, especially in the commercial sector, may produce a convergence near the centre but there is some movement over time, perhaps random, perhaps cyclical, perhaps representing some progressive learning process.[13] The media in several countries powerfully helped shape the transition from the technological to the conservationist values.

Given all this, can we say anything useful about the development of conflict between the established forces and new activist groups? At first sight, there is almost a polarization here between two opposed views. One, which could be called the radical establishment view, holds that the entrenched political-bureaucratic apparatus will try to manipulate participation for its own ends. In Arnstein's celebrated ladder of participation, there are eight rungs, of which only the top three (citizen control, delegated power and partnership) can truly be called citizen power. Three others (placation, consultation and informing) represent 'tokenism', in Arnstein's dismissive phrase. And the bottom two rungs (therapy and manipulation) represent no degree of participation at all.[14] But at the other extreme, a critic from the radical right, Aaron Wildavsky, sees the activist groups, too, as a threat to the real interests of the masses: 'The goal of this white, radical, privileged elite is clear: a society purged by them of the values, tastes, preferences and policies desired by the mass of Americans.'[15] According to this view, a part of the traditional upper class and upper-middle class have felt threatened by the growing affluence of the mass, which is felt directly as a loss of amenity. Thus the radical elite hates the traditional establishment, not because it exploits the masses, but because it does not repress their cultural desires enough: 'An aristocratic bid for power and prestige cannot succeed under the conditions of American life. But it can be dressed in democratic garb. The slogan of this white elite is 'participatory democracy'. Strangely enough, this doctrine, under which everyone is allegedly participatory, rules out the mass of working and middle-class Americans. The mass has to work.'[16]

One natural outcome is for this radical elite to ally itself with the underclass, which in American society is black. But on the environmental issue the radicals 'wish to force government to spend millions of public money to satisfy their aesthetic preferences',[17] and this naturally conflicts with social priorities. Thus, in America at any rate, the movement is split. In fact, there is no necessary conflict between Arnstein and Wildavsky. The existing establishment might well be playing a game of manipulation, while the radical opposition might equally be engaged in a conspiracy against the masses. To judge more closely, we would need to look at the real objectives of different actors in the political process, and those are not necessarily the stated objectives; we shall need to look very hard at outcomes too. That has been one of the major tasks of the case studies in Part One. The critical question at the end is: what are the *real* values of the masses, and who best represents them? To this intractable problem we shall return in Chapter 13. Meanwhile, what we do know is that most exercises in participation, however sincerely conceived, fail to involve more than a well-informed minority. Such exercises commonly show a very low level of perception of the question at issue, especially if this occurs at a large (non-local) scale and if it involves abstract choices.[18] In fact, in such cases most people are evidently not interested, even though the media may present the issue as one of crucial importance. This, for instance, was the experience of planners involved with the chosen site for the third London airport.[19] In the circumstances, it is small wonder that public opinion comes to be represented by professional lobbyists, who can safely claim to know the public view because no one will contradict them. Government needs such people because it needs views.[20]

This chapter has been concerned with positive theory, the discussion of what *is*; but it can hardly escape the question of what *ought to be*, which will be the main subject in Chapter 13. Logically, there can be only two answers: either the amount and quality of participation will need to be improved, or decision-makers need to find some way of bypassing the whole process and getting more reliable, less biased information directly from the real public – with all the problems of misperception and misinformation this may involve.[21] There is no easy way out.

CHAPTER 10

The Actors: (2) The Bureaucracy

Bureaucracies – including professional planning bureaucracies – form the second element of our decision-making triangle. We now understand their behaviour rather well. Research since the early 1960s has shown us that bureaucratic organizations have their own well-developed rules of behaviour, both formal and informal; and that the resulting behaviour is to a large extent predictable. Understanding these rules will take us a long way in the interpretation of planning disasters.

Most of this new knowledge comes from a select group of analysts in the United States. Some are psychologists by origin, some sociologists, some economists. From diverse origins, they come to a common set of themes. Their analysis is essentially socio-psychological: they seek to understand how rational individuals, concerned for their own advantage, will relate to other individuals in organizations. Their results give a picture quite unlike the usual stereotypes of a large organization.

THE FIRM: A THEORY OF ITS BEHAVIOUR

The starting-point must be the work of the school of behavioural analysts at Carnegie-Mellon University in Pittsburgh: Herbert Simon, Richard Cyert and James March. Their classic statement is the behavioural theory of the firm, developed by Cyert and March.[1] Firms – defined by Cyert and March as large organizations working in the market for profit – prove to be not homogeneous, unitary organizations with single goals; rather they are coalitions of sub-groups, each with their own partial goals, imperfectly rationalized in terms of general goals. Thus they proceed not in a rational mode, but rather via a series of compromises. The point is that in this regard, public non-profit-making organizations behave much like private profit-making ones. Among the most important features of decision-making, in both such organizations, are the following.

1. *Quasi-resolution of conflict.* Conflicts (between the different goals of the sub-groups) are never really resolved. The goals themselves are seen as constraints on the aspirations of the organization. Most are continuous, conventional, operational goals such as maximizing output or profit, maximizing or increasing market share, maintaining inventories at satisfactory levels, and so on. Conflicts between goals are resolved by various means: problems are decomposed into sub-problems each handled by sub-units, thus simplifying them (local rationality); decision-making rules do not demand total consistency; goals are approached sequentially. switching to one and then another.

2. *Avoidance of uncertainty.* Organizations see this as a problem because, usually, the uncertainty in their environment is more than they are capable of handling – and the proportion of firms with such 'turbulent environments' is constantly rising.[2] Firms deal with the problem first by reacting to feedback on a short-run crisis management basis rather than by anticipating trouble in advance; secondly by arranging a stable negotiated environment, with plans and operating procedures that are self-confirming.

3. *Problemistic search.* Faced with a pressing problem, firms will find a fairly immediate solution. Such searches are simple-minded; they depend on simple models of causality. They are biased by the training, experience and goals of participants. They will stop when a solution is found that satisfies the goals. If not, the goals will have to be revised – but this is a last step.

4. *Organizational learning.* This takes place in three ways. First, goals are adapted in the light of experience, of either the firm's past or that of other organizations. Secondly, the organization may change its 'attention rules' both as to measuring goal achievement and to analysis of the competitive environment. And

thirdly, it may adapt search rules, changing the order in which alternatives are considered in the light of previous successes or failures.[3]

All this must lead, so Cyert and March suggest, to organizational inertia. The goals of the organization, especially at the higher levels, must satisfy many conflicting sub-goals. Alternatives must be considered sequentially, concentrating only on areas where there seem to be immediate problems. Uncertainty must be avoided by following regular procedures, reacting to feedback rather than forecasting the future environment. Operating procedures must be standardized. Thus research allocations will come to reflect only gross comparisons of the marginal advantages of the alternatives; searches among alternatives will be made just before a commitment is needed; computations of expected consequences will be based on simple questions (Is it feasible? Is the money available? Is it better than what we are doing now?); bias will enter into expectations of sub-units.[4]

The critical key in this seems to be the analysis of decision-making sub-units within large organizations. M. A. Kaplan shows[5] that such units tend to acquire internal solidarity; their members come to believe in their own objectives, so that divergence is increasingly seen as deviancy. Conflicts are thus unlikely to occur within the unit, but rather will occur between sets of units. Most units have some degree of internal insulation, which inhibits communication and integration between members: thus in a strongly hierarchical chain-of-command unit the senior persons will be insulated, while units that delegate functions or reward other units will be insulated against other units. In general, Kaplan concludes, the longer a unit exists the more it will tend to show solidarity, thus tending to inertia and poor perception of new disturbing factors in its environment.[6]

THE DOWNSIAN ANALYSIS OF BUREAUCRACY

Building in part on these foundations, Anthony Downs has given us a complete theory of the behaviour of bureaucracies.[7] So complete is this theory, indeed, that it is difficult to summarize it within a short compass. But some of the central concepts are essential for any understanding of failures in the public planning process.

Bureaux, for Downs and for writers who have followed him, are by definition large organizations producing goods and services outside the market. Downs starts by assuming that officials in these organizations pursue their goals rationally, but that these goals are significantly affected by self-interest. He concludes that the birth, growth and decline of bureaux are largely due to external factors. New bureaux will be created by purposeful agitation of people interested in promoting programmes. As bureaux grow, they will attract individuals interested in climbing, and their recruitment in turn will help accelerate organizational growth. But as this happens, the energies of the climbers will be devoted progressively to internal politics and rivalry rather than to the performance of their functions *vis-à-vis* the outside world. Reverse trends may occur, but in general accelerators and decelerators in a bureau's life work on a ratchet principle; hence, bureaux tend to become larger over time.

Thus all bureaucracies, Downs argues, have inherent tendencies to expand. Growth provides leaders with extra power, income and prestige; it tends to reduce internal conflicts; and the incentive structure facing most officials provides much greater rewards for increasing expenditures than for reducing them. As bureaux age, the number and also the proportion of administrative officials in them tends to rise; the officials come to devote less time to carrying out the bureau's functions than to insuring its survival and growth. Bureaux faced with drastic shrinkage or extinction, because of the curtailment of their original functions, will seek to develop new ones so as to compensate.

As bureaux age, they also become more conservative unless for some reason they experience periods of rapid growth or internal turnover. Their officials also become increasingly conservers, interested in preserving what they have rather than in new aggrandizement. Such bureaucrats are biased against any change in the *status quo*. In growing institutions there are likely to be more individuals labelled by Downs as 'climbers', who try to invent new functions for their bureaux; these may be functions not performed elsewhere or they may be performed by existing bureaux, in which case the climbers will look for areas of low resistance to their colonizing activities. Climbers have a strong incentive not to economize in their budgets unless they can use at least some of the savings to finance an expansion of functions.

An important part of Downs's theory concerns the information that bureaucrats receive before they reach decisions. The great majority of all internal communications are subformal (or informal) in character; this will be especially true in organizations that have strong interdependencies, or that have great uncertainty in their operating environment, or that experience time pressures on operations. In large organizations with many officials, especially where they work in a hierarchy, significant distortion of information will take place as it goes from one official to another. Especially this will occur upwards: top officials will tend to hear what lower officials think they want to hear. Top officials may deliberately ignore the more significant qualitative (or weakly quantitative) information, especially where this is concerned with future events. And this in itself will make organizations vulnerable to unexpected changes in their working environment.

Large bureaucracies, according to Downs, not only have information problems; they also have control problems, and naturally these also are most serious for the top bureaucrats. For in any large, multi-level bureau, a very significant proportion of all activity is completely unrelated to the general goals of the bureau or of the top officials in it. Rather, many of the activities are aimed simply at maintaining the coalition of officials necessary to achieve the formal goals. Thus, in a large organization, no one has full control; the larger the organization, the poorer the control and the coordination between the parts. As an organization grows, the topmost official's capacity for direct action will rise but at a diminishing rate; more and more of total activity will consist of internal administration; and the proportion of wasted activity will also rise. Yet, if the topmost official does not bear any of the costs of adding subordinates to his staff, he will be motivated to expand the size of his organization indefinitely.

The irony is that the greater the effort at control from the top, the greater will be the efforts of subordinates to evade or counteract this control. Any attempt to control one large organization means the creation of another; and the quantity and detail of reporting required by monitoring bureaux tends to rise steadily, regardless of the amount or nature of the activity being monitored.

Further bureaucracies, in Downs's analysis, tend systematically to distort the process of search for alternative courses of action. They do not give enough attention to actions that involve large changes in the *status quo*, or that take account of future uncertainties. Especially where there is pressure for quick decisions, bureaux tend to consider a minimum number of alternatives; to give first attention to alternatives already thought out in advance and 'ready to go'; to restrict the number of decision-makers and the diversity of their views; and to use secrecy to guarantee this restriction. Thus if there are limited time, few decision-makers, little diversity of views, few skilled or trained people either involved in the decision or hearing about it, and few people isolated from the pressures of other decisions, few alternatives will be considered. This suggests that a bureau or bureau section, in order to concentrate on long-run planning, would need to be shielded from day-to-day pressures.

It follows from all this that many bureaux are extremely resistant to change. Large bureaux, where the power and functions of officials are well established, will tend to oppose changes, especially if these officials are conservers, as they probably will be. They also tend to have strong, autonomous support. Such a bureau may refuse to alter its behaviour even when agents in its power setting agree it should; instead, it may try to influence its agents' opinion; in particular it may tell agents that it is already doing what is suggested, though agents will deny this. Normally, bureau behaviour has long periods of drift interspersed by short phases of organizational catch-up. Bureaux are more liable to quick change if they exist in a turbulent external environment, or if they have high rates of personnel turnover (caused by demands from other organizations for scarce specialists, or fluctuating functions, or deliberate policy), or if they have innovation-proof technologies, or if they have functions in which it is easy to measure success in performance.

Bureaux have strong senses of territory; their officials exhibit strong loyalty to them. Every large organization is in partial conflict with other agents. New bureaux tend to arise in large, policy-dense areas of no-man's-land where many bureaux have peripheral interests but no one bureau is dominant. The longer a bureaucracy has been in existence, the more likely it is to have an ideology and the more elaborate the ideology is likely to be. Typically, bureau ideologies are narrower than party political ideologies; bureau ideologies stress the advantage of expanding the bureau's services and the positive benefits thus conferred, concentrating especially on general rather than sectional benefits; costs will be ignored. Bureau officials have longer time horizons but less sensitivity to public opinion than do politicians. Elaborate bureau ideologies are likely to arise in bureaucracies that are large, that recruit members with special characteristics, that provide only indirect benefits to large numbers of people, that require deep consensus on goals among their members, that are engaged in controversial *activities* that have functions overlapping with other agencies, or that are trying to expand. Single – or limited – purpose agencies such as aircraft suppliers or highway planners, are especially prone to such ideologies. Downs concludes that in modern complex society, the number and proportion of bureaucrats tend to rise; this arises due to division of labour, to conflicts between groups, to increased organizational size generally, to the 'tertiarization' of the labour force and to increasing wealth. Many citizens grumble about this but few, Downs claims, would abolish bureaucracy if given the chance.

ESCALATION OF BUREAU BUDGETS

Other observers of the process would agree with the facts but might contest the inference. For Kenneth Arrow,

... the nature and purpose of organizations create additional implications for the determination of agenda and, in particular, for sluggishness in the introduction of new items ... the combination of uncertainty, indivisibility and capital intensity associated with information channels and their use implies (a) that the actual structure and behaviour of an organization may depend heavily upon random events, in other words on history, and (b) that the very pursuit of efficiency may lead to rapidity and unresponsiveness to further change.[8]

Thus Arrow is extremely pessimistic about the possibilities of organizational change. While for Wildavsky, who has exhaustively studied the budgetary process in government, the conclusion is that all bureaucratic expenditures tend to ratchet up; they remain constant until a disturbance permits a higher level of taxation (thus wartime increases in defence; depression expenditures on recovery), yet the end of the crisis fails to bring a corresponding decrease.[9] One good reason for this is that the budget-making process is essentially rough and ready, is based on guesses, and is incremental in the sense that the largest determining factor in the size of this year's budget is the size of last year's.[10] An agency will come to expect some fair share of the total budget, based on previous experience; over and above this, current problems will provide a basis for extra demands, and in fact the agency will commonly be expected to exploit this.[11] Both bureaucrats and politicians find these simplifying rules a source of some comfort: budget-makers only have to consider a small number of alternatives at any time; these differ only marginally from what has gone before; each participant need consider only his preferences and those of a few powerful competitors.[12] Such an approach could mean that important interests come to be neglected; but Wildavsky argues that this will not be so, because someone will have an interest in taking them up fairly soon.[13] In fact, agencies may come deliberately to protect their more ill-organized client public.[14] In all this, bureaucrats have well-established rules and strategies. They must pitch their demands neither too low nor too unrealistically high. In an atmosphere of growth they may make token cuts in one area to show reasonableness and gain concessions elsewhere. Faced with cuts, they may slash popular programmes to cause an outcry, or make concealed transfers between items, or deliberately develop a crisis that demands spending. Usually, no agency chief will consider the general picture or the entire public interest; no one has a general interest in contributing to economies.[15] In fact, both legislators and officials reviewing a bureau budget positively expect that bureau to propose new activities and a higher budget; otherwise, they would not easily know how to perform their roles.[16] In other words, the monitors of the budget are at a permanent disadvantage, as is stressed by W.A. Niskansen.[17] The budget bureau, or equivalent, knows what size of budget it is prepared to grant for delivery of a certain quantity of services, but it does not know the minimum budget that would suffice, for it has neither the opportunity nor the incentive. The bureaucrat knows more than the monitor (or sponsor); the sponsor needs a lot of information but he can get very little, especially when he is, as is often the case, a part-timer.

THE ECONOMICS OF BUREAUCRATIC PRODUCTION

The result, in the extended earlier analysis by Niskansen,[18] is that bureaucratic organizations supply too much of their goods and services, at too high a cost to the customer. Much or all of their output is not sold in a market at all, but is paid for by periodic appropriations (i.e. budgets). A bureau's budget and output proposals, as already seen, will not reveal the true minimum marginal cost function because it will not suit the bureau to do so. The reason is that the bureau is often a monopoly producer of the service concerned. A profit-maximizing monopolist, as all economists know, would produce less output than would a competitive producer, thus selling at a higher price and reducing much of the free benefit (consumer's surplus) which the consumer enjoys in the competitive situation. (Compare the competitive output C and price C^1 with the monopoly output M and price M^1 in Figure 9). The bureau, in contrast to both these, produces amount B and sells it at the competitive price C^1. In this particular case, production as compared with perfect competition is double while the price is the same; the shaded amount is equal to the consumer surplus and can be described as social waste, since by definition it represents resources that could have been used to produce something the public desired more.

In actual practice, Niskansen argues, the situation will be very like that in the diagram; at constant marginal costs, bureaucratic organizations will tend to produce twice as much as a competitive industry, and the same will be true of the reduction of marginal costs in a budget-constrained area. Such a system, combined with majority rule and a proportional tax system, generates benefits

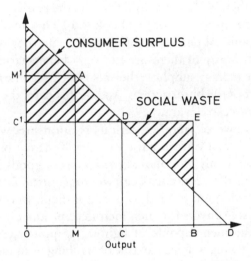

Figure 9: Competitive and Bureaucratic Outputs and Prices (Source: Niskansen).

only to the high-demand group that happens to want large quantities of the services concerned. The people in the low-demand group, most of whom are relatively poor, are absolutely worse off as a result, though the relatively worst off are high-income people with low demand (i.e. they have little need for education or the national health service). These non-beneficiaries have only two answers – emigration or revolution – neither of which they find easy. The most interesting group, though, are the middle-demand people (who are mainly middle-income too). They are somewhat indifferent or ambivalent, so the government (and the opposition) must woo them to ensure that they do not ally with the low-demand group. This is difficult since they tend to get some value out of the product, but less than they pay in taxes. They would therefore like less government; the system responds by constantly trying to produce more of the sort of services they would like in order to gain their acquiescence. How does the system succeed, then? Because, says Niskansen, the high-demand group controls it so successfully. Its members tend not to be the richest of the population (these buy their own private services); rather, Niskansen says, they are the readers of his book (and therefore, probably, of this book too). They tend to control both main political parties and the media, and they want bigger government. Many of them are not only beneficiaries from the services bureaucracy supplies; they also draw income from it, for they are part of the bureaucracy. And in this case, the Downsian analysis becomes relevant.

There is, however, another curious relationship, which again works in favour of bureaucratic expansion. Many bureaucratic agencies are not only *monopolistic suppliers* of goods or services, but also what the economists call *monopsonistic buyers* of the factors of production needed to produce them. In other words, they are the sole buyers for such factors of production as young, healthy young men capable of fighting or policing; or young, sympathetic young women capable of teaching or nursing; or airspace; or certain radio frequency bands. In some cases, bureaux simply assert a prior claim on such resources, paying less for them than private buyers of factors would have to pay (or even paying nothing at all). In other words, their cost curve is artificially lowered. But, so far as bureaux are able or even compelled to offer a competitive price for their factors (volunteer soldiers, policemen, aircraft, road contractors), these same factors may come positively to support bureaucratic expansion. There is no more fervent supporter of the BBC than the Musicians' Union, simply because the union knows that a high degree of bureaucratic monopoly in broadcasting is necessary to maintain the employment of its members. (This union has got nowhere with the commercial radio people.) Similarly with ASLEF, the NUF and many others, not to mention the road contractors, the aircraft suppliers and the manufacturers of hospital equipment. These bodies have noted from experience, even if they do not put it in formal economist's language, that a bureaucratic buyer aiming at a higher production level will tend to pay higher prices than a competitive producer, so long as supply prices are rising (which they often are). Thus a remarkable discrepancy of attitude exists between those factors strongly supported by sponsors, who want as much bureaucratic production as possible (regular army officers, highway contractors), and those factors weakly represented (young army conscripts, owners of land on a motorway line). Many classic conflicts, ranging from the Vietnam war debate in the United States to hundreds of motorway clashes, can be explained principally in these terms.[19]

Bureaucrats thus have a powerful incentive to increase production and a number of built-in advantages in trying to do so. The populace, for whom the services are provided, cannot keep their demands secret (partly because the media reveal them). There is a demand for expansion from special interest groups (the sellers of factors) and from the actual bureaucratic producers, all of whom have votes. The bureaucrats have all sorts of possible strategies to meet attacks, such as responding to expenditure cuts by slashing the best-loved or essential programmes to provoke an outcry. The only possible contrary factors, according to Tullock,[20] are that the legislature is not entirely ignorant of the bureaucratic production functions and, perhaps most hopefully, bureaucrats are too lazy to exploit all their advantages (or, in Downsian language, they are conservers). But this is small comfort. Tullock's practical answer, and Niskansen's, is a combination of deliberate competition between bureaux (ITV versus BBC, National Bus versus British Rail, Electricity versus Gas), plus private competition, plus contracting-out of services, plus a requirement for bigger majorities (say two-thirds) for budget proposals, plus deliberate incentives or rewards to bureaucrats for reducing the size of their operations and their budgets.[21]

These may or may not work in practice. Meanwhile, much of the analysis of contemporary bureaucracies merely tends to fortify the famous law, already expressed in more homely language by C. Northcote Parkinson in the mid-1950s, that: 'The rise in the total of those employed ... would be much the same whether the volume of work were to increase, diminish or even to disappear.'[22] Certainly, some later work tends to confirm Parkinson's original hypothesis: that the size of administrative staff may show a sharp increase at a time when, demonstrably, the functions of that particular bureau are contracting. (Parkinson quotes the twentieth-century British Admiralty and Colonial Office as excellent examples.) These are strong reasons to believe that, in the modern world, bureaucratic establishments and programmes will tend to grow by laws that have almost a natural force.

THE COST-ESCALATION SYNDROME

One particular aspect of bureaucratic budgeting behaviour, of particular interest to us here, is the fact that costs of projects often prove to be very badly estimated. We found this, for instance, in our case studies of the Concorde airplane and the Sydney Opera House. And already in Chapter 1 we found that careful comparative analysis of major civil projects suggested an *average* cost escalation of over 50 per cent, with applications of novel technologies running a good deal higher.[23] This failing is not unique to the private sector; the entrepreneurial historian John Sawyer has found many examples from the history of American enterprise in the nineteenth century. But Sawyer noted an important point: that many such cases were

undertakings of easily demonstrable economic utility ... for which a gross underestimation of the cost of the project was a condition of its inauguration or completion.... The most conspicuous cases are those characterized by heavy fixed investment and high indivisibility, in which the major capital commitments had to be made before returns began.[24]

Typically in such cases, the entrepreneur launched the project with either private or public funds on the basis of an estimate of capital requirements, construction time, and estimated earnings – with or without expert aid. Had the cost estimate been a multiple of the original – say five or ten times, which was what it often proved to be in reality – the project would never have been approved, or would have been abandoned or seriously postponed. But once approved and under way, the project invariably began to take longer, to cost more, to prove vastly more formidable than the original estimate. The original investors might then be asked to provide additional funds; by direct assessment, or under pressure of recouping something of their earlier investment, they would be forced to advance capital beyond anything they had originally desired or intended. This might happen more than once, until eventually new investors might have to be sought; finally, either before or after all private sources of funds had been tapped, there might be recourse to the legislature.[25]

The final irony in Sawyer's analysis, however, is that many such projects eventually justified their inflated costs, sometimes in terms of their total economic development on the community, sometimes even in terms of the narrower criterion of private profit. For this to happen, there must have been an underestimate of demand at least equal to the underestimate of costs. Sawyer quotes one such case: the Troy and Greenfield Railroad in New England. The original estimate of costs included a tunnel, more than four miles long, through Hoosac Mountain, pronounced easy to tunnel; in fact it was composed of soft rock and caused massive escalation in costs. Yet in the event, the Civil War and the opening up of the Midwest and Great Plains made the railroad unexpectedly a transcontinental link; by 1895, 60 per cent of Boston's exports came by this route, an event that was not expected in the original calculations of profitability. This was an example where eventually even the narrow profit criterion was satisfied, against all apparent odds. Sawyer argues that if one substitutes the broader criterion of contribution to economic development, then many early canals and railways in both England and the United States would fall into the category of unexpected successes.[26]

Building in large part on Sawyer's analysis, the development economist Albert Hirschman developed the principle of the *hiding hand*. Projects, Hirschman said, tend to be accompanied by two sets of developments which offset each other, partially or wholly: the first, a set of unsuspected threats to the project's profitability or existence; the second, a set of unsuspected remedial actions if the first threat should become real. Thus Hirschman argues: '... the only way in which we can bring our creative resources fully into play is by misjudging the nature of the task, by presenting it to ourselves as more routine, simple, undemanding of genuine creativity than it will turn out to be.'[27]

In conditions of uncertainty, Hirschman went on, decision-makers will tend to look for any help they can find – and they will find it particularly in two areas. First, *pseudo-imitation* of some existing recognized technique will help make an innovation seem less difficult. Secondly, a *pseudo-comprehensive programme* will indicate great powers of problem-solving in complex situations. Both, Hirschman claimed, can act as crutches to the uncertain decision-maker who cannot assess risks; in other words they will help risks.[28]

SOME POINTERS TO POLICY

Like the previous chapter and the one following, this study has been positive in character: it has sought to analyse the essence of the way people and institutions behave in the world now, not the way they might behave if rules and conditions were changed. Inevitably, perhaps, the conclusions have been implicitly critical, and even depressing. To use them as any kind of bridge to normative thinking, we need to gather together some of the key conclusions and then to ask what kind of changes might alter the behavioural rules.

The first is that most bureaucracies have a built-in conservatism and resistance to change. They exist to do what they are doing now. In Arrow's language, they have a determined *agenda*: that is, a selection of relevant decision variables: '... the nature and purpose of organizations create additional implications for the determination of agenda and, in particular, for sluggishness in the introduction of new items.'[29] Arrow concludes that, paradoxically, organizations which pursue efficiency may find themselves rigid and unresponsive to larger-scale change. Though organizations have a greater power to monitor their environment than individuals (and larger organizations ought to have greater power than smaller ones), they code the information to suit their own purposes and find it difficult to use in new situations; in particular, they cannot readily change from a passive to an active (information-seeking) rule.[30] However, it is clear that some organizations can and do seek information in an active way; they have organic forms of management, suited to dealing with unforeseen developments.[31] And organizations do in general respond to signals, if sluggishly, by changing their agenda.

The second main conclusion is that there exists a more or less permanent tendency to bureaucratic aggrandizement, especially in the supply of goods and services, so that these are produced in greater than optimal amount. To counteract this, a number of organizational and other checks have been suggested: competition between bureaux, private competition, contracting out of services, different decision rules for budget approval, above all the deliberate creation of monitoring or watchdog bodies which have a positive incentive to cut down the size of other bureaux. The 1977 report of the British Central Policy Review Staff, on the operation of the British diplomatic and related services, is a particularly good example of this last.[33]

The third conclusion is that public projects have a more or less built-in tendency to cost escalation, particularly where they represent the one-off or pioneer development of a new technology, or an existing technology in a new application. So many observations now exist to confirm this trend (and our earlier case studies have included a number of classic examples) that it has even been possible to develop a set of rules in order to form statistical estimates of the likely excess cost. To this point, as to others, we shall return in the last chapter of this book.

CHAPTER II

The Actors: (3) The Politicians

The politician is the third apex of our decision-making triangle. Invariably, the final decision is his. But he does not take the decision in a vacuum: he is faced with one set of pressures from voters, organized (more or less) into pressure and interest groups; and another set of pressures from bureaucrats or professionals-in-government.

THE BASIC PROBLEM

We need to make certain assumptions about the behaviour of these politicians, in order to build a theory for testing. Positive political science, following the lines of positive economists, assumes that politicians are motivated by self-interest. Just as producers want to maximize profits and consumers want to maximize welfare, so politicians want to maximize political support. At elections, therefore, they want to maximize votes (or, more strictly, useful votes). To say this is, of course, to simplify. Politicians have other motives too: as Henry Kissinger says, they will want to seek creative solutions to the general problems of society, which must bring them into conflict with the essentially risk-avoiding spirit of the bureaucracy.[1] But, in a democratic society, the politician will constantly be faced with the evidence of different groups with varying goals and interests, which he must seek to reconcile. As Tullock puts it, his motto might well be: 'The mob is in the streets. I must find out where it is going, for I am its leader.'[2] Precisely how he seeks to accommodate policies to different public values and priorities, in practice, is the main theme of this chapter.

We assume that most of these groups, or client publics, are centrally concerned with the supply of public collective goods – which, as we saw in Chapter 8, are goods which cannot be supplied to one person without being supplied in some measure to others. A sufficiently small and well-defined group may provide limited quantities and types of such goods for itself, by forming a club for the purpose. Private golf clubs, tennis clubs or sailing clubs are one such example; the squares in Bloomsbury and other old parts of London, managed by committees of residents, are another. Such groups can rely on voluntary action; those who want the benefits join, and pay the costs. But generally the problem with public goods is that not all members pay and benefit equally. Some care very much to have the goods in question, others less so. And the larger the group, the further it will fall short of providing an optimal amount for each member. Services like public transport or electricity supply can charge for their use; services like public parks or street sweeping or education are charged according to some quite separate criterion, such as liability to pay rates or taxes. In these circumstances, some will pay a great deal for very little; others may be virtual 'free riders', getting a great deal of service while paying very little for it.[3] At this point, those with a larger interest in consumption will tend to coerce others into membership. In most states, the principle of local government modifies this: different local governments can provide different mixes and quantities of services to suit local needs. But, with central pressure towards standardization coupled with transfers of revenues and central subsidies, this capacity is limited.

MARKET PLACE VERSUS BALLOT BOX

In practice, the adjustment between demand and supply of public goods is poorer even than this. For the supply on offer will be advertised only at occasional exercises in public choice, called elections, at which large indivisible bundles of public goods will be offered. It is rather as if, in the market economy, the buyer was forced to choose between a bundle consisting of a Mercedes car, a ton of bananas and a spin dryer, and another consisting of a bicycle, a ton of potatoes and a holiday in Spain, without any consideration of his preferences for any one item. Thus citizens get merely the choice of voting for the bundle with the highest aggregate attraction, or utility, even though it may well contain individual items that they dislike.

How, then, will politicians and voters behave? Politicians will try to maximize votes at elections; between times, they may follow other lines set by bureaucracies, their party faithful, or their own imaginations. But, in the need to win votes, they will generally tend to occupy a great deal of common ground with other politicians (with the other party, in a two-party system). They will then try to carve out some small part of this territory on which they can distinguish their own policies from those of their opponents, by offering more attractive bundles of public goods to some defined group or groups of voters. In most cases, this will consist in effect of a transfer of real income to that group. In most democracies, the tendency over a long time is to transfer from higher-income groups to lower (since the rich, like the poor, have only one vote each). But, as income tends more to equality, this tendency is severely limited – as present experience in countries like Britain and Sweden shows.

The voters, if they are intelligent, will react by certain kinds of behaviour. Generally they will be poorly informed about the true consequences to them of alternative policies. They will seek more information, but this can be costly (especially for lower-income groups; higher-income groups, in contrast, acquire more information and participate more, partly, of course, because they have more to lose). Those groups more directly affected by proposals, whether positively or negatively, will tend to work to acquire information. Producers will be better informed than consumers. And governments will tend to favour producers more than they do consumers.

The net result is that the mix of public goods and services will be far from optimal in an economic sense. The government's concern, to put it in terms of economic jargon, will be to equalize returns on its vote-income margin rather than on the voters' utility-income margin. Since the government can also use force to implement its wishes in a way the private decision-maker cannot, utility equilibrium must give way to vote equilibrium whether or not conflicts occur.[4] Thus the 'customers' of government are obliged to buy certain amounts of collective goods whether they want them or not. This arises partly from the ignorance of politicians and governments about what their individual voters actually want. But it arises far more from the Downsian paradox of vote-income margins versus utility-income margins.

BALLOT-BOX AND INTENSITY OF PREFERENCE

One particularly important expression of this is the paradox of intensity of preference. As Downs, Buchanan, Tullock and others have stressed, the one-person, one-vote system makes no allowance for intensities. In a market system, someone who wants something very much will be willing and also able to spend more of his income on it, so outbidding other potential buyers; but in an election he cannot. Not only is this sub-optimal for the individual; it is almost certain to be sub-optimal for the aggregate of those individuals. Consider a simple example: a three-person world. These three, who are neighbours, have to consider an improvement to their local environment – say, a tree-planting scheme. We can represent the surplus of net benefits, or utilities, over costs, by numbers representing pounds or dollars. Voter A would get great benefits from the scheme; but the other two get fewer benefits than from the non-planting alternative, so the scheme fails.

The point is that the social aggregate of net utilities is less than if the scheme had gone ahead: A is the 'passionate minority', who cares very much that something should happen, but he cannot assert this in the face of the 'weak majority' who can outvote him on the one-person, one-vote basis.

		A	B	C	Total	Outcome
Issue no. 1:	Plant	100	9	5	114	Minority
Tree Planting	Don't Plant	1	10	8	19	Majority

The only way out of this dilemma is by side-payments: that is, by permitting those citizens who feel strongly about an issue to compensate in some way those whose opinion is only weakly held. Thus A could pay B (whose aversion to the planting scheme is very mild) a bribe of as little as £2 to convert him into a supporter. The resulting net balance would then be.

		A	B	C	Total	Outcome
Issue no. 1:	Plant	98	11	5	114	Majority
Tree Planting	Don't Plant	1	10	8	19	Minority

Thus, with the aggregate of benefits minus costs remaining the same, the decision is reversed.

However, in practice a majority of voters tend to reject the whole principle of side-payments. But there is another method of achieving the same end: *logrolling*, or the exchange of votes. Suppose now that, in the example above, there is another issue – say, a proposal for better street lighting – on which the other voter, C, is in a minority. The full position can be stated:

		A	B	C	Total	Outcome
Issue no. 1:	Plant	100	9	5	114	Minority
Tree Planting	Don't Plant	1	10	8	19	Majority
Issue no. 2:	Light	9	9	20	38	Minority
Street Lighting	Don't Light	10	10	16	36	Majority

On Issue no. 2, again, the total social benefit is greater with the lighting solution, but the majority can outvote the minority voter. However, it is now possible for A and C to trade their votes, so that the *minority* view on both issues becomes a *majority*. This has the result that both A and C have a higher aggregate of benefits, or utility, than if the majority view had prevailed: A gets 100+9, or 109 (against 1+10, or 11); C gets 5+20, or 25 (against 8+16, or 24). This is a *coalition of minorities* and it demonstrates a most important way of overcoming the paradox of intensity of preference.

But there is a qualification: as well as requiring a majority of voters who are in a minority on some issues in a set, this happy outcome depends on the intensity of preference of the key voter, C. Suppose that on the second issue his preference had been very slightly different:

		A	B	C	Total	Outcome
Issue no. 1:	Plant	100	9	5	114	Minority
Tree Planting	Don't Plant	1	10	8	19	Majority
Issue no. 2:	Light	9	9	17	35	Minority
Street Lighting	Don't Light	10	10	16	36	Majority

Here, C will not trade his vote with A: the total benefit to him, 5+17, or 22, is less than if he stays with the majority, 8+16, or 24. The key here is that in total, the minority are less passionate about their views than the majority. The extreme preferences of A count for nothing, unless he can gain the support of a second voter who cares more about his minority position than he cares about the majority position. Thus the individual voter will consider the benefit to himself on the whole combination of issues. And the politician will appraise the willingness of each voter to trade the outcomes he prefers when in a majority for whose he prefers when in a minority.[5]

Very often in real life, logrolling takes place in a complex and disguised form. At elections, politicians offer a bundle of policies on different issues, in the hope that individuals or groups will identify issues on which they feel strongly, so that they will vote for that issue, even though they may have weak hostility towards many other items in the package. On many items in the package and for many voters this is likely to be true.

However, there is a resultant problem that needs to be understood and accepted, as a fact of political life. If interest groups can form coalitions through logrolling, then they may get what they most want, and hereby carry an election with an actual minority of votes. Again, a simple example will suffice. Imagine this time a society of twenty-five voters who organize themselves into five constituencies, each with five voters, to elect five representatives. Assume also, for the purpose, that once elected those representatives will vote as constituents wish – that is, they will fulfil their election promises faithfully. Then a measure favoured by nine voters, concentrated in only three constituencies, will be adopted. These nine voters are sufficient to control three representatives, who in turn constitute a majority of the five. Generalizing from this, Buchanan and Tullock show that, as the numbers of voters and constituencies rise, the minimum-sized coalition required for dominance under simple majority voting may fall from nine-twenty-fifths, or 36 per cent, in the example above, to 25 per cent as an absolute limit.[6] Or, in the formulation of Breton: in a state with an odd number of voters (N) and constituency representatives (R), control is possible with

$$\frac{(R+1)\ (N+1)}{4NR}$$

and as R and/or N increase, so this expression diminishes to 0.25.[7] But even this is not the limit of minority control. For, if we ally this 25 per cent rule with the logrolling rule, then it is easy to see that various minorities commanding much less than 25 per cent of total votes could enter coalitions. Indeed each one of the nine voters might be regarded as such an interest. It would then merely be necessary for each of the three voters in each of the three constituencies to agree on a programme and, secondly for each of the three representatives to ensure that this programme was compatible with those of the other two. (Even this condition would not be necessary if it was assumed that logrolling could take place between representatives after elections as well as during them; but this would threaten our artificial condition that representatives always acted on the mandates given them by their supporters.) If the issue in the programmes were purely local ones restricted to a single constituency, there is no theoretical reason why a winning coalition should not emerge, based on a pure combination of such local issues supported by very small minority groups.

In practice this is unlikely to happen: politicians have to show some consistency in policies across constituency boundaries, for reasons of equity and operating efficiency. But it is only necessary to identify some general issues on which minorities in different constituencies are prepared to ally, and couple these with local issues, to build a winning coalition. As a matter of fact, many planning issues are geographically concentrated in one constituency or in a limited number of constituencies. This is evidently true of urban motorways, power plants, mining schemes, airports or many of the controversial pieces of fixed investment that are the main burden of the case studies in this book. So the possibility of building on local interests in this way may be quite high.

This will be aided if (as in most local elections in Britain and some other western democracies) political apathy is rampant and the voter turnout is low. It will be aided even further if – as is commonly the case – a high proportion of constituencies are safe seats for one party or another, so that the outcome will be determined by a minority of marginal constituencies, which effectively constitute the true election. And in such cases (by no means rare) it may be possible for the outcome to be established by the views of a few determined people in a few areas, acting in coalition with like-minded people in a few other areas.

There is one other interesting reason why this is likely to be more common in local than in central government. It is that most local authorities are single-chamber governments. In bicameral legislatures, which characterize most central legislative assemblies, it is necessary to assemble a sizeable minority to pass a passionate-minority motion. But in a single chamber, the necessary figure may be as small as just over 10 per cent.[8]

Evidently, such minority power can achieve great successes;

in the case studies we have already seen some of them. And, in so far as they do express intensities, this may well be judged as a good thing. But it is worth stressing precisely how much minority government may be the result. As Buchanan and Tullock put it:

Thus, a logrolling bargain to obtain benefits from the political process need involve only about $\frac{1}{4}$ of the votes under a representative system. Therefore, representative institutions of this type are almost equivalent to permitting any group of $\frac{1}{4}$ of the voters in a direct democracy to form a logrolling coalition empowered to determine what roads will be repaired, which harbors dredged, and which interest groups will receive government aid.[9]

In practice, voters will find that there are costs involved in acquiring the necessary political information. They will therefore make a rough-and-ready calculation of how much effort is worth their while. The politician is likely to respond by making up fairly complex platforms which have a concentrated beneficial effect on small groups of voters, and a highly dispersed injurious effect on a much larger group (a classic instance being a proposal to make a modest increase in general taxation so as to benefit a defined group). Such a programme is likely to seem complex to most voters, but its benefits will readily be perceived by the lucky minority. Here the politicians can rely on the fact that logrolling itself is a complex operation, involving costs of acquiring knowledge, so that it is unlikely to engage more than a minority of all voters.

One other rule is relevant. It is the critical difference (to borrow again the language of Buchanan and Tullock) between *taking* action and *blocking* action. Psychologically, these have quite different values. In the extreme case of a jury, so-called majority rule is equivalent to minority rule of one or two, since these can effectively block a majority decision. In normal political life, the critical distinction is between a power to impose external costs on others (which is difficult) and a power to prevent external costs being imposed (which is much easier). This gives a built-in tendency for many political decisions to be conservative in character.

SOME FORMAL PROPOSITIONS

Our discussion so far leads to certain conclusions; they may logically be expressed (as previous workers in the field have done) in formal propositions.

1. In first-past-the-post voting systems, minorities command great power provided they can engage in logrolling.

2. This power will be greater if they are geographically concentrated in certain constituencies, and if the issues that excite them are similarly concentrated.

3. Generally, politicians will be more concerned to avoid imposing new costs on such defined groups than to benefit a majority at the expense of a group. Thus, on many proposals, they will tend to confirm the *status quo*.

4. Conversely, in so far as they impose new costs, they will tend to do so on the widest possible group, while concentrating the benefits on a small defined group.

5. They will rely on their solid supporters who are faithful to them, but in addition in two-party systems they will try to capture the vital middle ground occupied by floating voters. A third party, in contrast, will move away and try to stake out other ground.

6. Among these middle-ground voters, since costs of acquiring information are high, the richer members of the community are likely to be better informed. So are producer interests (rather than consumer interests).

7. Short of complete equality of income, there is always a difference between the distribution of income and the distribution of political power in a one-person, one-vote system. This gives governments a permanent incentive to follow Robin Hood-type policies. But, as incomes approach equality, there are limits to this.

It is easy to see how combinations of these rules might result in practical outcomes. Thus governments will be particularly solicitous to protect existing standards of living of workers by guaranteeing their jobs, especially where these workers are concentrated in particular contituencies. In so far as they are concerned with consumer interests, they will be particularly careful to preserve the existing levels and patterns of consumption of geographically defined constituency groups. If there are costs in these patterns of maintenance, they will try to spread these by general taxation among the community as a whole. If the costs are weakly perceived (that is, they are paid not directly in new financial imposts, but rather in more indirect ways, as through loss of time, or other kinds of inefficiency), they will be even more willing to follow these policies at the expense of the majority.

MINIMUM COALITIONS, INSTABILITY, AND DECISION COSTS

This makes the strategy seem simple. But in practice, political scientists have differed on important details. Anthony Downs, writing the first textbook in this field in 1957, asserted that politicians would strive to maximize vote support. William Riker, in a paper published in 1962,[10] questioned this: politicians would find, he said, that a minimum winning coalition would be best. Riker argued that, usually, coalition forming would be governed by a particular case of the Theory of Games (which will be treated more fully in Chapter 13): the n-person zero-sum game. In such a game, there is an unlimited number of possible players but the total gains are fixed: a gain to one player must be compensated by a loss to one or more others. Supposing participants in such a game could make side-payments to get support, Riker said, they would find in practice that they would maintain only a minimum coalition. If they went beyond that, they would find that there were too many conflicting interests in the coalition; none could get enough satisfaction. Therefore, some participants – the most dissatisfied – would withdraw. Actual American political history, according to Riker, showed that in periods of crisis, when outside opposition was great, internal conflicts would be minimized. But once the outside pressure diminished there would be less urgency to settle internal conflicts; and at that point, some members would withdraw.

The size of the coalition, Riker argued, would also depend on information levels. If information was poor, then coalition-makers would have to seek more than minimal allies; since a coalition traded promises against policies, if it did not know how its buyers would value the policies then it must offer more of them to make sure. Politicians would then logically seek to maintain a clear central ideology for the benefit of their minimal supporters, but would develop somewhat ambiguous policies for that part of the electorate for whom only low amounts of information were available.

Riker went on to draw a most important conclusion: that in contrast to economic life, which tends towards equilibrium, political life tends to disequilibrium. The basic reason was that 'players' in economic games perceived them as positive sum (i.e. they thought they would mean gains to many or even all), while players in political games invariably viewed them as zero-sum. Against this background, it is rare to find circumstances in which stability will occur. It might occur if there were two more or less permanent coalitions, each of which were able to block any tendency to aggrandizement on the part of the other. Or it might occur if there were two large and evenly balanced proto-coalitions plus one smaller balancing proto-coalition which reacted if a temporarily victorious winning coalition set its stakes too high. However, these conditions could easily be upset: either the weight of the major participants might change, or the winner might be willing to set high stakes. If these two occurred together, then disequilibrium could occur. In fact, so long as there were small proto-coalitions, they would often find it to their advantage to split away from a winning coalition. The problem, then, as Riker saw it, was to moderate politicians' perceptions of zero-sum situations, in order to give some stability to political behaviour.

However, such instability may be a price worth paying. For other political scientists stress the essentially inefficient nature of the political decision-making process. Since (as we have seen) choices are presented in a bundle, and since voters have only limited chances to express intensity of preference, all participants will pay high costs in terms of dissatisfaction. These costs are variously known as political externality costs,[11] constraints or

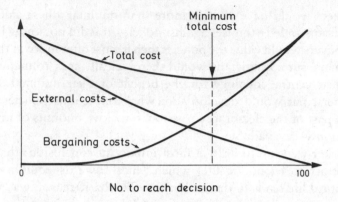

Figure 10: The Costs of Decision-Making (Source: Tullock).

coercion costs,[12] or the costs of expressing voice.[13] If a unanimity rule is adopted, these costs will be zero, but then the bargaining costs necessary to reach unanimity would be impossibly high. Thus bargaining costs rise as external costs fall, but not proportionally; the result is a U-shaped curve of total costs which had a minimum point (Figure 10). This point is usually well above the simple majority (51 per cent) point.

BACK TO THE COMMUNITY: THE PRESSURE GROUPS

So far this analysis has concentrated on the perceptions and behaviour of a group of people loosely called 'politicians' – the people who put together political platforms, persuade people to vote for them, and then (if elected) modify these programmes in the course of trying to get them carried through. It is also, however, instructive to recall Chapter 9, and to look at the role of pressure groups, or lobbies, in the whole process. Normally, these will seek to join either a winning coalition or a proto-coalition which can then ally with an existing coalition. The question must be what kind of political power they can command.

In an instructive study of a 1973 vote in California, where the principle of the referendum is enshrined in the state constitution, S.E. Finer has shown that an apparently popular measure to limit public spending to a fixed proportion of the state's income was voted down by 54 to 46 per cent on a minority (45 per cent) turnout. The likely reasons, Finer argues, were three. First, that it was easier to organize special interest groups who stood to lose from the measure (teachers, civil servants) than the general public. (This is in line with the formal proposition noted earlier, and first developed by Downs: that producer interests will be stronger than consumer interests.) Secondly, that there occurred what Finer called a Multiple Mirror Effect. Imagine, he wrote, a Nonconformist spinster of Welsh extraction who was in a high-income bracket, taught at university, drove a car and owned a dog. She was a member of seven minority groups, and if all these organized, then both to public and parliament they would appear as seven separate groups opposing a measure. In fact, they might largely consist of the same individuals. Pressure groups, in Finer's words, are a kind of stage army; and one American analyst has argued that if memberships of every pressure group there were to be added together, the population of the United States would seem to be seventy-five times greater than the census figures.

The third phenomenon in Finer's analysis is the contagion of fear. If the California proposition had been carried, the result must have been lower taxes overall – but not necessarily for everyone. No individual or group could be sure that they would not be the ones who paid out more as the result of the change. Therefore, they voted for the *status quo*.[15] (In 1978, of course, they overcame their fear on proposition 13. But even this could be interpreted as a desire to maintain the *status quo*.)

Finer's conclusions are of great importance for understanding how people will react on the substance (rather than the mechanics) of political decision-making. They interestingly confirm the results of work in the United States, which suggest that in practice citizens do not react rationally to the prospect of tax cuts, and that political parties show greater regard for those with greater resources, for the politically active, and for groups that express demand for public goods.[16] Most interestingly, they cast doubt on one of the basic propositions of political behaviour that Anthony Downs developed in his 1957 work: that politicians would seek to adjust to the preferences of the median voter, which on questions of income distribution would mean the median income earner.[17] But in fairness to Downs, it must be underlined that he also stressed the importance of the high political participation rates of higher income people and producer interests.[18]

THE NATURE OF POLITICAL POWER: ALTERNATIVE THEORIES

This logically introduces the question of the *substance* of political power – a question on which a separate, but related, literature has developed in modern political science. The relationship again comes through the study of bargaining processes. Suppose an individual (or group) with a particular interest (A) wishes to bring pressure to bear on a politician who is a member of a coalition (B). B essentially must consider how far he should accede to A's demands and thereby admit his interests to the coalition. This power of A over B has a number of dimensions: his *power base* (the number of votes he can deliver, his control over parts of the media); his *means of power* (appeals to supporters, actual mentions in the media); his *scope of power* (the list of specific political actions he may be able to get B to perform); his *amount of power* (the probability that B will do something if he asks; and his *extent of power* (the set of politicians B, C, D, etc. over whom he has power). All these elements must be judged by B in considering whether to accede to A's pressures. But there will be opportunity costs involved, equivalent to part of the bargaining costs discussed earlier in this chapter. The politician must continually make a very fine balance between the advantages of B's aid and the possible disadvantages for him – especially in terms of loss of other existing members of the coalition.[19] Such analyses as these are essentially based on what March calls *force models* of power. These assume that political power works in a kind of physical-mechanical way, so that the whole process can be modelled using analogies from classical mechanical theory. They assume that there is a fixed number of known power sources; the power of each has a given magnitude and direction; and that the result, in terms of social choice, is a sum of individual magnitudes and directions.[20] The problem with them is that there is evidence that power partly depends on the past exercise of power. To overcome these difficulties, variations in the activating mechanism take place, another in which power is increased by the fact of past exercise of power, yet another in which power is assumed to be a resource which depletes over time.

But all these, evidently, are members of an extended family of physical-analogue models; and the question must be whether all of them are unrealistic descriptions of the nature of power. (The same criticism may be applied to another kind of model, in which political choice is represented as a chance event unrelated to any exercise of power; such models have been little used in practice.) Rather, March suggests, it may be necessary to concentrate on a totally different kind of power models, which he terms *process models*. These assume that choice is substantially independent of power, but is not a chance event. Process models could take different forms: one in which preferences were expressed and aggregated through formal decision rules (such as winner-take-all elections); another where the outcome depended on information and skills; another depending on communication and diffusion of information; and yet another kind, involving actors who do not necessarily understand all aspects of the system they are trying to control.

The traditional concept of 'power', as understood by both the layman and the political scientist who manipulates mechanical models, does not in March's view contribute much to the understanding of political systems that could be reproduced in any one of the ways just outlined. If most systems are of this kind, then power would be a substantially useless concept. Power could be measured, but it would not be valuable for explaining or predicting outcomes.[21]

AN ECLECTIC MODEL

The truth might best be represented by some kind of eclectic theory. In it, power would be represented not in any crude way, but rather as a set of varied political resources, which actors may use as bargaining counters. The central part of the theory would be an account of this bargaining process, which would derive from the theory of games. It would essentially account for the behaviour of a set of constantly shifting coalitions, which sought to incorporate members of a much larger set of pressure or interest groups. These groups, and the individuals in them, would command different amounts or degrees of power, depending on such factors as income and information and relation to the production-consumption process. They would thus have different intensities of feeling on a number of political issues, and different abilities to translate these feelings into action.

But allied to this would need to be some account of the substantive issues involved: the agenda of the political process, the way it is generated, the manner in which issues wax and wane. American political scientists have developed the useful concept of the *mobilization of bias*: a set of values, beliefs, rituals and procedures that can be exploited by beneficiaries of the system to defend and promote their position. Since there will invariably be actual or potential challenges to the existing order, the dominant groups will seek to maintain and strengthen the existing mobilization of bias. Therefore, a shift in the pattern of mobilization (and in the resulting allocation of values) will usually require the acquisition of power and authority by previously disfavoured persons and groups, usually from movements or institutions outside the previously dominant group.[22] To borrow the different terminology of Schattschneider, the substitution of conflicts is the most devastating form of political strategy.[23] There will be strong interests in favour of maintaining existing alignments, along lines of cleavage. But new interests may manage to make new lines of division visible and meaningful, relating them at the same time to parallel lines of cleavage on other issues. This suggests that the emergence of new issues on the political agenda will seldom be drastic. It is far more likely to be incremental in character. Whatever the ingredients that make up the eclectic theory of political decision-making, it is clear that the essential ground rules are very different from those that govern bureaucratic behaviour. The theory would naturally lead to a concept of political behaviour that Schick has called *process politics*: a system that stresses bargains and strategies developed among interest groups intent on defending their own interests, with a broad degree of consensus on overall goals and with little interest in fundamental evaluation.[24] In such a concept, bureaucracies would play a passive role. But in contrast, there is a concept of *systems politics* based on systematic evaluation of alternative opportunities, with special emphasis on the distribution of public goods to different groups of the population. According to Schick, the 1960s in American political life saw a profound shift from process to systems politics, marked by the entry of a new kind of bureaucratic professional: the economist and the systems analyst. Possibly, by the late 1970s the pendulum was moving again in the opposite direction; and in building a normative model, it will be necessary to have some notion of the timing and force of such shifts.

CHAPTER 12

The Actors in Concert

This chapter will be brief. It will try to summarize and to interrelate the necessarily rather complex argument of the last three chapters, and to try to relate this analysis, in turn, to the case histories in Part One. It will seek to provide a general explanation of how planning decisions are in fact made, and of how planning disasters can arise. For details and for references, the reader should go back to the earlier chapters.

THE BUREAUCRATS: AGGRANDIZEMENT AND POLICY MAINTENANCE

In this part of the book, we began with the people because that seemed obvious. But it is now possible to see that the real starting-point should be the bureaucracy – including in that term all those, either in central or in local government, whether general administrators or specialized professionals, who maintain policies, who implement decisions, and who sometimes may initiate policy shifts by shaping the political agenda.[1]

We found in Chapter 10 a remarkable amount of agreement among observers as to the motives and the methods of the bureaucrats. Though they may contain within them some internal conflicts, which tend never properly to be resolved, bureaucratic organizations have well-defined agendas of their own. They exist to attack this agenda in terms of restricted definitions of problems and equally narrow ideologies of approach: what Hart[2] calls the factored mode of planning. Thus a ministry of aviation will tend to be interested in building aircraft and a national railway corporation will tend to be interested in maintaining railways. Few will have any interest in redefining the problems they are supposed to be attacking, in such a way as to open up the question of the justification for their own existence. Most such organizations have well-defined procedures which tend to produce inertia, both in the definition of problems and in the range of alternative answers.

However, change does occur in bureaucracies. But the way it occurs is a source of further problems. New organizations will tend to arise from political initiative, often as a result of a recognition of a new problem area. Once established, the new bureaucracy at first will tend to be expansionist, capitalizing on its political support; it will tend to contain a large number of aggressive, expansionist, bureaucratic climbers. Later, as the bureaucracy grows larger and its rate of growth slows, the organization will devote more of its energies to self-protection: it enters the stage of what Schon[3] calls dynamic conservatism. Its members will use established procedures to recycle problems, so that they will continue to have sufficient work. It will particularly react in this way to external threats, either from politicians bent on government economies, or from rival bureaucracies. Thus bureaucratic growth takes place on a ratchet principle: organizations grow rapidly in early stages but seldom decline, even when their ostensible purpose has diminished or disappeared.

In such large established bureaucracies, there are major problems of internal communication and control. The people at the top are seldom fully aware of what is happening throughout the organization. Much of the initiation of ideas takes place at lower or middle levels, and filters up to the top. This aids in the preservation and aggrandizement of sub-bureaucracies within the organization. Each of these, too, will be concerned to maintain its existing position and to guard against attacks. Therefore each of the parts will also tend to generate new agenda items, which are seldom really new but are more usually recycled, in order to maintain momentum.

Because of these mechanisms, there is a standard tendency for bureaucratic mechanisms to over-produce the supply of public goods. In particular, programmes once wound up are difficult to wind down. Further, because bureaucrats have little direct interest in the costs of their programmes – except when their careers are threatened by accusations of incompetence, which is rare – there is a general tendency for cost escalation in public projects.

Finally, there is an interesting symbiotic relationship between parts of the bureaucracy and particular client populations. These populations tend to be middle-income people who will benefit from more government, either as producers or as consumers. They control parts of the political parties and of the media. And their campaigns, against inadequacies in the public services, are frequently arranged in implicit concord with the bureaucrats and the key politicians who are ministers or chairmen of committees.

THE COMMUNITY: PRESSURE GROUPS AND PUBLIC RECOGNITION

Thus the bureaucrats emerge from the analysis as a group of generally conservative policy maintainers, chiefly concerned with the protection of themselves and their programmes. It is not a flattering picture. But neither is the one drawn in Chapter 9 of the community leaders.

The first important point is that these people constitute a minority, often a small one, of the entire population or electorate. They constitute interest groups, or classes in Dahrendorf's sense, with particular concerns. They develop because of the emergence of particular issues on the public agenda, sometimes apparently at random, but generally in response to broad socio-economic trends (for instance, the emergence of the environmental issue as *per capita* incomes rise). The object of any such group is first to have its issue generally recognized in the community (or that part of it that is actively concerned with issues anyway) which means shifting the political agenda. (Successful examples include environmental issues in the early 1970s, and cheap government in the late 1970s.) Then it is to influence the politicians to make policy shifts, often of a large and discrete kind (so as to block the possibility of reversal). Lastly, and most difficult, it is to ensure implementation by the bureaucracy: difficult, because by then the immediate political initiative may be lost and the issue may be disappearing from view. It is at this point that bureaucratic inertia may effectively block change, causing an almost imperceptible reversion to earlier policy – as in the case of the abandonment of Maplin.

In trying to get political support, activists have various options: they commonly bring marginal pressure on one or more parties or they may enter a coalition with one of them (or even set up a new coalition of their own). But, in all this, the activists also need to understand the bureaucracy, and even to penetrate it. This is perhaps the most difficult issue of all. For, while some observers see the bureaucrats as manipulating community participation for their own ends, others see the community activists as equally unrepresentative minority groups, having little in common with the values of the great mass of the people. Whichever the case, it is certain that only a minority of people ever become actively engaged on any issue; and that, given the costs of acquiring information, these people are likely to be disproportionately the better educated and better informed (hence, in general, higher income) members of society. Hence new political movements especially in the planning field, tend to reflect current middle-class preoccupations.

THE POLITICIANS: POLITICAL CALCULUS AND MINORITY LEVERAGE

The politicians, in the somewhat unflattering view of the positive school of political science that was portrayed in Chapter 11, seek to maximize votes just as consumers aim to maximize utility or producers profits. They can do this, in general, by remaining somewhere near the middle ground but by then trying to seize a particular part of it so as to broaden their base of support. They will achieve this by offering increases in real income to particular groups. On the whole they will find that these groups are more concerned about losses of welfare than about gains; that they are more interested in their money income as producers than in their income (often psychic) as consumers; but that the first principle may outweigh the second, especially where environmental losses are involved. The resulting vote equilibrium is likely to be far different from a welfare equilibrium, since in principle it does not allow for the expression of intensity of preference.

However, in practice this reservation is subject to drastic modification. Where small numbers vote in elections, where most constituencies are safe for one or another party and only a few will decide the outcome, where issues are concentrated in such constituencies, where these involve active minority pressure groups, and where these minorities can form active coalitions, relatively small groups can exert immense political leverage.

In general, since potential losses are perceived as much more important than perceived gains, and since fear of loss is a very potent emotional trigger to action, this kind of politics tends powerfully to maintenance of the *status quo*. The professional politicians will be particularly concerned to avoid imposing new costs on any group. For these reasons, major disturbances to the physical environment – a new motorway, a new airport – will be avoided. If, however, they cannot be avoided, and often of course that happens, then the professional politicians will take care to spread the costs as widely and as vaguely as possible, while concentrating any benefits very noticeably on certain groups. Fortunately the principle of paying for particular programmes through general taxation allows them to do this without too much trouble.

The result of this kind of democratic politics, in general, is a great deal of instability. Coalitions and crypto-coalitions will form and re-form around particular issues and groups. Small groups will be able to exert intense leverage on local and even national elections. Any decision threatening the established interest of any group will be difficult to make, and even more difficult to follow through. Only where the decision benefits a distinct local group, while the objectors are dispersed and have little to lose personally and directly, will policy maintenance be possible in the face of opposition. This may occur particularly if the local beneficiaries are the producers of a good, while the general objectors are claiming merely a generalized environmental loss.

THE ACTORS IN CONCERT

Thus the resulting system contains curious contradictions. At its heart is a bureaucracy, generally massive and well established, concerned with policy and programme maintenance. It is intensely conservative except during those periods, generally early in institutional life, when political pressure creates the demand for rapid expansion and new policy initiatives. At its edge is a series of activist pressure groups, forming sometimes in response to the development and recognition of new issues, sometimes in response to immediate pressures generated by outside forces. These groups, invariably involving quite small minorities, seek to exert leverage on professional politicians; they are often surprisingly successful in doing so, because of the particular circumstances that attend many controversial issues. Lastly the politicians, dominated by their need to maximize votes by strategic groupings at or near the centre of opinion, will seek to accommodate the demands of one or another of these groups either by responding to pressure or by forming coalitions. The resulting system will tend to be unstable in its decision-making, especially where decisions are involved that are unpopular with particular groups. Here, the underlying conservatism and permanence of the bureaucracy is the only counterweight. But the effect of this will be related to the actual balance of forces, and in particular to the relationship – geographically and within the production-consumption cycle – of gainers and losers.

This analysis helps powerfully to explain many of the most puzzling features of the great planning disasters described earlier in this book. For instance, it helps to provide a part-explanation of the tendency to cost escalation in many public projects, especially where these projects benefit particular groups of producers or consumers and are paid for by the taxpayer at large. It also explains how an established bureaucracy can resist pressure for a major policy shift, even one supported actively by pressure groups, by simply letting the issue subside and gradually working for the *de facto* reversal of a decision; the return to Stansted is a classic case. It further explains how some decisions, involving small but entrenched pressure groups, are reversed again and again; this is the story of the National Library. It shows how politicians can respond to political pressures by taking what they see as popular initiatives to increase their coverage of the middle ground, often without adequate analysis or even with suppression of the facts; and how established bureaucracies, committed to these initiatives because they serve the interests of the organization, will then seek to maintain the momentum, in the face of rising criticism from the pressure groups and even from rival bureaucracies. One of the sub-plots in this book is how to outwit the Treasury – as examined by Wildavsky.[4]

It adds up to a convincing explanation of how decisions are bungled, but not of how they might be taken with more foresight and more careful evaluation. For that, we need to move into the territory of prescription, which up to now this book has eschewed.

CHAPTER 13

Towards Prescription

In this final chapter, we come to the most difficult problem of the book. How might a society work if not to remove, then at least to mitigate, the effects of planning disasters like these? Could it seek to develop early-warning systems for planning failure?

It might as well be said straight away: there is no magic formula, no all-embracing model that will perform this miracle. At best, we are looking for piecemeal improvements that can be stitched together to provide some normative guidelines. They fall logically into two main areas.

First are improvements in forecasting the future world, in which the results of the decision would work themselves out. We need in particular to know how people will judge the results of the decision. Will they like living or working in it (a new housing estate, a new town or city) or visiting it (a country park, an opera house)? Will they use it and pay for doing so (a new airplane, an airport, a rapid transit system)? And will they enjoy using it? For if they do not like what they have, then at very least there will be dissatisfaction and malaise, and at the worst a planning artefact that nobody wants and nobody uses.

Secondly, suppose that we could obtain forecasts (or guesses) of likely developments, including people's own judgements. Then a separate question would still arise. Imagine two or more alternatives in the present each with chains of likely consequences: on what criteria would we seek to make our choice now? How would we seek to measure one individual's or group's gains against another's losses? How would we trade greater efficiency against greater equity in distribution of the product? How would we rank gains in the near future against losses in the more distant future, or vice versa?

These two questions are intimately linked in practice. But it is useful for analysis to separate them. The first and shorter part of this chapter is concerned with forecasting. The second and longer (because even more intractable) is concerned with evaluation.

FORECASTING: THE ART OF IMAGINATIVE JUDGEMENT

In Chapter 1 we already saw that forecasts, often conceived as a mechanical exercise in projecting trends, invariably went wrong for just that reason. In the rest of this book, we have seen numerous examples of the truth of that – and of the value of the distinction by Friend and Jessop: between three types of planning uncertainty. Basic uncertainty in the relevant *planning environment* (UE) leads to errors in projecting numbers of people or jobs or production. Beyond that, Uncertainty in *related decision areas* (UR) means that forecasts go wrong because they fail to take sufficient account of the actions of other actors, especially those in other decision-making groups or organizations – whether in bureaucracies, or community groups, or legislatures. Finally, and closely related, *uncertainty about value judgements* (UV) arises when decision-makers fail to anticipate shifts of value among other actors, especially members of the public and associated opinion formers; these failures too are likely to result in false forecasts.

The different uncertainties can be tackled, and the resulting poor forecasts improved, in different ways. But it is important to remember the rule from Chapter 1: that a particular problem of uncertainty, first perceived as UE, may on a closer look prove to be UR or UV or both.

Where there are true UE errors, they can best be reduced by alternative projections of basic variables, to provide the basis for judgement about which is most likely. Cost escalation, another UE syndrome, can be approached by systematic analysis of past

experience in comparable projects, which, as the work of Merewitz shows, often proves to have a measure of consistency.[1] But
beyond that point, better treatment of the UE demands a closer
look at the other two kinds of uncertainty. In particular a basic
and unexpected shift, such as the fall in the birth-rate in advanced
industrial countries, fairly clearly results from a shift in values
towards children and conventional family life. If demographers
had been less obsessed with demography and had paid more
attention to social change, their demographic forecasts might
have been better – and might still be.

UR and UE problems, then, have to be tackled in a different
way. Systematic, numerical projections will play a subsidiary
role, though the forecasts may eventually have numbers put on
them. The heart of the problem is to produce scenarios to suggest
how events – technological, economic, social, cultural, political
– will unfold and interrelate in the future. (As an example: with
benefit of hindsight, we can see how economic forecasting ought
to have taken account of the impact of OPEC on the energy crisis
of 1973–4 and indirectly on the course of the world economy.)
This kind of activity is the stuff of history, and it needs a good
historian to capture it, so as to write history in reverse.

There are some techniques in the pages of the futurologists'
textbooks that can offer limited aid here. Mechanical projections
may offer useful suggestions, so long as researchers respect their
limitations. Recent advances in mathematical theory, which
suggest that well-established trends can be upset by sudden cata-
strophes, may have their uses. Morphological analysis, invented
by Fritz Zwicky in Switzerland in the 1930s, has long been used
in technological forecasting to outline 'feasible' new technologies; maybe it could equally well define feasible new social
states. Diffusion times, widely employed to measure the spread
of new technologies, could also be used to plot the spread of new
social norms and values among classes, religions and countries.
Cross-impact analysis, again widely used in technological forecasting, could similarly be applied usefully to the analysis of
social behaviour. Delphi techniques, which synthesize individual
expert judgements about the likelihood of future events, might

also be useful so long as the participants have a sense of historical possibility; otherwise there is a risk of their degenerating into isolated forecasts of different events, without underlying historical rationale.[2]

The important point is to accept that no one technique, or even a bundle, will provide a substitute for the broad knowledge of social change and the ability to understand how some historical processes influence other processes. The scenario-writer must capture how decisions in one area, by one set of bureaucrats and politicians, affect decisions in another area. He must also try to predict the cultural shifts that may result in changes in values, or (more usually) the spread of new sets of values from one social group to others. The skills needed for this are not the traditional hard techniques of the past, but rather imagination and creative understanding coupled with judgement – the qualities associated with the 'divergent mind' of the arts graduate rather than the scientist.[3] Above all it requires appreciative judgement about the present state of the system and about what facts are significant to appreciate.[4]

Some writers, including G. Vickers, take this further. They want not only ways of scanning the future as accurately as possible, but they also want to try to stop or slow down reality so as to prevent it from moving too fast. Vickers calls for checks and balances to be imposed, before the planning environment imposes them on the planner.[5] Friend and Jessop call for 'robust' planning solutions: ones that leave the widest possible set of full solutions still available by providing flexibility in the face of uncertainty.[6]

But sometimes this is not easy advice to follow: planning, as we saw in several case studies in this book, occasionally has to take big discrete, go-no-go decisions. Here it is possible to adopt the celebrated mixed scanning approach of Etzioni. Big, so-called *contextuating decisions* are made through exploration of main alternatives, with details blurred. Small bit decisions are taken incrementally, in the light of fundamental decisions. Chess players, Etzioni points out, play this way. Applied to the kind of decision analysed in this book, mixed scanning means that first strategic decisions are taken by eliminating all but one alternative – the one that has fewest objections to it. But then, before implementation, this is split if possible into discrete steps, each with a resource commitment; implementation occurs in such a way that costly or reversible decisions appear later; and at key points, the decision-maker can still come back to the original strategic decision.[7]

Donald Michael's Long-Range Social Planning really incorporates all these approaches. It involves following through a number of steps. First, as with Etzioni, the planner chooses a plan after speculating about the future context, after setting goals, and after evaluating costs and benefits of alternatives. Then he considers the possible impact on the plan of the UE element. Then he works out the plan in detail, in terms of sequences of action. Finally, he monitors the working-out of the plan, so that these steps can be recycled if necessary. In all this the planner seeks to explore the nature of the problems to be solved, rather than providing tidy, one-shot solutions; to trace out conflict rather than to stop it.[8]

All this suggests an organization for planning with at least one (and preferably more than one) independent and critical institute for exploring the future. Some organizations – DATAR in France, the Science Policy Research Unit in Britain – are beginning to adopt this kind of approach for different areas of forecasting. They will combine quantitative and non-quantitative methods, but above all they will be exploratory and self-critical. Such methods will not cause us overnight to avoid the kinds of errors that have been chronicled in this book. But they can help develop our powers of critical evaluation.

THE PROBLEM OF EVALUATION: INTER-PERSONAL
COMPARISONS

But forecasting the future environment, including the problems of related areas and of values, is only part of the problem. Even were it possible to forecast accurately, that would still not produce decisions of itself. Planning centrally involves the consideration of alternative courses of action, and a resolution among them by means of some process of evaluation. Any course of action will involve some commitment of resources that might have been spent on something else. It will bring a set of consequences (provided they can be calculated), some of which will be seen as benefits, others as costs. Though described as benefits and costs, they need not all be capable of expression in monetary terms. There is thus a central problem of aggregation and comparison. And behind this there is the dilemma that the costs to some individuals or groups may be benefits to others. However it is expressed, the problem here is to obtain what the economists call a social welfare function. How does a society, composed of different individuals with different tastes and preferences, form rules that allow rational decisions to be made about the supply of public goods? To see whether it is even possible to derive a solution, it will be necessary to know how economists – and their latter-day political science offspring – have grappled with the problem.

The starting-point is the difficulty – perhaps the impossibility – of comparing one person's utilities and disutilities with another's: if my wife says she has a terrible headache, how do I compare that with my grumbling digestive system? Since we cannot get directly into other people's hearts and minds, we have no way of expressing intensities as between people. Income distribution compounds the problem: the rich have come to *need* diamonds or fast cars, or the good environment most of them seem to inhabit. But even in an egalitarian society, doubtless some would express their pleasures and pains more extravagantly than others – and who is to deny them their feelings?

Because of this, economists traditionally have tried to avoid comparing one person's utility directly with another's. They have avoided calculations based on *cardinal* utilities, where one person's measurements can be compared with another's even though they might be on different scales (like degrees Fahrenheit and degrees Centigrade). Instead they have used *ordinal* scales, where it is not clear what one scale means in relation to another, and where the scale can be transformed into any other as long as the orderings are preserved (as 1,3,5 into 101, 129, 147). So for a finite set of numbers the ordinal scale is really a disguised ordering;[9] if we use it to compare the utilities of different people, all we are saying is that one prefers *a* to *b* and another *b* to *a*.

Early in the twentieth century the Italian economist and sociologist Vilfredo Pareto established a classic principle for deriving a social welfare function from ordinal statements. (The earlier best known attempt, Bentham's felicific calculus, was based on cardinal measurements and fell on that fact; ironically, it provides the basis of modern cost-benefit analysis.) Suppose, said Pareto, that every person has ordinal valuations from a number of alternative situations: each person knows what is good for him, but no one knows what this means for anyone else. Then start from the existing situation, and consider an alternative. Each person could say whether he preferred it, or not. If it was preferred by just one person and no one found it less preferable, then move to that alternative; if not, stay at the existing position. Thus, by pairwise tests, society can arrive at a state where no further movement is possible: here, no one could become better off without someone else being worse off. This is the Pareto optimum.

Unfortunately, it has snags. The biggest is that the rule is very restricted. Most decisions about public spending are really about the distribution of real income. In such cases of dividing the national cake, as Sen puts it, every solution is Pareto-optimal since all would like more. Here, it is necessary to specify additional rules (such as majority decisions). But, unless combined with the possibility of payments by one voter to another, this may be the recipe for extreme conservatism; the weakly motivated majority may block the wishes of the passionate minority. It is the same with the so-called unanimity for change principle: if some prefer *x* to *y* and no one regards *x* as worse, then choose *x*, but if not choose the *status quo*, *y*. As Sen puts it, this solution has the paradoxical result: 'If preventing the burning of Rome would have made Emperor Nero feel worse off, then letting him burn Rome would have been Pareto-optimal. In short, a society or an economy can be Pareto-optimal and still be perfectly disgusting.'[10]

This is why economists have been forced to consider the possibility of side-payments. The Kaldor-Hicks principle, developed independently by its two inventors in 1939–40, suggests an alternative or additional principle: if *a* would be willing to compensate *b* for a change whereby *a* would be better off and *b* worse off, then, even if the compensation never occurred, the change would be optimal. The problem is that in practice few individuals are in a position to give or receive compensation. And in any case, as E. Mishan has shown, the outcome will depend on the rules of the game. Imagine an area affected by aircraft noise. Under one set of rules, residents could be allowed to subscribe £30,000,000 to get the airport moved, but this is £10,000,000 less than the airlines will be prepared to accept. Under another set, the airlines would be asked to pay the residents £50,000,000 for the privilege of flying, but in fact they will pay only £20,000,000. Then if the costs of implementation are more than £10,000,000, the airlines would move under the second rule but not under the first.[11]

Lastly, the Pareto principle conflicts with a principle of philosophic liberalism, including the weak liberal rule: that at least two individuals, faced with at least two alternatives, should have their personal preferences reflected in a social preference. In Sen's example, A and B consider three alternatives:

a: that A should be able to read pornography.
b: that B should be able to read pornography.
c: that neither should be allowed to.

A (a traditional moralist) prefers *c* to *a* to *b*. B (a trendy liberal) prefers *a* to *b* to *c*. Now, though both prefer *a* to *b*, there is no agreement beyond that: whether *b* is preferred to *c* or *c* to *b*, one individual will be worse off than at the start, so there is no optimal choice.[12] Even if we try to avoid this by never comparing more than two alternatives at once, we shall run up against the problem that the result does not conform to the principle of acyclity: that, if *a* is better than *b* and *b* better than *c*, then *c* must be at least as good as *a*.

In 1951, investigating these problems, the economist Kenneth

Arrow published his famous impossibility theorem.[13] He showed that it was impossible to derive a social welfare rule that simultaneously met four reasonable conditions. First, *collective rationality*: that a collective choice function could be developed by an ordering of individual orderings. Secondly, the *Pareto principle* already put forward. Thirdly, the *independence of irrelevant alternatives*: the social choices are to depend only on the orderings of alternatives within the environment under consideration. Fourthly, *non-dictatorship*: there is no individual whose preferences are automatically society's preferences, independently of the preferences of other individuals.

Arrow shows that with three alternatives (A, B and C) then:

$\frac{1}{3}$ of the individuals prefer A to B to C
$\frac{1}{3}$,, ,, ,, ,, B to C to A
$\frac{1}{3}$,, ,, ,, ,, C to A to B

and from this it can be seen that

$\frac{2}{3}$ prefer A to B
$\frac{2}{3}$ prefer B to C
$\frac{2}{3}$ prefer C to A

so that no ordering is possible. Arrow states his general theorem:

> There can be no constitution simultaneously satisfying the condition of Collective Rationality, the Pareto principle, the Independence of Irrelevant Alternatives, and Non-Dictatorship.[14]

Economists have been trying to resolve the paradox ever since, without too much success. (Planners, for the most part, proceed in blithe ignorance of the Arrow theorem, unaware that it had destroyed their entire basis of action). In fact, as Arrow himself suggests, the only way out is to drop one of the conditions. The most popular candidate is the independence of irrelevant alternatives, since often these do allow some estimate of intensity of preference. Thus if

> A prefers *a* to *c* to *d* to *e* to *h*, while
> B prefers *b* to *a* to *c* to *d* to *e*,
> then in a choice between *a* and *b* it would be fair to prefer

a to *b*, since A's intensity of preference is clearly so much greater.[15] As Sen puts it, the Arrow theorem:

> ... undoubtedly demands too much, and in actual planning we may be quite happy with a Social Welfare Function that is incomplete but does yield a social ordering with the type of individual orderings that are in fact likely.[16]

Towards cardinal measurement: the Theory of Games

Meanwhile, before Arrow, an attempt had already been made to break out of the constraint that welfare economics had imposed on itself by showing a way whereby cardinal utilities could legitimately be used. The problem, already seen, is that ordinal utilities make no proper allowance for intensity of preference. Suppose two people are deciding on the division of a cake: A prefers 70 : 30 in has favour, B 51 : 49 in his. Using ordinal measurement, we can say only that each has a first preference to give the bigger share to himself. We cannot even say that A is better off under the 70 : 30 arrangement than B is under the 49 : 51 arrangement.[17]

The Theory of Games, first published in complete form in 1944,[18] was a particularly ingenious way of introducing cardinal measurement while still avoiding basic questions of interpersonal utility comparison. As well as the ordering of utilities, it demands that the observer measures the ratios of the difference between pairs of utilities. Consider a simple example:[19] a game offers the players a choice between a certain prize of \$100, and a 50 : 50 chance of a gain of \$50 or a gain of \$150. By observing the player's behaviour, we can establish that at a bet of (say) \$120, he is indifferent between the two gambles. So the utility of \$120 is equal to half the utility of \$50 plus half the utility of \$150. And the difference between the utility of \$120 and the utility of \$50 is the same as the difference between the utility of \$150 and the utility of \$120. So it is possible to establish ratios between two different scales: the difference between \$50 and \$120 on one scale is the same as the difference between \$120 and \$150 on the other. This can be generalized in a rule applicable in any case. First: assign arbitrary values of utility to the least and the most favoured outcomes. Secondly, find, for any other outcome, the crucial probability such that the chooser is indifferent between two lottery tickets, one offering alternative C for certain, the other offering A with the probability Pc and the other offering B with the probability 1-Pc. The utility value of C is then the expected value of the lottery with which it is judged indifferent.[20]

This is a powerful advance. But, as authors have been pointing out ever since, it still gives formidable problems in practice. One is that the 'players' may adopt different strategies depending on

Table 16
ALTERNATIVE STRATEGIC CRITERIA FOR GAMES AGAINST NATURE

		Game:			Best Strategy according to criteria:
Strategy:	1	2	3	4	
1	2	2	0	1	Maximum average probability
2	1	1	1	1	Minimax (minimizing worst)
3	0	4	0	0	Hurwicz formula*
4	1	3	0	0	Minimax regret, i.e. minimize gap between payoff and potential payoff if true state of nature were known.

* Maximize result of A + (1 −) a where a = smallest and A = largest outcome.

Source: J. Milnor, 'Games against Nature' in M. Shubik, *Game Theory and Related Approaches to Social Behaviour* (New York, 1964), p. 122.

their own preferences. Thus the minimax principle seeks to minimize the maximum loss that might be made, while the minimax regret principle chooses the outcome with the smallest difference as against the best outcome (Table 16). A related problem is that people vary a great deal in their attitude to risk; not everyone will act on the basis of the expected monetary value of a gamble, and for these people it is necessary to find out how highly they rank certainty.[21] Yet another is that not all pay-offs can necessarily be expressed in money terms, and that people may be less consistent in their judgements when multi-dimensional judgement is involved.[22] It is not even clear whether people's preferences remain fixed, nor that individuals can perceive their preferences with the necessary accuracy.[23]

But there are even larger snags, which make the practical applications doubtful indeed. One is that even simple games are apt to involve very large numbers of strategies, that is, summary programmes of all the possible moves in the game. This is simply because of the very large numbers of possible combinations involved. Even noughts and crosses contains almost 1 billion (million million) strategies, while the first move in chess involves strategies which, written 100 to a page on paper stacking 100 to an inch, would mean a stack of paper 40,000 light years thick.[24] Another is that the Theory of Games becomes progressively more difficult once the analyst leaves the area of what are called two-person, zero-sum games (that is, pure competitive games where one player gains what the other player loses). Most games relevant to planning involve more than two players and are mixed in form, part competitive and part co-operative;* they would prove highly intractable – especially if the players failed to understand mathematics.[25] Schelling analyses in detail the bargaining element which is inherent in such games; he argues that it can contribute to normative theory since it will show that rational players may take advantage of bargaining and strategic devices.[26] But to apply this in practical situations is difficult indeed. All in all, the Theory of Games still remains a theoretical tool for planning decision-makers, rather than a working device.

---

* The well known 'Prisoner's Dilemma' is an example of such a game. Consider two prisoners separately being interrogated with the offer of a reduced sentence if they confess. Imagine that the payoff matrix is:

	B confess	B not confess
A confess	−5, 5	10, −10
A not confess	−10, 10	5, 5

Without collusion, both will confess and get rather severe commuted sentences. But if both can assume that the other will also recognize his self-interest, both will not confess and will be found not guilty.

THE PROBLEM OF INCOME DISTRIBUTION

There is at least one other problem with the Theory of Games. Like every other attempt to derive a social welfare function, it has to assume that 'players' start with the income they have. For this will presumably affect their judgement of utility and even their judgement of uncertainty. In other words, like the Pareto criterion it assumes either that the distribution of income is the one that we have now, or that it is some entirely theoretical other one. It provides no normative guidance on what a just distribution of income ought to be. But for planners, who in recent years have become increasingly obsessed with the effects of their plans on the distribution of real income, this seems a fatally restrictive limitation.

If every proposed new public good gave a surplus of benefit over cost for every individual involved, this would still present no problem. But in practice, of course, this is rare. One way out of the dilemma is to assume roughly that people will go along with a large number of public decisions that they individually do not much like, simply because they recognize that opting out of the system is impracticable; they will group their disapprovals into an overall decision at election time. But this does not help much in individual cases. If, in such cases, aggregate social preferences must be determined, then there are major problems. One is that efficiency must be judged against equity, for often in principle they may suggest opposite prescriptions. Implicitly, economists in the past have given a much higher weight to efficiency as against equity; this was the burden of the criticism of cost-benefit analysis in the third London airport inquiry. For the future, assuming that decision-makers take their stand on what the market seems to want, a weighting system might be developed either on the basis of analysis of past decisions (as indicating implicitly what society really wants) or perhaps through public opinion data. But even then the decision-maker may be forced to choose between interests on the basis of some criterion. In a democracy, the median view will tend to prevail (as Downs and others have shown) while in a pure theory based on willingness to pay the opinion of the mean voter should be decisive. But even if the decision-maker follows the quasi-market route he will not necessarily choose for society what he would choose for himself (for instance, he may support the war though rejecting military service for himself) while individuals in groups may do things that they would not do by themselves (like, for instance, supporting anti-discrimination laws). There is no absolute compulsion on governments to follow the market in this way; they may and do seek to forge and to lead public choice, but in this case the criteria for action are still unclear.[27]

One answer is that it may be impossible to reach firm and unambiguous criteria, but that at least the decision-maker should be able to quantify the trade-off between efficiency and equity. Thus, in a classic study of a real decision of where to build a new bridge in the city of New Orleans, Mumphrey and Wolpert found that on straight majority voting a majority would be for a bridge, and that a majority would have it built at a location which would bring losses to low-income people and gains to high-income people. These can be quantified; and so, assuming that this location is the more efficient one, it is possible to calculate either the taxation of net gains that should be levied on the rich or the compensation to be paid to the poor. But before doing this, society should re-evaluate this 'efficient' location in the light of the additional administrative costs of compensation.[28]

This goes some little way; it still does not suggest criteria for a just distribution of income. For this we must look away from economics and towards ethics. Cost-benefit analysis, with its emphasis on maximizing the net surplus of benefits, says nothing about how to resolve conflicts of interest; it seems appropriate only where the interests of all groups coincide, which will be rare. And, as already seen, the Hicks-Kaldor compensation formula is unreal because the compensation all too seldom occurs. The maximin theory from the Theory of Games does focus on distributional criteria, but suggests a conservative *status quo* solution rather like the Pareto one.[29]

Because no one had previously met these problems in an adequate way, the work of John Rawls is potentially of the greatest significance to planners. The point about it is that Rawls is a philosopher who uses the language of the welfare economists, but who has managed to derive entirely original principles for distribution. Rawls calls his book *A Theory of Justice*, but much of it concentrates on social justice. He argues that in a so-called original position, where no individual can know what lies in store for him in life (the so-called Veil of Ignorance), then all will accede to two critical criteria. The first is that individual liberty will have priority over any question of the distribution of other social goods. The second is a maximin principle of a special kind, called by Rawls the Difference Principle: that all will choose to maximize welfare at its minimum level, or in other words they will permit inequalities to occur only if they happen to improve the conditions of the least well-off. In the words of Rawls: 'All social primary goods – liberty and opportunity, income and wealth, and the bases of self-respect – are to be distributed equally unless an unequal distribution of any or all of these goods is to the advantage of the least favoured.'[30]

This provides a very powerful principle, rigorously derived from a conception of what people would themselves desire in the original position; in other words, it moves logically from the positive to the normative. It has of course excited critical comment, albeit of a highly sympathetic kind. Thus Arrow doubts that, in practice, a society would want to spend on medicine to keep someone barely alive if this involved keeping everyone else in poverty; he questions how society would identify the worst-off, since this again raises the whole hornet's nest of interpersonal comparison (albeit only on an ordinal basis). Most importantly, behind their veil of ignorance people must know the laws of the physical and social worlds, which seems contradictory.[31] Again, Nozick argues that Rawls ignores the historical principles which suggest that past circumstances and actions can cause different entitlements. To this Rawls would argue that differences in natural endowments and assets are undeserved and therefore morally arbitrary, so they should be nullified. But, Nozick argues, he nowhere provides a positive argument for this.[32]

To some extent, the protagonists in this argument seem to be arguing from different premises about different things. Rawls assumes that behind the veil of ignorance men would not know about their natural differences in ability; nor would they have any motive to engage in strategic behaviour, as some have argued. Equally, his critics have assumed that they would indeed know and that they would begin to play strategies. Thus the poor in the United States have not been the main recipients of redistribution; the middle classes have, for the simple reason that it pays a coalition of middle-income people to outbid the rest; if people, behind their veil of ignorance, do not know in which percentile income group they will fall, then surely they would expect that they might gain from joining the 51 per cent top-down group rather than the 51 per cent bottom-up group.[33] The answer to that seems to depend on empirical assessment of how people rank their own abilities and the risks involved in a gamble.

Beyond this, Rawls's position may give rise to unanswered dilemmas in practice. In stressing the welfare of the worst-off, it may ignore other issues involving the not-quite-so-badly-off. This in turn is related to its ordinal character, which makes comparison of magnitudes (and hence calculations of trade-off) impossible.[34] In this respect, it behaves curiously like a reverse version of the Pareto optimum. But at least it claims to be consistent in its psychological derivation – and that, presumably, could be tested empirically, by asking people to play games.

This in fact may prove to be a long way forward. Many of us would want to try to reach normative solutions rather than merely repeat positive analyses, if we possibly could. The way to do that is through ethical recommendations that are based on what we should recommend if we had an equal chance of being in someone else's shoes. There are good reasons for wanting to consider those; for one thing, we study collective choice partly because we are worried about the existing state of affairs.[35] The question then becomes: how best to develop ethical models?

One way is to refuse to be beaten by the considerable theoretical problems involved in developing a social welfare function, and to do the best one can. As Sen points out, weaker assumptions than Arrow's can generate some social decisions that do not have to consider all states of the world. Consider for instance three individuals, A, B and C, facing three alternatives x, y and z. The pay-offs are:

	x	y	z
A	1	0.90	0
B	1	0.88	0
C	0	0.95	1

In this case, utilitarianism (the sum of welfare) would give y preferred to x preferred to z. The majority decision rule would give x preferred to y preferred to z. There is no Pareto-optimal solution. The problem in this case is how far it is legitimate to weight the results in favour of one of the people rather than another. Assume for instance the effect of doubling the weight of each participant on the result. Start with the differences in welfare calculated from the table above:

	x versus y	y versus z	z versus x
A	0.10	0.90	−1.00
B	0.12	0.88	−1.00
C	−0.95	−0.05	1.00
Sum	−0.73	1.73	−1.00

Then, considering x versus y, it is possible to double the weight of A and B, and to halve that of C, but still to obtain the result that y is best. Similarly, for the comparison y versus z, halving A and B and doubling C will still produce y as the best result. True, on the z versus x comparison, halving A and B and doubling C will produce the result that z is better than x. But this is irrelevant if y is shown better than x or z. So, within these limits, there is a unique best element, y. Sen, who develops this example, argues that it demonstrates how to produce a 'very well behaved sequence of quasi-orderings'.[36]

The alternative answer is to try to produce new ways of arriving at preferences.[37] Economists have tended to restrict themselves to a highly narrow concept of value, based on observations of behaviour in the market. But, Clark argues, it would be equally

Table 17

BUDGET PIE: ALTERNATIVE RESOLUTION RULES

Rule	Criteria for preference: possible benefits				
	Intensity of preference measured	Budget constraint imposed	Honest preferences elicited	Cardinal measures obtained	Opinion leaders designated
Binary choice majority Rule	N	N	P	N	P
Mean of budget pie sectors	Y	Y	P	Y	N
Mean of continuous scale items	Y	N	P	P	P
Median of budget pie sectors	P	Y	P	N	N
Median of continuous scale items	P	N	P	N	P
Other mathematical operations	P	P	P	P	P

Y = yes, N = no, P = probably

Source: Clark, 1974, 24.

legitimate to look at other approaches, such as the individual (through questionnaires, tests and experiments) and the cultural (as seen in examination of cultural values). This last is unlikely to give very precise measures; it is the domain of the sociologist. But individual values may well be gauged more precisely. The so-called Budget Pie method, which asks an individual to spend imaginary amounts of money on a number of choices, in effect measures intensity of preference, in which sense it is superior to voting. But, strictly, it is a measure of readiness to spend rather than of actual utility; there may be gaps between people's stated preferences, even in a simulation, and their behaviour.[38] In particular, there may be a problem of strategic behaviour in playing the game, though this can be met in part by certain methods, such as (perversely) increasing uncertainty about the rules and the information that is needed.

Budget Pie methods are still in their infancy. They do not give an automatic best answer: the result depends on the decision rule adopted, each of which has certain advantages and disadvantages (Table 17). The point is that the method could be extended to encompass some problems now discussed at a purely theoretical level. There seems no reason, for instance, why Budget Pie games should not be used to gauge the empirical soundness of Rawls's difference principle.

The truth is that no one method, on its own, is going to achieve a miraculous breakthrough in equitable decision-making. What we do need is a conscious effort to apply the vast amount of literature in economic theory, and in related fields of ethics, to actual decision-making problems. This fairly obvious advice has been ignored up to now, for the simple reason that the theoreticians have been more concerned with theory than with any possible application, while the practical planners for the most part have had little inkling of the theory. To try to build this bridge is the most important advance that applied planning theory could now make.

A SUMMARY: ANTI-DISASTER METHODOLOGY

To repeat at the end the message at the outset: in the present state of the art, there is no one easy and reliable way by which in future we could avoid the errors we made in the past. The decision-maker will still find his task confused by the uncertainty of the future for which he is planning; by the complex relationships between his own actions, and those who affect the decision but are in turn affected by it; by the basic difficulty of reaching a solution that seems to combine efficiency of resource allocation with even rough justice as to equity between these groups and by the way this problem is compounded by the long time scale, over which the decision must work itself out. All these problems have been present for a long time in society, and will be with us for a long time yet. All we can do is to try to develop various methods of approach, a combination of which may help to appreciate and obviate the grosser errors.

First: planners need to make a more conscious effort to forecast the world (or rather the alternative possible worlds) in which the decision may be made and in which its consequences will then be felt. This involves much more than the mechanical exercises in statistical trend-extrapolation which now pass for forecasts in planning. It involves much more even than the general appreciation of international and national trends, which now precedes the trend projection exercises in more pretentious plans today. Indeed, an important part of the exercise could not reasonably be achieved by any single plan team; it would necessarily be derived from one or more general exercises in creative forecasting. Its essence would be a somewhat heroic attempt to trace the likely future evolution of the economy, of technology, of society, of culture and of values – first internationally and nationally, then in its regional and local application to the problem at hand.

Such basic work would be done by one or more independent teams of specialists, who would be united by a common competence, and common interest, in historical method. Ideally there should be at least two, in order to guard against too easy acceptance of some single orthodox interpretation. Econometric forecasting, though it represents the kind of sophisticated numerical projection that is inappropriate here, provides a model in this respect: in Britain, the National Institute for Economic and Social Research, the London Business School, and the Cambridge University Department of Applied Economics all work independently and all submit each others' work to intense critical scrutiny.

The detailed application might, however, appropriately be the work of local specialized teams, seeking to apply the more general forecasts to the problem in hand. How much further work should be done at that stage depends on some assessment of the costs of a bad decision. The greater the likely losses arising from a mistake in the initial decisions, the greater the resources which can justifiably be applied before it is taken.

But this already introduces the other critical area in which improvement is needed: the production of some kind of better balance sheet of costs and benefits. The impacts of the decision need to be viewed in terms of the valuations of individuals (or better, groups of individuals) as they will be expressed during the lifetime of the thing that is being planned. The problem here is to try to gauge not merely the individuals' valuations for themselves, but also their equity judgements, which will be needed to produce the social welfare function that will aggregate the individual valuations. If possible, these valuations should be expressed in some common measurement, such as money. If impossible, then they should be expressed in the best measure available – even as an arbitrary scale, if nothing better is possible. Such a mixed method is well developed in the Planning Balance Sheet developed in a number of studies by Nathaniel Lichfield, and adopted for use by the British government for the evaluation of major highway schemes.[39]

As stated earlier, economists have tended to rely exclusively on a behavioural approach to derive individual values. They distrust statements, listening only to actual evidence of behaviour: what people want is what in practice they get. But, for estimating *future* valuations, this approach is by definition unhelpful and irrelevant. We are therefore forced into role-playing games of the Budget Pie type, with the complication that the players will be asked to simulate not merely themselves now, but other people at different dates in the future. The simulations of the future, that are in any case being developed for the forecasting part of the exercise, will of course provide the basis here.

However this is done, the final part of the exercise is to marry the forecasting and the valuation elements. In the classic operations-research-based American school of decision-making uncertainty, two steps were involved: first, the assessment of probabilities of outcomes; secondly, assessment of the utilities of those involved. This, without the attempt at precise quantification, has to be the model here. The theory of games, as already seen, allows the decision-maker to understand how these people will choose between alternative courses of development, each with a probability of occurrence and with a certain pay-off. Applied to our problem, that means first that the decision-maker must assess the probability of certain outcomes. For instance, in the case of a major investment he must calculate the probability of total failure, of various degrees of cost escalation, and of failure to deliver the stated performance. He must also try to estimate pay-offs to various individuals or groups that may use, or be affected by, the investment, and he will need to bear in mind that, for some groups at some times, these pay-offs may well be negative.

Put this way, the objective is not strictly attainable. From all that has been said, probabilities cannot be calculated so finely; nor can utilities be computed, for future groups of people who may not even yet exist, in such a precise way. The best we can hope to achieve is an illustrative exercise. We can use a combination of systematic analysis of relevant past experience, and expert judgement, to derive probabilities – perhaps on some simple scale, as from 0 to 10. And then, by a combination of game-playing techniques and some expert judgement, we can arrive at similar broad estimates of utility. We shall have to reckon with the fact that people will disagree in their assessments of both probability and utility, and that they may not act consistently with their stated utility preferences.[40]

If that could be done, what would be the result? It would start with a choice between two or more alternatives: they could be as simple as do this or do not do this, they could involve more complex choices as between amounts and kinds of investment. Each of these would have estimates attached to them of their likely cost and feasibility. These would be calculated on a basis of probabilities. Where necessary, these would be further calculated for different time points during the likely lifetime of the development. Then, further calculations would be made, for different groups, of the utilities attached to these probable outcomes, including negative utilities where relevant. Then, a balance sheet would be drawn up for a number of selected time points. Then, one or more alternative aggregation rules (social welfare functions) would be adopted, perhaps with the aid of further game-playing research. This would be unlikely to yield an unambiguous preferred result, both because the utilities will not have been calculated on a single numerical scale and because there may be no evident preference for one aggregation function as against another. Judgement and debate would still be the basis of selecting the preferred course of action.

There are several points to be made about this method. First, as stressed more than once already, it is not neat or tidy. It does not assume that one can feed a whole set of quantities into some mixing machine, homogenize them and get a precise comparison in which one alternative unambiguously rings up the highest number. On the contrary, it assumes that judgement will be needed every step of the way. In this it departs from the classic tenets of cost-benefit analysis, and approaches closely to the planning balance sheet of Lichfield and the British Leitch Committee. But secondly, it goes beyond previous exercises in this genre by introducing probabilities, and also by seeking to evaluate at various points in the time path of the investment.

Thirdly, and most importantly, it is still cast in the mould which earlier (Chapter 8) was called the economizing or rational mode. That is, it assumes that decisions can and should be reached by studying the welfare of individuals as they themselves measure it (whether through their behaviour, as is traditional, or through survey or game-playing, as is more experimental). In other words, it by-passes the whole morass of political behaviour – whether by politicians themselves, or bureaucrats, or community action groups – analysed in Chapters 8–12. The final and least tractable question is: are we right to ignore political behaviour in this way? Should we not take explicit account of it?

I think that this question has to be left open; it is strictly a question of value judgement. At one extreme, if a planner ignores political behaviour, his decisions will be simply unrealistic and therefore incapable of implementation. At the other, if he leans over backward to accommodate political behaviour, he will cease to be a planner, or a decision-maker of any kind; he will be rather like the politician who never takes initiatives because he is too conscious of all the pressures, and so never achieves political greatness. The planner is paid to make decisions (or to make strong recommendations to politicians in favour of decisions); but equally, he has to do this in the light of the likely reactions.

The best course would probably be to incorporate political action into the analysis at the level of probability. We can say that it is likely that at such a stage this proposal would run into opposition from Group A, but that Group B would continue strongly to support it; we can calculate the likely strength of the two pressures at that time. But we want to do this partly in order to measure the likely divergence between the strength of these pressures and the pattern of perceived welfare of different groups. For that may even suggest a determined attempt by planners and politicians to fight the opposition in the interests of the public or indeed to fight the supporters, if that appears right.

Lastly, by its nature it does not at all necessarily involve one-shot decisions. On the contrary, it will often suggest a risk-avoiding strategy, based on minimal commitments at each stage where a decision is necessary. This would generally mean an incremental or adaptive approach to development of any kind, rather than a major new departure; it would suggest enlargement and adaptation of existing airports rather than building new ones, piecemeal improvement of roads at their most congested points rather than new motorways, and incremental upgrading of existing aircraft or rail technology rather than the invention of completely new concepts. The problem, of course, is that sometimes the new technology – the jump in the dark – is necessary and optimal. But that choice can at least be subjected to rational evaluation by the method outlined here.

DISASTERS RE-EXAMINED

Suppose all that had actually been done for the disasters outlined in the first half of this book. What would have been the likely result? It is beyond the object of this book to answer that question in detail, but some contentious suggestions might be made.

In the *Third London Airport* decision, the decision-makers are

the British government (since this is clearly a collective Cabinet decision). They have to balance a number of considerations of a general nature, having to do with the welfare of air travellers and the general economic health of the country and its dependence on trade and tourism, with some contradictory considerations concerning the particular loss of welfare of small but well-organized and influential interest groups. In resolving this, the worst possible outcome (for the government) would be to run out of airport capacity, with the inefficiency and nuisance and political opprobrium that would bring. That means finding the solution that falls within certain critical parameters (including location and cost) and that is capable of implementation by some defined date. Against this background, there are two strategies:
1. Develop existing airports to their maximum physical capacity, on the basis that, despite opposition, people around these airports will be more prone to accept high nuisance levels than those elsewhere. Develop each according to the level of local political opposition. At the least used, build aircraft movements up slowly at first, so that local people become gradually habituated. At the critical point, when opposition builds up, overcome it politically by the argument that crisis point has been reached: that this is now the only feasible solution. This is a somewhat high-risk strategy, but in view of its relatively low resource cost it may be preferred. The decision-makers may also judge that despite the apparently high level of risk they can bluff their way through to success with it. Admit the high level of risk in the first solution, and find the less controversial new site, preferably one with minimal environmental impact on people. Develop this at first as an overspill airport, later increasingly as a third main element in the London airport system.

The first of these strategies, clearly, is the one that has been pursued for most of the two decades 1960–79. The second is the one that was pursued from 1970 to 1973. It may appear that the first, in the event, proved to be based on a shrewd estimate of the likely scenario: with increasingly intolerable pressure at existing airports, government would be able to ignore local protests by what, after all, was a small minority of people in the country or in the south-east region. And over time, increasing habituation should mean that these people's perception of their own disutilities would diminish. So the incremental solution was optimal.

The only problem with it is that it assumes the decision-makers to belong to a homogeneous group, which they do not. Between 1970 and 1973 the government position was in direct conflict with that of the CAA, the BAA and the airlines. It could be in conflict again, given a government sympathetic to pressures from Stansted residents. And if this occurred in the early 1980s, the disaster outcome could occur. It may still well prove that Maplin would have been optimal for everyone – but by then it would be too late.

In the case of the *London Ringways* it should have been clear from the start that any scheme, above all any large and visible scheme, would have aroused intense and well-organised opposition in middle-class areas. The decision-makers, who were actually people with a functional interest in building roads and/or improving London's environment by comprehensive improvement – at least, as they saw it – should have adopted a more incremental strategy: first developing improved and new stretches of roads in industrial or railway or warehousing areas where opposition was at a minimum; secondly ensuring that generous compensation laws were in operation before any attempts were made to extend the scheme into well-established owner-occupied housing areas. At the same time compromises should have been made in design standards, and in directness of route, in order to allow the roads to snake less injuriously between and around the inner residential suburbs. In the most sensitive areas, more expensive solutions, like tunnelling, might have been justified, especially if the programme had been extended over a longer period of time. In this way, the highway builders could have expected to benefit from the almost certain emergence in the 1980s of an anti-congestion movement, aroused by the increase in traffic. The choice here was between building some roads earlier and some later, with certain penalties for drivers and other road users, and certain losses for residents; and building no roads at all, with much fewer losses for residents but far greater losses for users. The solution was to build no roads, which may have been highly sub-optimal.

Concorde is in some ways the easiest case. A careful projection of the economic and political environment the plane would inhabit – including its commercial prospects in the age of the big jets and also the intense environmental opposition – should have caused the project to be abandoned at a very early stage of feasibility testing. Even later, abandonment would almost certainly have been economic at any stage in the history of the project. In order to provide an alternative use for the relatively fixed assets in the British aircraft industry, resources should have been committed to an incremental technology with strong commercial prospects. The European A300 Airbus, which proved ideally adapted to an era of high fuel costs – an era which should have been perfectly predictable as a high probability from the mid-1960s onwards – was the obvious alternative use for these supplies of plant, capital and labour.

The BART *system*, a closely comparable investment, has similar lessons. Realistic analysis of the likely commercial demand to use the service – based on a combination of experience in other American cities, plus simulation games – would have suggested that there were poor possibilities of taking people out of their cars and that the riders would be drawn disproportionately from those who now used buses, to the detriment of the entire system of public transportation in the Bay Area. A systematic analysis of cost-escalation records would have suggested that the system could not be built for the original estimates, further affecting the commercial prospects. A relatively small part of the total investment could have been used to upgrade the existing bus systems with new kinds of vehicle and with priority for public transport at congested times, giving a service that would have performed much better overall, in terms of door-to-door speeds and comfort, at a fraction of BART's cost.

Lastly, the *Sydney Opera House* could have been presented to the public as a classic case of high-risk investment, with a very large variation between likely minimum and maximum costs. The people of New South Wales could have chosen between such a high-risk investment and a safer, more prosaic design. They could also have been invited to express a preference for methods of funding. Ironically, it is always possible that faced with this choice they would have voted for the high-risk solution to be financed by risk-takers in a state lottery – which, through desperation, is what they got.

In some of these cases, therefore, the outcome might not have been very different. In others, it might have been the reverse of what actually happened. But, in all, the decision would have been taken more consciously, more rationally, with greater knowledge of likely consequences, and in the last resort more democratically. The methods would still have been far from perfect: they would not have stilled criticism or debate or even heated controversy. But they would certainly have allowed politicians and planners and people, in Britain and in California and in Australia, to do much better than they did, even then. We could certainly do better with what we know now, let alone with what we could soon put together with the aid of some more research and experiment. There may be some excuses for great planning disasters, but there are not nearly as many as we think.

Notes

CHAPTER 1
1 P. Hall, *Theory and Practice of Regional Planning*; P. Hall, *Urban and Regional Planning*.
2 These include P. Bromhead, *The Great White Elephant of Maplin Sands*, D. McKie, *A Sadly Mismanaged Affair* and P. Self, *Econocrats and the Policy Process* on the third London airport; D.A. Hart, *Strategic Planning in London* on London's motorways; J. Costello and T. Hughes, *The Battle for Concorde* and A. Wilson, *The Concorde Fiasco* on Concorde; S. Zwerling, *Mass Transit and the Politics of Technology* and M.M. Webber, *The BART Experience – What Have We Learned?* on BART; M. Baume, *The Sydney Opera House Affair* and J. Yeomans, *The Other Taj Mahal* on the Sydney Opera House.
3 J.K. Friend and S.N. Jessop, *Local Government and Strategic Choice*.
4 G. Chapman, 'Economic Forecasting in Britain 1961–1975'; P. Hall (ed.), *Europe 2000*, ch. 1.
5 L. Merewitz, *How Do Urban Rapid Transit Projects Compare in Cost Estimating Experience?* and 'Cost Overruns in Public Works'.
6 A. Hirschman, *Development Projects Observed*.
7 A. Mumphrey and J. Wolpert, *Equity Considerations and Concessions in the Siting of Public Facilities*; Hart, *Strategic Planning*; J. Grant, *The Politics of Urban Transport Planning*.
8 A. Downs, *An Economic Theory of Democracy*.
9 D.A. Schon, *Beyond the Stable State: Public and Private Learning in a Changing Society*.
10 D.H. Meadows *et al.*, *The Limits to Growth*.

CHAPTER 2
1 McKie.
2 L.D. Stamp, 'Nationalism and Land Utilisation in Britain' and *The Land of Britain*, p. 431.
3 McKie, p. 30.
4 P. Abercrombie, *Greater London Plan 1944*, pp. 79–80.
5 McKie, pp. 43, 63–5.
6 Ibid., p. 47.
7 Ibid., p. 72.
8 GB House of Commons, Estimates Committee, *Fifth Report*.
9 GB Ministry of Aviation, *Report of the Inter-Departmental Committee on the Third London Airport*, pp. ix–x.
10 GB Board of Trade, *The Third London Airport*, p. 12; J.W.S. Brancker, *The Stansted Black Book*, p. 32.

Notes

11 GB Board of Trade, p. 12.
12 Standsted Working Party, *The Third London Airport*, pp. 3–4.
13 Brancker.
14 Ibid., p. 18.
15 Ibid., pp. 29–31.
16 McKie, pp. 128–141.
17 Self, p. 11.
18 GB Commission on the Third London Airport, *Report*, pp. 33–4.
19 Ibid., p. 137.
20 Ibid., pp. 149–51.
21 Ibid., p. 151.
22 Ibid., p. 149.
23 Ibid., p. 153.
24 GB Department of the Environment, *The Maplin Project; Surface Access Corridor*; GB Department of the Environment, *The Maplin Project: Designation for the New Town*.
25 Lord Boyd-Carpenter, *Airport Planning in the UK*, pp. 2–3.
26 Bromhead; McKie, p. 222.
27 McKie, pp. 218–20.
28 GB Department of Trade, *Maplin: Review of Airport Project*, pp. 4–5.
29 Ibid., p. 77.
30 Ibid., pp. 9–11.
31 R. Doganis, *A National Airport Policy*.
32 GB Department of Trade, *Airport Strategy for Great Britain*.
33 Ibid., I, pp. 27–8.
34 Ibid., p. 5.
35 Ibid., p. 7.
36 GB Secretary for Trade, *Airports Policy*.
37 Ibid., p. 29.
38 P. Hall *et al.*, *The Containment of Urban England*.
39 C. Foster *et al.*, *Lessons of Maplin*.

CHAPTER 3
1 Greater London Council, *London Road Plans 1900–1970*.
2 Ibid., pp. 19–23.
3 Hart, pp. 59–63.

4 G. Dix, 'Little Plans and Noble Diagrams', p. 332.
5 Hart, pp. 66–78.
6 Ibid., p. 36.
7 GB Ministry of Transport, *Traffic in Towns*.
8 Hart, p. 112.
9 Greater London Council, *Movement in London*, p. 39.
10 Greater London Council, *London Traffic Survey*, Vol. II, p. 184.
11 Ibid., pp. 48–9, 184.
12 Greater London Council, *London Road Plans*; Hart.
13 Hart, p. 136.
14 Ibid., p. 116.
15 Greater London Council, *London Traffic Survey*, Vol. II, p. 145.
16 Ibid., p. 85.
17 Greater London Council, *Movement in London*, p. 53.
18 Ibid., pp. 53–5, 68, 74.
19 Greater London Council, *London Road Plans*, p. 45.
20 Greater London Council, *Movement in London*, p. 66.
21 Greater London Council, *Greater London Development Plan. Public Inquiry*, Stage 1. *Transport*.
22 Freeman Fox, Wilbur Smith and Associates, *London Transportation Study, Phase III*.
23 Greater London Council, *Movement in London*.
24 Greater London Council, *GLDP*, Stage 1, p. 59.
25 Ibid., p. 104.
26 Greater London Council, *Greater London Development Plan: Statement Revisions*, p. 29.
27 GB Department of the Environment, *Greater London Development Plan: Report of the Panel of Inquiry*, Vol. 1: *Report*, p. 268.
28 London Motorway Action Group and London Amenity and Transport Association, *Transport Strategy in London*.

29 J.M. Thomson, *Motorways in London*; S. Plowden, *Towns Against Traffic*.

30 Plowden, *Towns Against Traffic*, p. 116.

31 Thomson, *Motorways in London*, pp. 160–3.

32 Ibid., p. 165.

33 Plowden, pp. 112–13.

34 Thomson, p. 151.

35 London Motorway Action Group, *Transport Strategy*, pp. 90–1.

36 Thomson, p. 125.

37 London Motorway Action Group, *Transport Strategy*, pp. 65–6.

38 GB Department of the Environment, *GLDP: Report*, Vol. 1, p. 257.

39 Ibid., p. 285.

40 Ibid., pp. 442–4.

41 Ibid., pp. 451–7.

42 GB Department of the Environment, *Greater London Development Plan: Statement by the Rt. Hon. Geoffrey Rippon, QC, MP*, p. 10.

43 Hart, pp. 159–60.

44 Ibid., p. 175.

45 GB Department of the Environment, *Greater London Development Plan: Statement by the Rt. Hon. Anthony Crosland, MP*, p. 6.

46 Grant.

47 Hart, pp. 183–94.

CHAPTER 4

1 GB House of Commons. Expenditure Committee, *Sixth Report: Session 1971–72*, Q. 175, 367.

2 Ibid., Q. 375.

3 Ibid., Q. 376.

4 Costello and Hughes, *The Battle for Concorde*, pp. 6–7.

5 GB, House of Commons. Expenditure Committee. Report, Q. 1144.

6 J. Barry, P. Gillman and R. Eglin, 'The Concorde Conspiracy'.

7 Edwards, *Concorde*, pp. 9–10; Costello and Hughes, p. 11.

8 Edwards, pp. 9–10.

9 GB House of Commons, Estimates Committee, *Second Report: Session 1963–64*, Q. 1127, 1137.

10 Ibid., Q. 1179.

11 GB House of Commons, Estimates Committee, *Seventh Report: Session 1963–64: With Minutes of Evidence*, p. 8.

12 GB House of Commons, Estimates Committee, *Second Report*, Q. 1130.

13 Ibid., xxiv.

14 Ibid., xxvii.

15 Ibid., xxciii.

16 Barry, Gillman and Eglin, 'The Concorde Conspiracy'; Wilson, *The Concorde Fiasco*, pp. 30–1.

17 GB House of Commons, Estimates Committee, *Second Report*, Q. 1446.

18 Quoted in Costello and Hughes, p. 156.

19 GB Lords Hansard, Vol. 244 *Debate on Concorde* (London, 1962), col. 572.

20 Ibid., col. 571.

21 Ibid., col. 600.

22 GB House of Commons, Committee of Public Accounts, *Third Report*, p. 11.

23 GB House of Commons, Committee of Public Accounts, *Third Report*, p. 9, Q. 639–45.

24 GB House of Commons, Committee of Public Accounts, *Sixth and Seventh Reports*, xiii, Q. 1631.

25 Ibid., xvi–xx.

26 Ibid., Q. 2135.

27 Ibid., Q. 2135.

28 Ibid., xiv.

29 Ibid., xxiv.

30 Ibid., Q. 1789–90, 1795, 1827–32.

31 GB House of Commons, Committee of Public Accounts, *Second Report*, xvi.

32 GB Commons Hansard, *Written Answers on Concorde Noise*,

Notes

Vol. 847, col. 451; Edwards, pp. 31–3.

33 J.G.U. Adams and N. Haigh, 'Booming Discorde', pp. 663–6.

34 Wilson, p. 36; Barry, Gillman and Eglin.

35 Wilson, pp. 46–8.

36 GB Commons Hansard, *Concorde Aircraft Act*, 2nd *Reading*, Vol. 848, col. 850; 3rd *Reading*, Vol. 850, col. 1593.

37 Costello and Hughes, p. 79.

38 Costello and Hughes; House of Commons. Expenditure Committee, *Sixth Report: Session 1971–2. With Minutes of Evidence*, p. 32.

39 GB House of Commons, Expenditure Committee, *Sixth Report*, p. 32.

40 Wilson, pp. 99–100, 101.

41 Edwards, p. 27.

42 GB House of Commons, Committee of Public Accounts, *Sixth and Seventh Reports*, xxvi.

43 Wilson, p. 151.

44 Edwards, pp. 26–7.

45 GB House of Commons, Committee of Public Accounts, *Sixth and Seventh Reports*, xxvii.

46 Edwards, p. 15.

47 P.H. Levin, *Government and the Planning Process*, p. 241.

48 GB Ministry of Technology, *Report of the Steering Group on Development Cost Estimating*, p. 74.

49 GB Ministry of Technology, *Report*, p. 71.

50 Ibid., p. 3.

51 GB House of Commons, Expenditure Committee, *Sixth Report*, Session 1971–2, Q. 361, 375.

52 GB Committee of Inquiry into the Aircraft Industry, *Report*, pp. 7–9.

53 Ibid., pp. 36–8.

54 Ibid., pp. 38, 59–61.

55 Barry, Gillman and Eglin.

56 Costello and Hughes, pp. 27–9, 115–17.

CHAPTER 5

1 For instance, N. Kennedy, *San Francisco Bay Area Rapid Transit: Promises, Problems, Prospects*; California Legislative Analyst, *Investigation of the Operations of the Bay Area Rapid Transit District with particular reference to Safety and Contract Administration*; Zwerling, *Mass Transit*.

2 Parsons, Brinckerhoff, Hall and Macdonald, *Regional Rapid Transit 1953–1955: A Report to the San Francisco Bay Area Rapid Transit Commission*, p. 3, Kennedy, *San Francisco BART*, p. 5.

3 California. Legislative Analyst, *Investigation*, pp. 51–3.

4 C.G. Burck, 'What We Can Learn from BART's Misadventures', p. 105.

5 California, Legislative Analyst, *Analysis of BART's Operational Problems and Fiscal Details with Recommendations for Corrective Action*, pp. 10, 17.

6 Webber, *The BART Experience*.

7 Parsons, Brinckerhoff, Tudor, Bechtel, *The Composite Report*.

8 Webber, p. 10.

9 Ibid., p. 18.

10 California, Legislative Analyst, *Analysis of the Current and Proposed (1976–77 and 1977–78) Operating Budgets of the BARTD*, p. 1.

11 Webber, p. 22.

12 Ibid., p. 28.

13 California, Legislative Analyst, *Financing Public Transportation in the San Francisco Bay Area Three County BART District*, pp. 15–16.

14 California, Legislative Analyst, *Financing*, pp. 3–6; Webber, p. 35.

15 Webber, p. 35.
16 Ibid., p. 33.
17 Ibid., p. 34.
18 Parsons, Brinckerhoff, *Regional Rapid Transit*, p. 3.
19 Parsons, Brinckerhoff, *The Composite Report*, pp. 82–3.
20 Zwerling, p. 27.
21 Ibid., p. 30.
22 Metropolitan Transportation Commission, *A History of the Key Decisions in the Development of Bay Area Rapid Transit*, pp. 11–29.
23 K.M. Fong, 'Rapid-Transit-Decision-Making', p. 83.
24 Fong, pp. 81–90; Metropolitan Transportation Commission, *A History*, p. 42.
25 Fong, p. 95.
26 Ibid., pp. 103–14.
27 Ibid., p. 130.
28 US Congress Office of Technology Assessment, *San Francisco Case Study*, pp. 11–12, 21, 37–41.
29 Merewitz, *Urban Rapid Transit Projects*, p. 485.
30 US Congress Office of Technology Assessment, *San Francisco*, p. 24.
31 Merewitz, 'Cost Overruns', p. 279.
32 P.N. Bay and J. Markowitz, *Bay Area Rapid Transit System – Status and Impacts*, p. 1.
33 US Department of Transportation, *1974 National Transportation Report: Current Performance and Future Prospects*, V–7.
34 US Department of Transportation, *A Study of Urban Mass Transportation Needs and Financing*, III–15–19.
35 US Congress Office of Technology Assessment, *Washington DC Case Study* (An Assessment of Community Planning for Mass Transit. Vol. 10), pp. 29–32.
36 H. Bain, *New Directions for Metro: Lessons from the BART Experience*, pp. 2–3.

37 US Congress, Office of Technology Assessment, *Atlanta Case Study*, p. 37.
38 US Congress Office of Technology Assessment, *Denver Case Study*, Vol. 5.
39 R.M. Fogelson, *The Fragmented Metropolis: Los Angeles 1850–1930*, p. 250; S.B. Warner, Jr, *The Urban Wilderness: A History of the American City*, pp. 137–8.
40 P. Marcuse, *Mass Transit for the Few: Lessons from Los Angeles*, p. 2.
41 Southern California Rapid Transit District, *A Public Transportation Improvement Program: Summary Report of Consultant's Recommendations*, p. 43.
42 W. Elliott, 'The Los Angeles Affliction: Suggestions for a Cure', *The Public Interest*, 38, pp. 122–4.
43 Marcuse, *Mass Transit for the Few*, pp. 15–20.
44 Marcuse, pp. 2, 15–20; M. Wachs, *The Case for Bus Rapid Transit in Los Angeles*, p. 11.
45 Southern California Association of Governments, *Regional Transportation Plan*.
46 US Congress, Office of Technology Assessment, *Los Angeles Case Study*, p. 47.

CHAPTER 6
1 Quoted in Baume, *The Sydney Opera House Affair*, p. 120.
2 Quoted in Baume, p. 120.
3 Quoted in Baume, p. 120.
4 Yeomans, *The Other Taj Mahal*, p. 54.
5 Baume, pp. 3–4, 9; Yeomans, pp. 58–9.
6 Yeomans, p. 77.
7 Baume, pp. 131–2.
8 Yeomans, p. 80.
9 Quoted in Baume, p. 122.

10 Baume, p. 125; E.D. Cohen, *Utzon and the Sydney Opera House: A Statement in the Public Interest*, pp. 15–16.

11 Baume, pp. 26–7, 29, 38.

12 Yeomans, pp. 140, 145–6.

13 Cohen, pp. 31, 46–58.

14 Yeomans, pp. 168–87.

15 Ibid., pp. 196–8.

16 Quoted in Baume, p. 123.

17 Quoted in Baume, p. 125.

18 Hall, quoted in Yeomans, pp. 190–2.

CHAPTER 7

1 California, Liaison Committee of the State Board of Education and the Regents of the University of California, *A Master Plan for Higher Education in California, 1960–1975*.

2 California, Liaison Committee, *Master Plan*, p. 109.

3 T.C. Holly, 'California's Master Plan for Higher Education, 1960–75', p. 9.

4 A.G. Coons, *Crises in California Higher Education*, pp. 24–5, 30–1.

5 Ibid., pp. 77–82.

6 California, Liaison Committee of the State Board of Education and the Regents of the University of California, *A Study of the Need for Additional Centers of Public Higher Education in California*, pp. 82–94.

7 University of California, Office of the President, *Unity and Diversity: The Academic Plan of the University of California, 1965–1975*, pp. 34–5.

8 San José, City Planning Department, *Study on Suggested Sites for a University of California Campus*; Santa Cruz – City and County, *A University of California Campus at Santa Cruz*; Livingston & Blayney (Consultants), *A University Community in the Almadén Valley*, pp.

27, 28; University of California: Santa Cruz, *Long Range Development Plan* (John Carl Warnecke & Associates), p. 11.

9 University of California: Irvine, *Long Range Development Plan* (William L. Pereith & Associates), pp. 4–5.

10 University of California: Office of the President, *Unity and Diversity*, pp. 41–2.

11 D.R. Gerth, J.O. Haehn and Associates, *An Invisible Giant: The California State Colleges*, pp. 197–200.

12 California, Department of Finance, *California Population 1971*, i, p. 10; California Postsecondary Education Commission, *Agenda*, 14–15 October, pp. 2, 13–14.

13 F.E. Cheit, *The New Depression in Higher Education: A Study of Financial Conditions in 41 Colleges and Universities*, pp. 17, 91–3, 101–4, 112–18.

14 C. Kerr, *The Uses of the University*, pp. v–vi, 1, 53–4.

15 Cheit, p. 155.

16 US President's Commission on Campus Unrest, *Report*, pp. 25–8.

17 M. Heirich, *The Spiral of Conflict: Berkeley 1964*, pp. 417–18.

18 Heirich, pp. 373–6; *Facts on File*, p. 266.

19 US President's Commission on Campus Unrest, *Report*, pp. 61–9, 70–6, 78–83; R. Nisbet, *The Degradation of the Academic Dogma: The University in America, 1945–1970, passim*.

20 US President's Commission on Campus Unrest, *Report*, pp. 32–4.

21 J.R. Searle, *The Campus War*, ch. 1 *passim*, p. 109; Nisbet, The Degradation of the Academic Dogma, p. 194.

22 Searle, pp. 108–9.

23 *Facts on File*, 1970, p. 711.

24 Ibid., pp. 696–7.
25 California, Coordinating Council for Higher Education, *The California Master Plan for Higher Education in the Seventies and Beyond*, pp. 3, 32–3, 104.
26 California, Legislature, *Report of the Joint Committee on the Master Plan for Higher Education*, pp. 38–40.
27 California, Coordinating Council for Higher Education, *Annual Report of the Director*, 1969, p. 1.
28 California, Coordinating Council for Higher Education, *Annual Report of the Director*, 1970, p. 1.
29 California, Coordinating Council for Higher Education, *Annual Report of the Director*, 1971, p. 17.
30 California, Coordinating Council for Higher Education, *Annual Report of the Director*, 1972, p. 9.
31 California, Postsecondary Education Commission, *Agenda*, 14–15 October, 1974, pp. 2, 13–14; California, Postsecondary Education Commission, *Planning for Postsecondary Education in California: A Five-Year Plan, 1976–81* (Sacramento, 1975), passim.
32 A.G. Coons, *Crises*, p. 207.
33 California, Liaison Committee, *Master Plan*, p. 168.
34 P. Abercrombie and J.H. Forshaw, *County of London Plan* (London, 1943), p. 52.
35 London County Council, *County of London Development Plan* (London, 1951), p. 46.
36 *The Times*, 15 March 1951, p. 7.
37 Ibid., 28 April 1955, p. 7; 15 July 1955, p. 5.
38 Ibid., 15 July 1955, p. 9.
39 Ibid., 11 April 1956, p. 5.
40 Ibid., 21 February 1961, p. 12; 23 February 1961, p. 6.
41 Ibid., 1 November 1962, p. 21 December 1962, p. 4.

42 Ibid., 27 October 1967, p. 9.
43 Ibid., 31 October 1967, p. 11.
44 Ibid., 25 November 1967, p. 9.
45 Ibid., 27 October 1967, p. 8.
46 Ibid., 14 December 1967, p. 81.
47 GB National Libraries Committee, *Report*, p. 150–1.
48 Ibid., pp. 93–6.
49 *The Times*, 14 January 1971, p. 4; 27 February 1971, p. 14.
50 GB Paymaster General, *The British Library*, p. 7.
51 *The Times*, 24 January 1974, p. 8.
52 Ibid., 6 August 1975, p. 2.

CHAPTER 8
1 M. Olson Jr, *The Logic of Collection Action*, p. 172.
2 P. Steiner, 'The Public Sector and the Public Interest', p. 26.
3 M. Olson Jr, 'Economics, Sociology and the Best of all Possible Worlds', p. 108; Steiner 'The Public Sector', pp. 30–2.
4 J.P. McIver and F. Ostrom, 'Using Budget Pies to Reveal Preferences: Validation of a Survey Instrument', pp. 87–8.
5 A.O. Hirschman, *Exit, Voice and Loyalty*.
6 M. Olson Jr, 'On the Priority of Public Problems', pp. 318–19.
7 Cf. R.A. Bauer, 'The Study of Policy Formulation: An Introduction', p. 9.
8 J.D. Stewart, *Management in Local Government: A Viewpoint*, p. 30; Y. Dror, *Public Policymaking Reexamined*, p. 132; G. Chadwick, *A Systems View of Planning*, p. 68; C.W. Churchman *et al.*, *Introduction to Operations Research*, pp. 118, 127.
9 R.L. Ackoff and M. Sasieni, *Fundamentals of Operations Research*, pp. 44–5.
10 R. Zeckhauser and E. Schaefer,

Notes

'Public Policy and Normative Economic Theory', p. 107.

11 A. Etzioni, *The Active Society: A Theory of Societal and Political Processes*, p. 265.

12 H.W.J. Rittel and M.M. Webber, 'Dilemmas in a General Theory of Planning', p. 160.

13 Etzioni, pp. 283-5.

14 Ibid., p. 284.

15 A. Eddison, *Local Government: Management and Corporate Planning*, p. 23.

16 G.T. Allison, *Essence of Decision*.

17 D. Bell, *The Coming of Post-Industrial Society*, pp. 283-4; Olson, pp. 110-17.

18 J.M. Simmie, *Citizens in Conflict*, pp. 59-60.

19 Ibid., pp. 60-2.

20 J.L. Bower, 'Descriptive Decision Theory from the "Administrative" Viewpoint', pp. 129-32.

21 Ibid., p. 142.

22 K. Newton, 'Community Politics and Decision-Making', pp. 11-22.

CHAPTER 9

1 E.E. Schattschneider, *The Semisovereign People*.

2 R. Dahrendorf, *Class and Class Conflict in Industrial Society*, p. 213.

3 J.S. Coleman, *Community Conflict*, pp. 4-6.

4 Ibid., pp. 6-8.

5 Ibid., pp. 10-13.

6 Ibid., pp. 21-22.

7 Schon, *Beyond the Stable State*, pp. 138-40.

8 G. Tullock, *Toward a Mathematics of Politics*, pp. 129-30.

9 P. Bachrach and M. Baratz, *Power and Poverty*, pp. 59-62.

10 W.A. Cozzens, *Client-focused Policy Research*, pp. 26-8.

11 R.A. Dahl, *Pluralistic Democracy in the United States*, pp. 429-30.

12 E.C.B. Schoettle, 'The State of the Art in Policy Studies', pp. 163-7.

13 Tullock, pp. 89-94.

14 Eddison, p. 130.

15 A.B. Wildavsky, *The Revolt against the Masses and Other Essays on Politics and Public Policy*, p. 29.

16 Ibid., p. 31.

17 Ibid., p. 44.

18 T.M. Cowling and G.C. Steeley, *Sub-Regional Planning Studies: An Evolution*, p. 98.

19 B. Perkins and G. Barnes, 'A Planning Choice', pp. 97-8.

20 Downs, *An Economic Theory of Democracy*, p. 91.

21 Stewart, *Management in Local Government*, pp. 82-5.

CHAPTER 10

1 R.M. Cyert and J. March, *A Behavioral Theory of the Firm*.

2 R. Lawrence and J.W. Lorsch, *Organization and Environment*, pp. 153-8.

3 Cyert and March, pp. 116-24.

4 Ibid., pp. 78-81, 113.

5 M.A. Kaplan, *System and Process in International Politics*.

6 Ibid., pp. 106-12.

7 A. Downs, *Inside Bureaucracy*.

8 K.J. Arrow, 'On the Agenda of Organizations', pp. 215-16.

9 A.B. Wildavsky, *The Politics of the Budgetary Process*, pp. 124-5.

10 Ibid., p. 13.

11 Ibid., pp. 17, 18.

12 Ibid., p. 130.

13 Ibid., pp. 156-7.

14 Ibid., pp. 156-7.

15 A.B. Wildavsky, 'Budgeting as a Political Process', p. 194.

16 A.B. Wildavsky, *The Politics of the Budgetary Process*, pp. 160-5.

17 W.A. Niskansen, *Bureaucracy: Servant or Master?*

18 W.A. Niskansen, *Bureaucracy and Representative Government.*
19 Ibid., pp. 48–52; Niskansen, *Bureaucracy: Servant or Master?*, p. 18.
20 G. Tullock, *The Vote Motive*, pp. 33–4.
21 Niskansen, *Bureaucracy and Representative Government*, pp. 195–223; Tullock, *The Vote Motive*, pp. 38–9.
22 C.N. Parkinson, *Parkinson's Law, or the Pursuit of Progress*, p. 5
23 Merewitz, *Urban Rapid Transport Projects*; Merewitz, 'Cost Overruns'.
24 J.E. Sawyer, 'Entrepreneurial Error and Economic Growth', p. 200.
25 Ibid., p. 200.
26 Ibid., pp. 202–3.
27 Hirschman, *Development Projects Observed*, p. 13.
28 Ibid., p. 26.
29 Arrow, 'On the Agenda of Organizations', p. 215.
30 Ibid., pp. 228–9.
31 T. Burns and M. Stalker, *The Management of Innovation.*
32 GB Central Policy Review Staff, *Review of Overseas Representation.*

CHAPTER 11

1 H.A. Kissinger, *A World Restored*, p. 326.
2 G. Tullock, *The Politics of Bureaucracy*, p. 122.
3 M. Olson Jr, *The Logic of Collective Action*, p. 35.
4 Downs, *An Economic Theory of Democracy*, p. 204.
5 Ibid., pp. 64–5.
6 J.M. Buchanan and G. Tullock, *The Calculus of Consent*, p. 220.
7 A. Breton, *The Economic Theory of Representative Government*, pp. 44–5.
8 Buchanan and Tullock, p. 242.

9 Ibid., p. 22.
10 W. Riker, 'Voting and the summation of preferences: an interpretative bibliographic review of selected developments during the past decade'.
11 R.L. Bish, *The Public Economy of Metropolitan Areas.*
12 Tullock.
13 Hirschman, *Exit, Voice and Loyalty.*
14 Tullock, p. 55.
15 S.E. Finer, 'Proposition One', pp. 157–8.
16 W. Hoffman, 'The Democratic Response of Urban Governments', p. 71.
17 Tullock, p. 55.
18 Downs, p. 299.
19 M.J. Harsanyi, 'Measurement of Social Power'.
20 J.G. March, 'The Power of Power', pp. 54–6.
21 Ibid., p. 68.
22 Bachrach and Baratz, *Power and Poverty*, pp. 105–6.
23 Schattschneider, *The Semisovereign People*, p. 74.
24 A. Schick, 'Systems Politics and Systems Budgeting', pp. 138–41.

CHAPTER 12

1 W. Solesbury, *Policy in Urban Planning*, pp. 50–2.
2 Hart, *Strategic Planning in London.*
3 D.A. Schon, *Beyond the Stable State*, pp. 31–60.
4 A. Wildavsky, *The Politics of the Budgetary Process.*

CHAPTER 13

1 Merewitz, *Urban Rapid Transit Projects*; Merewitz, 'Cost Overruns'.
2 D. Bell, p. 207.
3 L. Hudson, *Contrary Imaginations*, pp. 49–67.

Notes

4 G. Vickers, *The Art of Judgement: A Study of Policy Making*, p. 67.

5 Vickers, pp. 82–3.

6 Friend and Jessop, pp. 166–7, 159.

7 Etzioni, pp. 286–7.

8 D.M. Michael, *On Learning to Plan and Planning to Learn*, pp. 45–6, 175.

9 A.K. Sen, *On Economic Inequality*, pp. 4–5.

10 A.K. Sen, *Collective Choice and Social Welfare*, p. 22.

11 E. Mishan, 'Pareto Optimality and the Law', p. 272.

12 A.K. Sen, *Collective Choice*, pp. 79–80.

13 K. Arrow, *Social Choice and Individual Values*.

14 K. Arrow, 'Public and Private Values', p. 18.

15 W. Riker, p. 904.

16 A.K. Sen, 'Planners' Preferences: Optimality, Distribution and Social Welfare', p. 205.

17 Sen, *Collective Choice*, p. 13.

18 J. von Neumann and O. Morgenstern, *Theory of Games and Economic Behaviour*.

19 A. Rapoport, *Fights, Games and Debates*, pp. 125–6.

20 Zeckhauser and Schaefer, p. 79.

21 H. Raiffa, *Decision Analysis*, pp. 57–60.

22 A. Simon and C. Stedry, 'Psychology and Economics', p. 276.

23 Shubik, pp. 57–8.

24 Rapoport, pp. 146–7.

25 T.C. Schelling, *The Strategy of Conflict*, pp. 113–15.

26 Ibid., p. 108.

27 Steiner, pp. 37–49.

28 Mumphrey and Wolpert, pp. 10–26.

29 D.J. Berry and G. Steiker, 'The Concept of Justice in Regional Planning: Justice as Fairness', pp. 418–20.

30 J. Rawls, *A Theory of Justice*, p. 303.

31 K. Arrow, *Rawls's Principle of Just Saving*, pp. 251–9.

32 R. Nozick, *Anarchy, State and Utopia*, pp. 216–26.

33 Ibid., pp. 274–5.

34 A.K. Sen, *Collective Choice*, pp. 138–40.

35 Ibid., pp. 121–3.

36 Ibid., p. 102.

37 T.N. Clark, 'Can You Cut a Budget Pie?', p. 7.

38 Ibid., pp. 12–15.

39 N. Lichfield, 'Cost benefit Analysis in Urban Expansion. A Case Study: Peterborough'.

40 R.M. Adelson and J.M. Norman, 'Operational Research and Decision-Making', pp. 401–8.

References

ABERCROMBIE, P. AND FORSHAW, J.H., *County of London Plan* (London: London County Council 1943).

ABERCROMBIE, P., *Greater London Plan 1944* (London: HMSO 1945).

ACKOFF, R.L. AND SASIENI, M., *Fundamendals of Operations Research* (New York: John Wiley 1968).

ADAMS, J.G.U. AND HAIGH, N., 'Booming Discorde', *Geographical Magazine*, 44 (1972), pp. 663-6.

ADELSON, R.M. AND NORMAN, J.M., 'Operational Research and Decision-Making', *Operational Research Quarterly*, 20 (1969), pp. 399-413.

ALLISON, G.T., *Essence of Decision: Explaining the Cuban Missile Crisis* (Boston: Little, Brown 1971).

ARROW, K.J., *Social Choice and Individual Values* (New York: John Wiley 1951).

—— 'Public and Private Values' in Hook, S., *q.v.*

—— *Rawls's Principle of Just Saving*, Technical Report No. 16, Institute for Mathematical Studies in the Social Sciences (Stanford, California: The Institute 1973).

—— 'On the Agenda of Organizations', in Marris, R., *q.v.*

BACHRACH, P. AND BARATZ, M., *Power and Poverty* (New York: OUP 1970).

BAIN, H., *New Directions for Metro: Lessons from the BART Experience* (Washington: The Washington Center for Metropolitan Studies 1976).

BARRY, J., GILLMAN, P. AND EGLIN, R., 'The Concorde Conspiracy', *Sunday Times*, 8 and 15 February 1976.

BAUER, R.A., 'The Study of Policy Formulation: An Introduction' in Bauer, R.A. and Gergen, K.J., *q.v.*

BAUER, R.A. AND GERGEN, K.J. (eds.), *The Study of Policy Formulation* (New York: Collier-Macmillan Free Press 1968).

References

BAUME, M., *The Sydney Opera House Affair* (Melbourne: Nelson 1967).

BAY, P.N. AND MARKOWITZ, J., *Bay Area Rapid Transit System – Status and Impacts* (Presented to Annual Meeting, Institute of Traffic Engineers, Seattle, August 1975, Mimeo).

BELL, D., *The Coming of Post-Industrial Society: A Venture in Social Forecasting* (New York: Basic Books 1973).

BERRY, D.J. AND STEIKER, G., 'The Concept of Justice in Regional Planning: Justice as Fairness', *Journal of the American Institute of Planners*, 40 (1974), pp. 414–21.

BISH, R.L., *The Public Economy of Metropolitan Areas* (Chicago: Markham 1971).

BOWER, J.L., 'Descriptive Decision Theory from the "Administrative" Viewpoint' in Bauer, R.A. and Gergen, K.J., *q.v.*

BOYD-CARPENTER, LORD, *Airport Planning in the UK: Past, Present and Future* (Presented to the Fifth World Airports Conference, Brighton 1975, Mimeo).

BRANCKER, J.W.S., *The Stansted Black Book* (Dunmow: North West Essex and East Herts. Preservation Association 1967).

BROMHEAD, P., *The Great White Elephant of Maplin Sands* (London: Paul Elek 1973).

BUCHANAN, J.M. AND TULLOCK, G., *The Calculus of Consent* (Ann Arbor: University of Michigan Press 1962).

BURCK, C.G., 'What We Can Learn from BART's Misadventures', *Fortune*, July 1975, pp. 104–67.

BURNS, T. AND STALKER, M., *The Management of Innovation* (London: Tavistock Publications 1961).

CALIFORNIA, COORDINATING COUNCIL FOR HIGHER EDUCATION, *Annual Report of the Director* (Sacramento: The Council 1969, 1970, 1971, 1972a).

—— *The California Master Plan for Higher Education in the Seventies and Beyond*, Report and Recommendations of the Select Committee on the Master Plan for Higher Education to the Coordinating Council for Higher Education (Sacramento: The Council 1972).

CALIFORNIA, DEPARTMENT OF FINANCE, *Projections of Enrollment for California's Institutions of Higher Education 1960–1976*, prepared for the Master Plan Survey Team and the Liaison Committee of the Regents of the University of California and the State Board of Education (Sacramento: The Department 1960).

—— *Enrollment in California Higher Education*, Annual Return (Sacramento: The Department 1960–1977).

—— *California Population 1971* (Sacramento: The Department 1972).

288

CALIFORNIA, LEGISLATIVE ANALYST, *Investigation of the Operations of the Bay Area Rapid Transit District with particular reference to Safety and Contract Administration* (Sacramento: California Legislature 1972).

—— *Analysis of BART's Operational Problems and Fiscal Details with Recommendations for Corrective Action* (Sacramento: California Legislature 1974).

—— *Financing Public Transportation in the San Francisco Bay Area Three County BART District* (Sacramento: California Legislature 1975).

—— *Analysis of the Current and Proposed (1976–7 and 1977–8) Operating Budgets of the BARTD* (Sacramento: California Legislature 1977).

CALIFORNIA, LEGISLATURE, *Report of the Joint Committee on the Master Plan for Higher Education* (Sacramento: California Legislature 1973).

CALIFORNIA, LIAISON COMMITTEE OF THE STATE BOARD OF EDUCATION AND THE REGENTS OF THE UNIVERSITY OF CALIFORNIA, *A Study of the Need for Additional Centers of Public Higher Education in California* (Sacramento: California State Department of Education 1957).

—— *A Master Plan for Higher Education in California, 1960–75* (Sacramento: California State Department of Education 1960).

CALIFORNIA, POSTSECONDARY EDUCATION COMMISSION, *Agenda*, 14–15 October 1974 (Sacramento: The Commission 1974).

—— *Planning for Postsecondary Education in California: A Five-Year Plan, 1976–81* (Sacramento: The Commission 1975).

CHADWICK, G., *A Systems View of Planning* (Oxford: Pergamon 1971).

CHAPMAN, G., 'Economic Forecasting in Britain 1961–1975', *Futures*, 8 (1977), pp. 254–60.

CHEIT, F.E., *The New Depression in Higher Education: A Study of Financial Conditions in 41 Colleges and Universities,* for the Carnegie Commission on Higher Education and the Ford Foundation (New York: McGraw Hill 1971).

CHURCHMAN, C.W. *et al., Introduction to Operations Research* (New York: John Wiley 1957).

CLARK, T.N., 'Can You Cut A Budget Pie?', *Policy and Politics*, 3 (1974), pp. 3–31.

COHEN, E.D., *Utzon and the Sydney Opera House: A Statement in the Public Interest* (Sydney: Morgan Publishers 1967).

COLEMAN, J.S., *Community Conflict* (New York: The Free Press of Glencoe 1957).

COONS, A.G., *Crises in California Higher Education: Experience*

References

under the Master Plan and Problems of Coordination, 1959 to 1968 (Los Angeles: The Ward Ritchie Press 1968).

COSTELLO, J. AND HUGHES, T., *The Battle for Concorde* (Salisbury: Compton Press 1971).

COWLING, T.N. AND STEELEY, G.C., *Sub-Regional Planning Studies: An Evaluation* (Oxford: Pergamon 1973).

COZZENS, W.A., *Client-focused Policy Research: Identifying Slippage in a Hierarchy of Governments*, Research on Conflict in Locational Decisions, Discussion Paper No. 18 (Philadelphia: The Wharton School of Finance and Commerce 1972).

CYERT, R.M. AND MARCH, J., *A Behavioural Theory of the Firm* (Englewood Cliffs: Prentice Hall 1963).

DAHL, R.A., *Pluralistic Democracy in the United States: Conflict and Consent* (Chicago: Rand and McNally 1967).

DAHRENDORF, R., *Class and Class Conflict in Industrial Society* (London: Routledge and Kegan Paul 1959).

DIX, G., 'Little Plans and Noble Diagrams', *Town Planning Review*, 49 (1978), pp. 329–52.

DOUGANIS, R., *A National Airport Plan*, Fabian Tract 377 (London: Fabian Society 1967).

DOWNS, A., *An Economic Theory of Democracy* (New York: Harper & Brothers 1957).

—— *Inside Bureaucracy* (Boston: Little, Brown 1967).

DROR, Y., *Public Policymaking Reexamined* (San Francisco: Chandler 1968).

EASTON, D. (ed.), *Varieties of Political Theory* (Englewood Cliffs: Prentice Hall 1966).

EDDISON, A., *Local Government: Management and Corporate Planning* (London: Leonard Hill 1975).

EDWARDS, C.E., *Concorde: Ten Years and a Billion Pounds Later* (London: Pluto Press 1972).

ELLIOTT, W., 'The Los Angeles Affliction: Suggestions for a Cure', *The Public Interest*, 38 (1975), pp. 119–28.

ETIZIONI, A., *The Active Society: A Theory of Societal and Political Processes* (London: Collier-Macmillan 1968).

FACTS ON FILE, A monthly record of events.

FINER, S.E., 'Proposition One', *New Society*, 16 October 1975, pp. 157–8.

FOGELSON, R.M., *The Fragmented Metropolis: Los Angeles 1850–1930* (Cambridge, Mass.: Harvard UP 1967).

FONG, K.M., 'Rapid Transit-Decision-Making: The Income Distribution Impact of San Francisco Bay Area Rapid Transit' (Unpublished BA thesis, Harvard University 1976).

FOSTER, C. *et al., Lessons of Maplin: Is the Machinery of Government*

Decision-Making at Fault? (London: Institute of Economic Affairs 1974).

FREEMAN FOX, WILBUR, SMITH AND ASSOCIATES, *London Transportation Study, Phase III*, 4 Vols. (London: The Associates, Mimeo 1968).

FRIEND, J.K. AND JESSOP, W.N., *Local Government and Strategic Choice* (London: Tavistock Publications 1969).

GERTH, D.R., HAEHN, J.O. AND ASSOCIATES, *An Invisible Giant: The California State Colleges* (San Francisco: Jossey-Bass 1971).

GRANT, J., *The Politics of Urban Transport Planning* (London: Earth Resources Research 1977).

GB ADVISORY COMMITTEE ON TRUNK ROAD ASSESSMENT, *Report* (London: HMSO 1977).

GB BOARD OF TRADE, *The Third London Airport*, Cmnd. 3259 (London: HMSO 1976).

GB CENTRAL POLICY REVIEW STAFF, *Review of Overseas Representation* (London: HMSO 1977).

GB COMMISSION ON THE THIRD LONDON AIRPORT, *Report* (London: HMSO 1971).

GB COMMISSION OF INQUIRY INTO THE AIRCRAFT INDUSTRY, *Report*, Cmnd. 2853 (London: HMSO 1965).

GB COMMONS HANSARD, *Written Answers on Concorde Noise*, Vol. 847 (London: HMSO 1972).

GB COMMONS HANSARD, *Concorde Aircraft Act, 2nd Reading*, Vol. 848; *3rd Reading*, Vol. 850 (London: HMSO 1973).

GB DEPARTMENT OF THE ENVIRONMENT, *The Maplin Project: Surface Access Corridor* (London: The Department 1973).

—— *Greater London Development Plan: Report of the Panel of Inquiry*, Vol. 1 (London: HMSO 1973).

—— *Greater London Development Plan: Statement by the Rt. Hon. Geoffrey Rippon, QC, MP* (London: HMSO 1973).

—— *Greater London Development Plan: Statement by the Rt. Hon. Anthony Crosland, MP* (London: HMSO 1975).

GB DEPARTMENT OF TRADE, *Maplin: Review of Airport Project* London: HMSO 1974).

—— *Airport Strategy for Great Britain*, Part I, *The London Area*; Part II, *The Regional Airports: A Consultation Document* (London: HMSO 1975/7).

GB HOUSE OF COMMONS, COMMITTEE OF PUBLIC ACCOUNTS, *Third Report* (London: HMSO 1965).

—— *Second Report* (London: HMSO 1967).

—— *Sixth and Seventh Reports* (London: HMSO 1973).

GB HOUSE OF COMMONS, ESTIMATES COMMITTEE, *Fifth Report: Session 1960–61. With Minutes of Evidence* (London: HMSO 1964).

References

—— *Second Report: Session 1963–4. With Minutes of Evidence* (London: HMSO 1963).

—— *Seventh Report: Session 1963–4. With Minutes of Evidence* (London: HMSO 1964).

GB HOUSE OF COMMONS, EXPENDITURE COMMITTEE, *Sixth Report: Session 1971–2. With Minutes of Evidence* (London: HMSO 1972).

GB LORDS HANSARD, *Debate on Concorde*, Vol. 244 (London: HMSO 1962).

GB MINISTRY OF AVIATION, *Report of the Inter-Departmental Committee on the Third London Airport* (London: HMSO 1963).

GB MINISTRY OF TECHNOLOGY, *Report of the Steering Group on Development Cost Estimating*, 2 Vols. (London: HMSO 1969).

GB MINISTRY OF TRANSPORT, *Traffic in Towns* (London: HMSO 1963).

GB NATIONAL LIBRARIES COMMITTEE, *Report*, Cmnd. 4028 (London: HMSO 1969).

GB PAYMASTER GENERAL, *The British Library* (London: HMSO 1971).

GB SECRETARY FOR TRADE, *Airports Policy*, Cmnd. 7084 (London: HMSO 1978).

GREATER LONDON COUNCIL, *London Traffic Survey*, Vol. II (London: The Council 1966).

—— *Movement in London* (London: The Council 1969).

—— *London Road Plans 1900–70*, Greater London Research, Research Report No. 11 (London: Greater London Research and Development Unit 1970).

—— *Greater London Development Plan: Public Inquiry. Statement Evidence*, Stage 1, Transport (London: The Council 1970).

—— *Greater London Development Plan: Statement Revisions* (London: The Council 1972).

HALL, P., *Theory and Practice of Regional Planning* (London: Pemberton 1970).

—— *Urban and Regional Planning* (Harmondsworth: Penguin Books 1975).

—— (ed.), *Europe 2000* (London: Duckworth 1977).

HALL, P., THOMAS, R., GRACEY, H. AND DREWETT. R., *The Containment of Urban England*, 2 Vols. (London: George Allen & Unwin 1973).

HARSANYI, M.J., 'Measurement of Social Power' in Shubik, M. (ed.), *q.v.*

HART, D.A., *Strategic Planning in London: The Rise and Fall of the Primary Road Network* (Oxford: Pergamon 1976).

HAVEMAN, R.H. AND MARGOLIS, J. (eds.), *Public Expenditures and Policy Analysis* (Chicago: Markham 1970).

HEIRICH, M., *The Spiral of Conflict: Berkeley 1964* (New York and London: Columbia UP 1971).

HIRSCHMAN, A., *Development Projects Observed* (Baltimore: Johns Hopkins UP 1967).

HIRSCHMAN, A.O., *Exit, Voice and Loyalty* (Cambridge, Mass.: Harvard UP 1970).

HOFFMAN, W., 'The Democratic Response of Urban Governments: An Empirical Test with Simple Spatial Models', *Policy and Politics*, 4 (1976), pp. 51–74.

HOLLY, T.C., 'California's Master Plan for Higher Education, 1960–75', *Journal of Higher Education*, 32 (1961), pp. 9–16.

HOOK, S. (ed.), *Human Values and Economic Policy* (New York: New York UP 1967).

HUDSON, L., *Contrary Imaginations* (London: Penguin 1967).

KAPLAN, M.A., *System and Process in International Politics* (New York: John Wiley 1964).

KENNEDY, N., *San Francisco Bay Area Rapid Transit: Promises, Problems, Prospects* (Presented to Society of Automotive Engineers – Australasia, Convention, Melbourne. Mimeo October 1971).

KERR, C., *The Uses of the University* (Cambridge, Mass: Harvard UP 1963).

KISSINGER, H.A., *A World Restored* (London: Gollancz 1973).

LAWRENCE, R. AND LORSCH, J.W., *Organization and Environment: Managing Differentiation and Integration* (Boston: Harvard University Graduate School of Business Administration 1967).

LEVIN, P.H., *Government and the Planning Process* (London: George Allen & Unwin 1976).

LICHFIELD, N., 'Cost Benefit Analysis in Urban Expansion: A Case Study, Peterborough', *Regional Studies*, 3 (1968), pp. 123–55.

LINDZEY, G. AND ARONSON, E. (eds.), *The Handbook of Social Psychology* (Reading, Mass.: Addison-Wesley 1969).

LIVINGSTON AND BLAYNEY (Consultants), *A University Community in the Almadén Valley* (Mimeo 1961).

LONDON COUNTY COUNCIL, *County of London Development Plan* (London: London County Council 1951).

LONDON MOTORWAY ACTION GROUP AND LONDON AMENITY AND TRANSPORT ASSOCIATION, *Transport Strategy in London* (London: The Group 1971).

MCIVER, J.P. AND OSTROM, F., 'Using Budget Pies to Reveal Preferences: Validation of a Survey Instrument', *Policy and Politics*, 4 (1976) pp. 87–110.

MCKIE, D., *A Sadly Mismanaged Affair: A Political History of the Third London Airport* (London: Croom Helm 1973).

MARCH, J.G., 'The Power of Power' in Easton, D. (ed.), *q.v.*

References

MARCUSE, P., *Mass Transit for the Few: Lessons from Los Angeles* (Los Angeles: UCLA, School of Architecture and Urban Planning 1975).

MARGOLIS, J. AND GUITTON, H., *Public Economics* (London: Macmillan 1969).

MARRIS, R. (ed.), *The Corporate Society* (London: Macmillan 1974).

MEADOWS, D.H., *et al.*, *The Limits to Growth: A Report for the Club of Rome's Project on the Predicament of Mankind* (New York: Universe Books 1972).

MEREWITZ, L., *How Do Urban Rapid Transit Projects Compare in Cost Estimating Experience?*, Proceedings of the International Conference on Transportation Research, Bruges, Belgium, June 1973 (Berkeley: California University, Institute of Urban and Regional Development, Reprint No. 104, 1973).

—— 'Cost Overruns in Public Works' from Niskansen, W., *et al.*, *Benefit Cost and Policy Analysis Annual* 1972. Berkeley: California University, Institute of Urban and Regional Development. Reprint No. 114 (Chicago: Aldine 1973).

METROPOLITAN TRANSPORTATION COMMISSION (McDonald & Smart Inc.), *A History of the Key Decisions in the Development of Bay Area Rapid Transit* (San Francisco: Jossey-Bass 1973).

MICHAEL, D.M., *On Learning to Plan and Planning to Learn* (San Francisco: Jossey-Bass 1973).

MILNOR, J., 'Games Against Nature' in Shubik, M. (ed.), *q.v.*

MISHAN, E., 'Pareto Optimality and the Law', *Oxford Economic Papers*, 19 (1967), pp. 255–87.

MUMPHREY, A., AND WOLPERT, J., *Equity Considerations and Concessions in the Siting of Public Facilities*, Research on Conflict in Locational Decisions, Discussion Paper 17 (Philadelphia: Wharton School of Finance and Commerce 1972).

NEWTON, K., 'Community Politics and Decision-Making: The American Experience and the Lessons' in Young, K. (ed.), *q.v.*

NISBET, R., *The Degradation of the Academic Dogma: The University in America, 1945–1970* (New York: Basic Books 1971).

NISKANSEN, W.A., *Bureaucracy and Representative Government* (Chicago: Aldine-Atherton 1971).

—— *Bureaucracy: Servant or Master?*, Hobart Paperback No. 5 (London: Institute of Economic Affairs 1973).

NOZICK, R., *Anarchy, State and Utopia* (Oxford: Basil Blackwell 1974).

OLSON, M., JR, 'Economics, Sociology and the Best of all Possible Worlds', *The Public Interest*, 12 (1968), pp. 96–118.

—— 'On the Priority of Public Problems' in Marris, R. (ed.), *q.v.*

PARKINSON, C.N., *Parkinson's Law or the pursuit of Progress* (London: John Murray 1958).

PARSONS, BRINCKERHOFF, HALL AND MACDONALD, *Regional Rapid Transit 1953–1955: A Report to the San Francisco Bay Area Rapid Transit Commission* (San Francisco: The Consultants 1956).

PARSONS, BRINCKERHOFF, TUDOR AND BECHTEL, *The Composite Report: Bay Area Rapid Transit* (San Francisco: The Consultants 1962).

PERKINS, B., AND BARNES, G., 'A Planning Choice', *The Planner*, 61 (1975), pp. 96–8.

PLOWDEN, S., *Towns Against Traffic* (London: André Deutsch 1972).

RAIFFA, H., *Decision Analysis* (Reading, Mass.: Addison-Wesley 1968).

RAPOPORT, A., *Fights, Games and Debates* (Ann Arbor: University of Michigan Press 1960).

RAWLS, J., *A Theory of Justice* (Cambridge, Mass.: Harvard UP 1971).

RIKER, W., 'Voting and the Summation of Preferences: An Interpretative Bibliograph review of selected developments during the Last Decade'. *American Political Science Review*, 55, 900–11.

RITTEL, H.W.J. AND WEBBER, M.M., 'Dilemmas in a General Theory of Planning', *Policy Sciences*, 4 (1973), pp. 155–69.

SAN JOSÉ, CITY PLANNING DEPARTMENT, *Study on Suggested Sites for a University of California Campus* (San José: Mimeo 1958).

SANTA CRUZ, CITY AND COUNTY, *A University of California Campus at Santa Cruz* (Santa Cruz: The City 1960).

SAWYER, J.E., 'Entrepreneurial Error and Economic Growth', *Explorations in Entrepreneurial History*, 4 (1952), pp. 199–204.

SCHATTSCHNEIDER, E.E., *The Semi-Sovereign People: A Realist's View of Democracy in America* (New York: Holt, Rinehart & Winston 1960).

SCHELLING, T.C., *The Strategy of Conflict* (Cambridge, Mass.: Harvard UP 1960).

SCHICK, A., 'Systems Politics and Systems Budgeting', *Public Administration Review*, 29 (1969), pp. 137–51.

SCHOETTLE, E.C.B., 'The State of the Art in Policy Studies' in Bauer, R.A. and Gergen, K.J., *q.v.*

SCHON, D.A., *Beyond the Stable State: Public and Private Learning in a Changing Society* (London: Temple Smith 1971).

SEARLE, J.R., *The Campus War* (Harmondsworth: Penguin 1972).

SELF, P., *Econocrats and the Policy Process: The Politics and Philosophy of Cost-Benefit Analysis* (London: Macmillan 1975).

References

SEN, A.K., *Collective Choice and Social Welfare* (San Francisco: Holden-Day 1970).

—— *On Economic Inequality* (Oxford: Clarendon Press 1973).

—— 'Planners' Preferences: Optimality, Distribution and Social Welfare' in Margolis, J. and Guitton, H., *q.v.*

SHUBIK(M. (ed.), *Game Theory and Related Approaches to Social Behavior* (New York: John Wiley 1964).

SIMMIE, J.M., *Citizens in Conflict: The Sociology of Town Planning* (London: Hutchinson 1974).

SIMON, A., AND STEDRY, C., 'Psychology and Economics' in Lindzey, G., and Aronson, E. (eds.), *q.v.*

SOLESBURY, W., *Policy in Urban Planning* (Oxford: Pergamon 1974).

SOUTHERN CALIFORNIA ASSOCIATION OF GOVERNMENTS, *Regional Transportation Plan: Towards A Balanced Transportation System* (Los Angeles: The Association 1975).

SOUTHERN CALIFORNIA RAPID TRANSIT DISTRICT, *A Public Transportation Improvement Program: Summary Report of Consultant's Recommendations* (Los Angeles: Southern California Rapid Transit District 1974).

STAMP, L.D., 'Nationalism and Land Utilisation in Britain', *Geographical Review*, 27 (1937), pp. 1–18.

STAMP, L.D., *The Land of Britain: Its Use and Misuse* (London: Longmans, Green 1962).

STANSTED WORKING PARTY, *The Third London Airport: The Case for Re-Appraisal* (Chelmsford: The Working Party 1967).

STEINER, P., 'The Public Sector and the Public Interest' in Haveman, P.H. and Margolis, J., *q.v.*

STEWART, J.D., *Management in Local Government: A Viewpoint* (London: Charles Knight 1971).

THOMSON, J.M., *Motorways in London* (London: Duckworth 1969).

TULLOCK, G., *The Politics of Bureaucracy* (Washington: Public Affairs Press 1965).

—— *Towards a Mathematics of Politics* (Ann Arbor: University of Michigan Press 1967).

—— *The Vote Motive*, Hobart Paperback No. 9 (London: Institute of Economic Affairs 1976).

UNIVERSITY OF CALIFORNIA OFFICE OF THE PRESIDENT, *Unity and Diversity: The Academic Plan of the University of California, 1965–1975* (Berkeley: The University 1965).

UNIVERSITY OF CALIFORNIA, SANTA CRUZ, *Long Range Development Plan*, John Carl Warnecke & Associates (Irvine: The University 1963).

UNIVERSITY OF CALIFORNIA, IRVINE, *Long Range Development Plan*, William L. Pereith & Associates (Irvine: The University 1963).

US PRESIDENT'S COMMISSION ON CAMPUS UNREST, *Report* (Washington: Government Printing Office 1970).

US CONGRESS OFFICE OF TECHNOLOGY ASSESSMENT, *San Francisco Case Study*, An Assessment of Community Planning for Mass.: Transit, Vol. 10 (Washington: Government Printing Office 1976).

—— *Washington DC Case Study*, An Assessment of Community Planning for Mass Transit, Vol. 2 (Washington: Government Printing Office 1976).

—— *Los Angeles Case Study*, An Assessment of Community Planning for Mass Transit, Vol. 6 (Washington: Government Printing Office 1976).

US DEPARTMENT OF TRANSPORTATION, *1974 National Transportation Report: Current Performance and Future Prospects* (Washington: Government Printing Office 1974).

—— A Study of Urban Mass Transportation Needs and Financing (Washington: Government Printing Office 1974).

VICKERS, G., *The Art of Judgement: A Study of Policy Making* (London: Chapman and Hall 1965).

VON NEUMANN, J. AND MORGENSTERN, O., *Theory of Games and Economic Behaviour* (Princeton: Princeton UP 1944).

WACHS, M., *The Case for Bus Rapid Transit in Los Angeles* (Los Angeles: UCLA, School of Architecture and Urban Planning, Mimeo 1976).

WARNER, S.B., JR, *The Urban Wilderness: A History of the American City* (New York: Harper and Row 1972).

WEBBER, M.M., *The BART Experience – What Have We Learned?*, Monograph No. 26 (Berkeley: Institute of Urban and Regional Development and Institute of Transportation Studies 1976).

WILDAVSKY, A.B., *The Politics of the Budgetary Process* (Boston: Little, Brown 1976).

—— 'Budgeting as Political Process', *International Encyclopedia of the Social Sciences*, 2 (1968), pp. 192–9.

—— The Revolt Against the Masses and Other Essays on Politics and Public Policy (New York: Basic Books 1971).

WILSON, A., *The Concorde Fiasco* (Harmondsworth: Penguin 1973).

YEOMANS, J., *The Other Taj Mahal: What Happened to the Sydney Opera House* (Camberwell, Victoria: Longmans 1973).

YOUNG, K., (ed.), *Essays on the Study of Urban Politics* (London: Macmillan 1975).

ZECKHAUSER, R. AND SCHAEFER, *Public Policy and Normative Economic Theory* in Bauer, R.A. and Gergen, K.J., *q.v.*

ZWERLING, S., *Mass Transit and the Politics of Technology: A Study of BART and the San Francisco Bay Area* (New York: Praeger 1974).

Index

Index

Index

Index

personal rapid transit systems, 132
Peters, G.H., 54
Phoenix, 133
Piccadilly Circus redevelopment, 9,
83
planning, defined, 1–2
Planning Balance Sheet, 269
Plowden, Stephen, 74, 76
Plowden Committee, 106–7
political activists, 204–7
politicians, 197, 224–41, 245–7; cost
of decision making, 235–6; eclectic
theory of political decision
making, 239–41; election and
intensity of preference, 227–32;
influence of politics on decision
making, 193–4; logrolling, 228–32;
market place versus elections,
225–7; minimum coalitions, 234–
6; mobilization of bias, 240;
nature of political power, 238–9;
pressure groups, 236–8; process
politics, 241; systems politics, 241;
vote maximization, 224–5, 226,
234, 245, 247
pollution, see noise
polytechnics, 169
population forecasts, 6, 10
positive analysis, 189–98
Powell, Enoch, 94
pressure groups, 10–11, 236–8, 244–
5, 247
'Prisoner's Dilemma', 260n
process politics, 241
public goods, economics of
bureaucratic production, 216–20;
elections and supply of, 225–7;
non-equality in payment and
benefit, 225; supply of, 187–9
Publishers' Association, 174

Radcliffe, Lord, 177, 178
radical elite, opposition, 206–7
Rapid Transit Commission, 110, 112
rapid transit systems, American
debate on, 128–36; personal, 132;
see also Bay Area Rapid Transit
rational actor paradigm, 192, 194

Rawls, John, 262–4, 267
Reading University, 87
Reagan, Ronald, 126, 161, 163
Rex, John, 195
Riker, William, 234–5
Rippon, Geoffrey, 78, 107, 176
Roads Campaign Council, 62
Robson, William, 57
Rohr, 116, 117
Rolls Royce, Boeing 757 engines,
108; Concorde engines, 91, 98–9
Roskill Commission, 15–16, 24, 29–
38, 39, 51–5; cost/benefit analysis,
31, 32–7; methodology, 29–33;
recommendations, 34–8
Royal Aircraft Establishment,
Farnborough, 89, 107
Royal Institute of British Architects,
80

Saarinen, Eero, 139, 141
Salt Lake City, 133
San Diego, 133
San Francisco, Embarcadero
Freeway, 83; see also Bay Area
Rapid Transit
Sandys, Duncan, Concorde project,
91, 93, 107; urban containment,
53
Sawyer, John, 220–1
Schelling, 260
Schick, 241
Schon, Donald, 12, 203, 243
Schumacher, E.F., 11
Science Museum Library, 178
Science Policy Research Unit, 253
Science Reference Library, 180, 183
Self, Peter, 29
Sen, 255, 258, 264
Shoeburyness, 27, 34
Shore, Peter, 44
Simon, Herbert, 208–10
SNECMA, 91
Southend Airport, 27
Southern California Rapid Transit
District (SCRTD), 133–5
Stamp, Dudley, 16
Stanford Research Institute, 112

306

Index